DISCARD

LEARNING
RESOURCE
CENTERS
Selected Readings

Edited by

Neville P. Pearson
University of Minnesota
and

Lucius A. Butler
University of Hawaii

BURGESS PUBLISHING COMPANY   •   MINNEAPOLIS, MINNESOTA

Copyright © 1973 by Burgess Publishing Company
Printed in the United States of America
Library of Congress Card Number 72-78260
SBN 8087-1632-8

1   2   3   4   5   6   7   8   9   0

FOREWORD

The current dilemmas that face public education become crystalized most completely as it becomes apparent that there is not a major school district in the United States which is not facing financial difficulties. This condition is said to be due to a combination of increasing costs, overwhelming influxes of young people who wish to participate in education — kindergarten through the university level; and, the inability to meet these problems through the application of traditional staffing and school building patterns.

As professional educators confront the decade of the seventies, there are portents of change and innovation which give promise that creative solutions are forthcoming through which to solve some of the old dilemmas.

Among the most dramatic of all of these is the ground swell of interest in, research about, and demonstrations of what has grown to be recognized as the field of "educational communications."

From the advent of federal financing of media learning research in the mid-fifties, we can today envision the flowering of multimedia learning systems strategies as an important way for providing effective learning opportunities to those who wish this — and within the limitations of current manpower supplies and dollar budgets.

Recently I had the opportunity of spending a sabbatical year examining innovations in educational media utilization on the mainland and in Europe. I was impressed by the unanimity of concern for searching for and evaluating the efficiency of new methods of communicating information to increasing numbers of young people. Though described by a variety of terms, educators are approaching the problem of the improvement of instruction through systematic analysis of learner needs, examination and selection of useful communications, and the appropriate use of large, small, and individualized multimedia learning experiences which would yield the highest kind and most appropriate learning opportunities for youth and young people. Regardless of the means of communicating — whether it be television, language laboratory, sound-motion picture films, community study, graphics, charts, or open-school learning opportunities in which students have an increased voice in helping to decide on the nature and availability of experiences even outside of traditional school walls — learning by mediated experiences is being subjected to a searching analysis by people who must work at the problem: school administrators, subject supervisors, learning psychologists, *and* educational communications specialists.

As the decade of the seventies unfolds, the professional educator will contemplate a dramatic reawakening of planning for, acting about, and, evaluating new means for employing electronic and non-electronic learning resources as a means of providing much of the cognate and skill experiencing needed by increasing numbers of learners.

This volume entitled *Learning Resource Centers*, presents a broad spectrum of articles which suggest how the above may be accomplished. In the midst of current changes, it is not at all certain that the learning resource center, as it is known today, will bear any resemblance to what it must and can become in the forseeable future if the proper deployment of manpower, multimedia learning resources and pupils is to result in a new kind of learning opportunity. An analysis of the titles included in this anthology will reveal the latitude, and, at the same time, the intensive care and efforts that the authors, Dr. Neville P. Pearson and Dr. Lucius A. Butler, have made in order to bring together for the reader the kinds of background understanding which can become the foundations for future action. Understanding gains from a study of these articles can be built into the foundation for the pyramid which must be constructed in the next ten years.

I congratulate the authors, and, I enjoin my colleagues in examining the contents of this volume.

University of Hawaii   WALTER A. WITTICH
Honolulu, Hawaii   Professor of Educational Communications
September 1, 1972   Department of Education

PREFACE

For years our schools have had libraries — collections of mostly print-type material supplementing the textbooks which have traditionally structured the curriculum.

The use of more than one text, the addition of enrichment material which gave greater depth and greater breadth, the recognition of the very real need for materials meeting the wide range of needs of the individual student, have brought very considerable change to the old book collection.

The more recent addition of audio-visual materials has resulted sometimes in an unwilling combination, sometimes in a happy marriage into the new instructional material centers.

Hopefully, the IMC brings to all the students in the school all the media materials the school can provide: materials for basic information, materials for supplementary information, materials for depth, materials simply for enrichment. In fact the IMC has the materials that provide the base, the depth, and the breadth that are needed to do the job.

In charge of the IMC is a qualified staff which is integrated completely with the regular teaching faculty.

There has been a widespread development of IMC's in concept and in operation, but there is still less than 100 per cent use of these collections.

So, the Learning Resources Center, immediately adjacent to the Science Department, or the Math Department, or whatever subject area, came into being. The regular science teacher, with the help of the media specialist in the IMC, has materials to present to his students; the student whose motivation may be momentary only has to go next door to find the special materials that increase the motivation and help him understand, help him to pursue his own special interests — and may direct him to the IMC and the media personnel there who can assist his pursuit still further.

The LRC tries to meet individual needs — when the individual feels a need!

In this collection of readings we have tried to find ideas on the elementary and secondary level resource centers — centers for many subject areas, centers which point the way to techniques for better communication, a better communication which results in more learning, better understanding. We express our appreciation to the authors and publishers who have granted permission for the republishing of these articles. May they help you explore the area of the resource center and help you establish centers that will work. We express appreciation also to the Burgess Publishing Company staff who have assisted us and to Lorna Borman who has served us well as proofreader.

October, 1972   Lucius A. Butler
                                                                      Neville P. Pearson

CONTENTS

SECTION ONE / CONCEPT AND THEORY

A Look at the Progress and Prospects of Electronic Education

Edgar Dale

Educational technology is a means, not an end. But what is the end — the goal we are trying to achieve?

We face the age old question: What knowledge is of greatest worth? My answer would be: That knowledge is of greatest worth which enables us to learn our worth; which enables every man, woman, and child to achieve his potential.

We are a long way from achieving that goal. But something new has happened. Modern media of communication have enabled the disadvantaged to learn that their potential is underdeveloped and caused them to look longingly at any form of governmental or economic arrangement which promises to help them achieve that goal. Further, among the affluent today in the United States, and especially among the young, there is a feeling that they, too, have not achieved their potential; that perhaps the goals they have tried to achieve were not the most worthwhile. They are asking: Instead of trying to get ahead of the others in school, college, business, or professional life, wouldn't it make more sense to try to get ahead with the other fellow? They are asking: Wouldn't the circle of friendship and cooperation which helps everybody be better than the ladder of competition where it is every man for himself?

It is in such an atmosphere that we discuss the topic, educational technology. The problem really is not whether we shall use film, filmstrip, radio, recordings, computers, overhead projectors, television, simulation devices, etc. That issue is settled. We are going to use every possible means to help learners achieve their potential. The problem is how and when you combine their use with a live teacher.

Electronic media, including programmed materials, will not replace teachers but will help replace them and enable them to play the important role of guide, counselor, motivator, organizer, integrator, critical questioner, intellectual gadfly — the things that only a live and lively teacher can do in personal, face-to-face communication. The teacher can become a model of the thinking man or woman instead of being the administrator of learning tasks easily handled by a mediated teacher. The teacher can spend more time designing and programming the learning environment of the student so that he can become an independent learner.

A teacher is one element in a learning situation — sometimes an indispensable one. But sometimes the learner doesn't need a classroom teacher at all. Indeed, our best, most creative learning will not take place in the presence of a

Reprinted from *Ohio Schools*, January 1968, by permission of Edgar Dale and the publisher.

teacher. Furthermore, all instruction aims to prepare the student to learn outside the physical presence of a teacher.

The able teacher tries to make himself dispensable. He helps his students move from dependence to independence. We should let the teacher perform the uniquely human tasks that require mature, compassionate guidance. The teacher should not spend time or energy on those aspects of learning which can be efficiently learned by other means. If a book or filmstrip can really substitute for a teacher, let's use these ways of communicating with students.

Another question that we must face as we try to think through the problem of educational technology is the place where learning should take place. We have a stereotyped notion that most learning will take place in the school and college in a formal learning atmosphere. But the places where we learn informally are legion.

We can get our instructions on what to learn, how to learn, and why we learn from a live teacher or instructor. But some of these instructions may be secured by telephone, telelecture, or closed circuit television to homes or dormitory rooms — from a distant teacher. The learning may take place in the Museum of Natural History in Dayton, at a Shakespearean play at Antioch, or in many other settings.

It is clear that the conditions of learning are going to change a great deal in the next few years. What we must do is to make much greater use of our teaching staffs to program this learning. In such a program we would not wait until the child came to nursery school or kindergarten before we worked with the parents on a language development program. The teacher would become a consultant to parents and help them set up an effective learning environment in the home.

As we try to program this instruction, we shall have to face some tough, hard questions about goals and objectives. We need a basic educational taxonomy; a classification of the kind of behaviors we want. Do we expect the student to memorize what the teacher or book says, or do we want the learner to discover the implications and the applications of this knowledge? When we decide on the whole range of behaviors we shall try to reach, we have committed ourselves to a radical change in our educational program.

We also need a radical change in the entire testing programs of our schools. Most school and college tests are largely on questions of fact, but they contain very little questioning of fact. Students are usually required to answer questions they never asked. They are told to answer questions but less commonly are they taught to question answers.

The author visualizes the time when our testing program will be a functioning part of the learning program. Now it is an after-piece. We now discover what students don't know at the end of the unit instead of having them discover at the beginning what they don't know and then remedy their ignorance.

I see a testing program which will be so simple and so easily available that any child or any adult could take a test on a computer or by some other means almost any time he wants to and discover his attainments on any of several phases of a subject. He could take a vocabulary test and discover those aspects of important life experience where he is weak and where he is strong. Further, the computer may actually print study materials for him or refer him to books, pamphlets, recordings, or programmed instructional materials.

It follows that we must have easily accessible sources of learning materials which fit the needs and abilities of a wide range of children. Here we turn to a new type of library — the learning materials center.

These centers are concerned with all the media which carry important messages — print, film, filmstrip, computer, photograph, painting, radio, recording, videotape, television, radiovision, telelecture. The Meadowbrook Junior High School in Newton, Mass., has four major learning centers, one each for math, science, and language, and a large combined center for English and social studies.

ALL FIVE SENSES

In a classroom of tomorrow now being built in the Centennial School District, Warminster, Pa., there will be a special experiences center to be used for teaching through all five senses — sight, sound, smell, feel, and even taste.

Some of these learning materials centers will have built in dial access systems. At Ohio State University, for example, a student can dial in from 368 different locations, 27 of which are in fraternity and sorority houses. A catalogue indicates what is found in the center. The magnitude of this service is indicated by the fact that an average of 40,000 calls is received each week. Video is being tied into the center and it is no exaggeration to say that eventually a dial access system will put the world's best ideas at the learners' finger tips and present it in a form that they can easily understand.

New systems of distributing ideas are also available in the amplified telephone lecture, the radiovision program which can be tied in with telephonic feedback.

Properly programmed, the computer can present varied and flexible experiences to the individual learner. It can diagnose his level of learning and fit the new experiences to this background. It can give him messages by a typewriter, by a film, a television sequence, a slide, or a recording. It can receive or react to messages by pressing knobs, by a light pencil, a cathode ray tube, or by a typed message. Computers are being developed that react to spoken stimuli.

We may mistakenly conclude that the computer will convey only rote and drill material, and nothing dealing with the higher mental processes. This need not happen. For example, certain elements in learning to write expository prose will be taught by computer. By means of the light pencil on the cathode ray tube, the learner can rearrange the structure of a "disorganized" paragraph. The computer could ask the learner to analyze and discriminate between various paragraphs and pick the best one.

No one expects the computer to make a brilliant writer out of a learner. But the computer can present and juxtapose writing choices which require increasing levels of discrimination. Computer-assisted instruction can provide more quickly, and perhaps more effectively, some of the basic background of skills and insights needed for the complicated higher mental processes involved in effective writing and reading.

Professor O. K. Moore has experimented with the use of a computerized typewriter as the first tool which children use in writing the letters of the alphabet. The children freely explore the computerized typewriter and when they strike the key, the computer calls the name of the letter or the symbol struck.

Modern life is too varied and too complex to meet and understand all of it at first-hand. In curriculum-making, we must study those educational situations most likely to help us solve our basic personal and social decisions and be most generative of new ideas. Following this selection, we can then set up learning programs which simulate these situations and then evaluate how well students can solve these problems.

Simulation is being used in an administrative training program developed by the University Council for Educational Administration which simulates and checks the decisions of an elementary school principal in a suburban community. The simulations provide the necessary reality by including filmstrips, sound motion pictures, and tape recordings.

Donald R. Cruickshank and Frank W. Broadbent have developed what is called *Teaching Problems Laboratory* where "real" situations are presented to teachers in training or in-service. This is available from Science Research Associates.

RASH OF SIMULATIONS

We may now expect a rash of simulations to be available at all levels of education. One is called *Inter-Nation Simulation*. Another is titled the *Game of Farming* and presents problems faced by the Kansas farmer in three sharply varying historical periods.

Teachers will have to make some important decisions about learning by simulation. The critical question is this: Does the simulation teach the intended learning economically and efficiently? How elaborate must the equipment be to give a feeling of reality, to avoid the feeling of merely play acting? Since simulation will play a large part in the education of the future, we should now put a number of task forces at work to evaluate this new approach to instruction.

In summary, I would present these conclusions:

- Progress in the use of certain media has been widespread but our students and teachers do not yet have easy access to the excellent films, filmstrips, and recordings already produced. Nor do we have access to the best that has been printed — the kinds of materials that should be found in learning materials centers.
- The programming of instruction and the developing of instructional systems are still undeveloped fields. There is much yet to do in helping students learn how to learn and to develop a taste for learning. Our taxonomies are inadequate. We do not have the necessary tests to determine whether learning has taken place and to provide a diagnosis and remediation for what has not been learned.
- There is too sharp a disparity, too great a lag, between what we know how to do in education and what we are actually doing. We need to use the new media to help us shorten this lag.
- The great revolution going forward today in our schools means a shift in the role of the teacher from a Jack or Jill-of-all-trades to taking on the role of a sophisticated organizer, administrator, counselor, guide, and simulator of learning. The new role promises to be more complex but certainly more professional. We have the choice of staying where the inaction is or moving into the excitement and challenge that always faces the pioneer.

The Instructional Materials Center: A Theory Underlying Its Development

Kenneth I. Taylor

The major characteristic of school library development in this decade is the library's increasing identification with the school's total educational program. Today, the school library is frequently called an instructional materials center by educators in order to give emphasis to its important supportive role. In this context, the instructional materials center, or IMC, may be defined as a school department which supplies well-selected curriculum-related printed and audio-visual materials for students and teachers. Equipment, facilities, and professional services are offered to implement the use and production of materials for individuals and for groups of various sizes.

Very little has yet been written in professional literature on the relationships between the IMC, school objectives, and learning activities selected to achieve those objectives. Far more has been written on "how" to create a materials center than on "why" it is an essential part of the modern school.

In this article, a theory will be proposed which attempts to give meaning to recent changes in education and the rise of the IMC. The premise of the theory is that the basic function of the IMC program is to support schoolwide independent and group creative inquiry. Creative inquiry is accepted here as the major contemporary school objective. It is believed that by beginning with an examination of the nature of creative inquiry and of the conditions needed in a school for it to flourish, one should understand more clearly the collections, equipment, and facilities that are required in the IMC.

NATURE OF CREATIVE INQUIRY

A discussion of creative inquiry requires a review of two older objectives which may be viewed as its components. The first of these objectives, accepted for centuries, is the teaching of information, ideas, principles, and concepts discovered by men of previous times. Almost all parents and teachers agree that there is available to us a body of "established knowledge" which schools should transmit from one generation to the next as part of man's heritage. In each field, schools provide a sampling which is generally considered to be the mark of an educated man. This knowledge, having once been discovered, needs only to be transmitted to our young people. Schools have had little difficulty in achieving this goal. In fact, there is ample evidence, furnished by the Committee of the Taxonomy of Educational Objectives, to indicate that schools may have pursued it so well that they have spent a disproportionately large amount of time upon it, partly because knowledge as such is easy to teach and partly because its testing requires only simple recall by the student.

A second fundamental objective of the schools is the teaching of commonly accepted techniques for discovering knowledge. These techniques will vary with the discipline and are dependent upon the nature of knowledge within that discipline. Joseph Schwab has identified three genera of disciplines: the investigative (natural sciences), the appreciative (the arts), and the decisive (social sciences). Each discipline is characterized by its own proved procedures for discovering knowledge, determining new relationships, and reporting findings to others. The scientist, for example, works with hypotheses and selected data and reports conclusions so that replication may be attempted. The artist makes judgments about his work and that of others with reference to recognized critical standards. The social scientist reconciles natural and social data in areas of human activity that are neither black nor white.

As in the case of the first objective, schools may also be said to have achieved this second objective well. In earlier days, whenever one passed a rural school and saw the same paper snowflake on every window, he had evidence that the teacher was teaching a technique in art. In a laboratory where all students perform the same experiment, their teacher, too, is interested in technique. At this point in the laboratory, there is no place for a creative answer because evidence of successful performance of the learning activity requires uniform results of all pupils.

Each of these two objectives has played and will continue to play an important part in education. It is a thesis of this article, however, that schools must not stop at these two objectives alone. To do so would leave students at that stage where they have learned only what has already been learned by others. Our society today requires that schools go beyond this stage and develop students who are competent in fashioning new ideas to meet demands of novel situations.

The creativity that is needed at this point occurs if students are encouraged to draw upon "personal experience," the third component of creative inquiry. When students are encouraged to relate their pasts of, say, twelve or fourteen years, to the pasts of others, they are then in a position to develop new ideas and new products which are uniquely their own. Yet, because they have already studied previous performances of others, their ideas have substance and some basis in fact. When schools provide optimum conditions for this kind of creative inquiry, they cease to be agents of mass communication and begin to individualize learning.

CONDITIONS REQUIRED FOR CREATIVE INQUIRY

Under what conditions does creative inquiry occur within the school? There are at least four which are needed by the student for success in this activity:

The first condition is opportunity for mastery of established knowledge and traditional techniques for discovering knowledge. This mastery might be learned alone by the student through reference and informational materials of the IMC, but in practice a major portion of the knowledge and techniques transmitted by the school is customarily taught to groups. The groups, in most instances, are composed of twenty-five to thirty students, and they learn through lectures, textbooks, programmed books, and projected materials.

Taught in this manner, knowledge and techniques compose what schools consider to be a basic part of every student's education. Both have been and will continue to be accepted functions of our schools; and, as indicated in the previous section, both are viewed here as essential components of creative inquiry. In recent years, it has been discovered that much of this basic instruction may be taught equally as well to even larger groups of two, three, or four classes. This discovery is important to this theory because it is often found that, should a school attempt large group instruction, other conditions for creative inquiry are easier to provide.

A second condition needed for creative inquiry is solitude. A student must be alone in order to draw upon personal ideas and experiences. At this point in inquiry, he begins the development of something new by discovering relationships which previously were not perceived. In some articles, this activity has been called "independent study"; but as defined here, it is an isolated and unique exploratory or reflective activity where personal ideas may be introduced. It is not to be confused with text or laboratory manual study wherein all student activities are predesigned and alike. Although this latter type of study also occurs when the student is alone, it is more nearly related to condition one, basic instruction, than to condition two, the need for solitude. It is here that a student proceeds a step beyond that which is taught as known.

A third condition for creative inquiry is the sharing of one's ideas with one's age mates. Following reflection and the discovery of a new idea or product, a student often wishes to have an appraisal by his peers. The exchange offers a standard by which the student sees and measures his personal growth.

A fourth condition for creative inquiry is consultation with an expert. An expert bridges the gap between materials and the present; he saves time because he simplifies relationships within a field for greater clarity; and he individualizes learning. In many instances, the expert is the student's teacher, but for certain projects he is a resource person from the community.

These four conditions are to be encouraged at almost any time of the day within the school. Because there is no rigid sequence of steps in creative inquiry, a student will choose, when he is able, to move from one condition to another, working in one momentarily and at great length in the next. His ultimate goal is the discovery and development of what is, at least to him, a new product or idea.

The nature of knowledge and conditions for inquiry have been the concern of philosophers for centuries. In the previous two sections, the writer is especially indebted, however, to Herbert Thelen for his clarification of the role of personal experience in creativity and the interrelationships needed among conditions of inquiry.

THE INSTRUCTIONAL MATERIALS CENTER

A number of implications in this theory of creativity become apparent to the media specialist, particularly for IMC programs and design. Instructional innovations of recent years, such as large group instruction, small group discussion, and independent study, may in combination contribute very well toward providing conditions for creative inquiry. All of these areas, regardless of location, should be of interest to the IMC staff if materials are to be used with success. The IMC itself should also have comparable areas for large groups, small groups, and individuals, in which materials are used under optimum conditions.

Flexibility must become a characteristic of the school program, in time allocations and utilization of personnel. In the IMC, in similar fashion, there must be flexibility in student traffic flow and in patterns of material use. Because students learn in many ways, their exploratory pursuits should involve all manner of instructional materials within every setting available for inquiry.

Collections of traditional and newer materials must be combined and become more extensive than in previous years. Story information and reference books are required in greater numbers to provide larger samplings of the accelerating accumulation of established knowledge. Audio-visual materials must be accessible to students, as well as teachers, for contemporary viewing and listening experiences. Materials must be selected with reference to the curriculum and in relation to those texts and workbooks that are commonly used around the school. IMC staff members must also be aware of the numerous kits, recordings, filmstrips, models, maps, and study prints that are now furnished by publishers to supplement their basic texts.

In addition to these materials, professional personnel in the IMC must explore the potential of special materials, exhibited at present by the programmed book, which are and will continue in the future to be designed to promote behavioral change, especially for skill development in traditional techniques for discovering knowledge. Materials should be used in varied combinations for mutual reinforcement at any sequential condition of creative inquiry.

The final goal of creative inquiry, the development of an original idea by the student, gives special emphasis to a relatively new service of the IMC, the production of instructional materials. In fact, this may become the most rapidly growing area of the IMC in the future. Because the original idea of the student must be presented in some communicable form, the final product furnishes evidence that the idea has been fully developed. Today's students are as likely to make a sound tape, a set of transparencies and photos, or a three-dimensional model as they would have written an essay in earlier days. It is important to remember that the product must be created by the student himself rather than by someone else for him. For this reason, we expect to find production areas available around the school, with the equipment in the IMC generally restricted to what is too expensive to duplicate.

All IMC services to students are likely to increase with greater emphasis on individual creativity. Their effectiveness will best be determined as they are evaluated with reference to creative inquiry as the major education goal.

The Instructional Materials Center: A Changing Concept

Carolyn I. Whitenack

Dr. Gordon Ray, distinguished scholar, began his opening address to the 1966 ALA with a quotation from Dickens, "It was the best of times; it was the worst of times." The wealth of federal support and the paucity of trained school librarians and audio-visual specialists to aid in planning and directing programs has caused us to agree. We are in the best of times, in that we are obtaining sufficient money to work with; worst, in that we lack competent personnel to take full advantage of this financial support.

First of all, I would like to give you some of the philosophy behind recent developments in instructional resources.

Second, I would like to show you some favorable developments that are taking place in Indiana.

Third, I would like to suggest some of the qualities of leadership needed by persons who direct integrated programs of materials.

I will be speaking today from the following points of view:

1. Learning is a very private affair — personal and individual. Books, films and all library resources go straight to the individual.
2. The content of media is important, not the format.
3. Educational media or instructional materials means the entire range of materials, both print and non-print.
4. Books are among the best developed of our educational tools and are a very important medium today; they are versatile, adaptable and well respected in the world of audio-visual education, as well as in the world of library education.
5. The newer media are just as personal in instruction as books and are very useful tools in the management of information. It has been stated by well-known educators that the so-called new media have been proposed, promoted or projected for so many different reasons and for the solution to so many of our pressing educational problems that one could easily lose sight of the fact that they, like all teaching activities, are a means to one primary objective — instigating learning and appropriate changes of behavior in students.
6. The school principal is the programmer or planner of the learning behavior policy and the curriculum of the school. The teacher is the director of the learning process. The media librarian and/or AV specialist is a codirector of learning, an associate of the teacher.

Reprinted from *American Annals of the Deaf*, November 1967, by permission of the publisher.

Far-reaching changes have taken place in American society and education during the past ten years. Well-known social trends include: expansion of population, with a higher percentage in school; changing vocational and occupational needs leading to new expectations from the school; growing urban areas demanding more services; rapid mobility of people including international travel; mass organization and restructuring of knowledge presenting new problems; and greater concern for quality, as well as a demand for higher levels of education. This changing nature of modern society is changing educational goals, particularly as they relate to the instructional materials center concept.

The modern school program is confronted with a rich variety of resources for learning. These resources include a host of materials and devices from textbooks to television to computers. The aims of education can be defined as individual personal growth and the learning of specified content, or even more simply stated as *the teaching of students to think*. These aims are interrelated and the task of the teacher is the selection of the best combination of learning resources and experiences to achieve these aims.

The best learning occurs when the student is mentally active — selecting, responding, making discriminations and value judgments, and taking action upon important ideas, experiences, and resources as they relate to him personally — in such a way that learning takes place and that further learning is continued on his own initiative.

The greater degree of responsibility now placed on the individual for self-direction, self-learning and self-testing makes the services of an instructional materials center imperative. New arrangements of teacher and student deployment, with new roles for each in the learning process, are characteristic of good schools. One example is Project English which relies on the strength of an organized literature program. Another example is team teaching. Each person has a responsibility delegated by interest and choice, releasing other members of the team for preparation and study; and releasing students to pursue their interests in instructional materials centers. The extended school day makes new demands on the staff and resources of materials centers.

Teachers and materials specialists are deeply involved in reviewing and evaluating teaching and learning materials in all content areas. The many curriculum-content studies — e.g., AIBS, NCTE, PSSE — have developed a core of materials — films, filmstrips, books, tapes, and laboratory materials — which are being distributed nationally to materials specialists for their consideration. The center needs to provide reviewing services and examination copies, if service will be useful to the curriculum specialists for the improvement of instruction in each subject area. Better ways of grouping students, ungraded classes, ability grouping, advanced placement, accelerated groups, and enrichment classes all demand adequate learning resources to meet the diverse needs of these students.

New schools are being planned as clusters of centers, laboratories, and shops. Spaces for learning resources are in instruction materials centers, individual carrels, in classrooms, in laboratories, and wherever learning takes place.

Teachers, parents, peers and institutions are the sources of many ideas, experiences, and materials. Traditionally, books and libraries have been the primary means of recording and communicating ideas. In recent years there have been many audio-visual materials developments such as programmed learning, tapes, educational television programs, new kinds of projected materials, teaching machines, and other special teaching devices. Each type of material has a contribution to make to the educational process. The distinctive qualities of each resource should be recognized and all appropriate resources should be used in the learning situation.

New approaches in reading have enhanced the utilization of instructional resources. Well-designed and illustrated books and many quality paperbacks are available. A multimedia approach to learning demands a comprehensive program of materials with a collection of at least 30,000 items, including books, films, filmstrips, tapes, sets of pictures, slides, transparencies, globes, maps and charts, programmed materials and devices, audio and video tapes, and radio and television programs to meet the varying needs, abilities, and interests of all the students.

Paraphrasing Dr. C. Walter Stone of the University of Pittsburgh, the rationale of professional services from a resource center includes three sorts of professional responsibilities in educational media services: (1) To put at the disposal of the teaching faculty all media, technology, services, and systems which will enhance the effective communication of ideas in the presentation phase of learning; (2) To put at the disposal of the students all media, technology, services, and systems which will enhance the effective communication of ideas in a self-programmed phase of learning; and (3) To reinforce the importance of quality education for each child by showing the need for media services and the improvement of individual learning through a wide variety of materials and resources in each school.

On the basis of this rationale an instructional materials program serves the objectives of the total educational program of the school by:

1. Locating, gathering, organizing, coordinating, promoting, and distributing a rich variety of quality learning resources for use by teachers and students as individuals and in groups;
2. Offering leadership in motivation, utilization, and experimentation in best arrangements of materials for teaching and learning;
3. Making available facilities, services, and equipment necessary for the selection, organization, management and use of learning resources;
4. Furnishing facilities for and assistance in the production of instructional materials, displays, and demonstrations;

5. Counseling and guiding teachers and students in terms of the best media or arrangement of media for the particular situation;
6. Exploring the use of modern technology, including exploratory use of computers in attacking the control and synthesis of knowledge to encourage more learning in less time;
7. Exploring the desirability and cost of central services required in processing the varied learning materials for all the schools of the area.

Such a program must have staff, facilities, collections of materials, equipment, devices and funds. Learning resources include books, films, filmstrips, tapes, recordings, programmed learning, maps, globes, charts, sets of pictures, sets of slides, transparencies, models, realia, video tapes and the like with all the appropriate equipment.

● ● ●

Qualities of leadership are needed in persons who are going to direct a media program, or any kind of educational program. My six C's of leadership are as follows:

First of all, people who are *Committed*. I think that we must have commitments to the goals of education and we must believe in the teacher, the principal and the media person working together in a team effort with a commitment to education.

Second, persons who are *Competent*. Scholarship, life-long learning, maturity and judgment, making decisions and standing by them, further education in the field in which you are not competent are all attributes of a competent person. I say to librarians, you must get audio-visual training; I say to audio-visual people, you must get library training if you are going to be a media person.

Third, persons who are *Cooperative*. I think that education is not a process by itself. I think it is a team process, beginning with a superintendent, working through the principal, the teacher, and the specialist. All of these people must work together. This is a very difficult task for each of us.

Fourth, persons who are *Creative*. We need people who aim high and who aim to work in this team process to the best of their ability.

Fifth, persons of *Conscience*. I think one of the great problems of our time is the social revolution in which we are presently participating. This revolution calls for all the love and understanding that we may have to be people who work creatively to help these newly developing people in our own country and in other countries to have a better opportunity.

Sixth, if you are all of these five, then you must be *Courageous*. It takes courageous persons to accept a plan of operation, to direct this plan, and once convinced that this is your dream, to stand by it and push it. The task needs courage to be different, courage to drop some of the old ideas that we have had, courage to be concerned about the truth as we know it today, knowing that truth is ever changing.

I end with one of my favorite quotations from Virgil's "Aeneid," "Some of these things I saw, and some of them I was." I think in this audience there are many "I was" people, and I am delighted to be here. I hope to get to know each of you, and I look forward to visiting with you in the discussion groups. Thank you so much for this opportunity to talk with you.

IMC Concept Grows Here

Robert C. Wheeler

The educational air today is filled with comment about the "Instructional Materials Center Concept." (Call it the "Learning Resources Center," if you will. It's the same idea.) Some Wisconsin districts are building new schools with an IMC as the very hub of the entire plant. Others are remodeling existing facilities to accommodate the IMC concept.

A number of schools in the state have operated IMC's with varying degrees of satisfaction for the past four or five years. Education journals are replete with descriptions of proposed IMC's and discussions about the equipment and organization needed. Federal aid is lending assistance in furnishing them, and conferences are devoted to the details of their management.

Out of this milieu of planning, exploration and experience are arising some discoveries and convictions which bode well for improved instruction.

But first, what *is* an IMC?

At least three varieties are currently receiving much attention. The regional IMC is a coöperative venture serving teachers and learners of a number of adjoining school districts. The school district IMC serves as a supply depot and service agency for all of the schools in a single district. A single school's IMC is the successor to a school library and provides opportunities to learn from a whole galaxy of instructional materials.

Although an analysis of any one of the three might well be the theme of a separate article, this discussion centers around the third of these — the IMC serving an individual building.

In any of its forms, an IMC is a facility so located, so equipped, and so staffed as to foster a principle well established by research and observation:

Reprinted from *Wisconsin Journal of Education*, November 1967, by permission of Wisconsin Education Association.

Children learn best through rich educational experiences which include appropriate use of a wide variety of instructional materials. Access to a variety of good-quality materials can enhance learning opportunities for the gifted and the slow learner as well as the average student.

Newer instructional media have been called "democratizers" of instruction. Every experienced teacher has observed that some students learn easily from the printed page; some grasp ideas more easily from visual material; still others benefit most from a composite of learning activities. An IMC, well-equipped and well-managed, can offer a synthesis of learning experiences.

The American School Library Association at its annual convention in Miami Beach, Florida, in 1956 did much to set the stage for the establishment of IMC's when it formally resolved: "... that the school library, in addition to doing its vital work of individual reading guidance and development of the school curriculum, should serve the school as a center for instructional materials. Instructional materials include books – the literature of children, young people and adults – other printed materials, films, recordings and newer media developed to aid learning."

The resolution also contained the advice that, "Teaching methods advocated by leaders in the field of curriculum development and now used in elementary and secondary education call for extensive and frequently combined use of traditional along with many new and different kinds of materials." Since these methods depend for their success upon a cross-media approach to learning, a convenient way of approaching instructional materials on a subject or problem basis must be immediately at hand in each school.

A good summary of the intended function of an IMC and its personnel is contained in the following excerpt from a handbook, "The Instructional Materials Center in Action," distributed in Michigan by the Department of Public Instruction there: "This cross-media approach to learning both challenges and gives increased dimension to study and helps to meet the individual differences of children. It provides for the variety of learning abilities among the pupils and gives breadth and depth to the concepts being formulated by them.

"In summary, these activities in and materials from the Instructional Materials Center can aid in developing an entire classroom study unit:

1. The teacher confers with the director of the Center for general planning in the selection, evaluation and use of materials.
2. The materials available are determined with the possible dates for their use.
3. The kinds of materials found to be available for use include, among others:
   a. Books and other printed materials
   b. Free and inexpensive materials

    c.   Films, especially the 8 mm-cartridge-loaded variety
    d.   Study prints
    e.   Filmstrips and slide-sets
    f.   Recordings
    g.   Transparencies
    h.   Models and collections
    i.   Equipment

4.   Provision is made for individual differences, self-direction and interest
5.   The community is involved through field trips and by using resource people.
6.   A complete index to available materials is maintained to determine the type and quantity of materials available. (Frequently color-coded fo various types.)
7.   The skills necessary for the use of the materials and the equipment are taught by the teacher and the IMC specialist.
8.   The specialist is an active consultant in the classroom to answer questions, to suggest new materials, to help in making community contacts to assist in certain group activities and to aid in the development of individual skills through the production of original materials.
9.   The conferences between the teacher and the specialist are continued until the study is completed."

Kenneth I. Taylor, Director of Instructional Services for the Madison Public Schools, has advocated that the materials for an IMC be evaluated and described in terms of behavioral outcomes in order to implement their wise selection. An integral part of the rapidly emerging "systems approach" to instruction, this would appear to be sound advice. It persuades those making the selections to ask, "What are the anticipated needs of the learners who will use these materials and how, hopefully, will they benefit as a result?" Emphasis thereby shifts from subject matter coverage to the child's needs and interests.

Once selected, many schools are turning to color-coded card index systems to help with the task of directing students and teachers to desired materials.

Some large schools, apparently taking their cue from the military premise that battles are won with short supply lines, are developing "satellite" IMC's. This scheme seeks to place separate centers close by various classroom cluster representing certain areas of the curriculum. While the arrangement is expensive it has the obvious merits of time saving efficiency in large plants.

Also from the Michigan handbook comes a significant reminder for the school administrator:

"An Instructional Materials Center will be used effectively if the building administrator works to encourage his staff to understand and use the Instructional Materials Center wisely. Staff members will consider the Instructional Materials Center valuable if the building administrator —

- makes specific plans for in-service training, orientation and guidance to encourage teachers to use the Instructional Materials Center and its services in their teaching.
- views the instructional materials specialist to serve as a person who can and should contribute to the in-service training of teachers.
- invites the instructional materials specialist to serve as a member, with special information about materials, on curriculum communities.
- · involves classroom teachers in the selection and evaluation of materials under the guidance of the instructional materials specialist.
- encourages teachers to use the Instructional Materials Center for their own professional growth."

At least four pitfalls are becoming evident as some schools establish their new IMC's:

1. The former school library is converted into an "IMC" by scattering several filmstrip viewers and a record-player or two about the premises, giving the newer instructional materials a sort of shirt-tail position among the total collection of learning resources.

     The IMC concept envisions well balanced "cafeteria" offering of all resources with choices determined only by the nature of the subject matter and the appetites and needs of the patrons.

2. Management of the IMC is turned over to a single director who is trained, experienced and enthused either in the area of print or in the area of newer media. Frequently this specialist has only peripheral concern for the family of materials with which he is least acquainted.

     The matter of staffing appears to be the keystone of a successful IMC. Its effectiveness is directly related to such things as the skill, knowledge and enthusiasm of the person or persons directing its activities, the amount of released time provided for these specialists, and the clerical help provided. As in other sectors of the school enterprise, *people* make the IMC work. Space, materials, equipment and the attendant funding implement their efforts to provide improved instruction.

     It seems highly improbable that both the full range of library responsibilities as well as all of the functions of an audio-visual specialist can be performed satisfactorily in any sizable school (300 or more) by one person. Ideally, the IMC is managed by a team approach which features harmonious assistance by two or more professionals, each well-qualified in his respective field.

     The need for this new breed of specialist has strong implications for our teacher preparation programs. It is extremely doubtful, however, that even a specialist well trained in library science as well as newer media management can find the time and energy to do justice to a well-developed IMC in any sizable school. The multiplicity of duties tend to overshadow the number of hours on the clock.

3. Sometimes the school's IMC is made the sole repository of multimedia resources and the only place in the school where their combined advantages can be experienced. Classrooms are left to carry on "business as usual."

Actually, the IMC is a place where all types of resources, equipment, and well-qualified personnel combine forces to offer opportunities for learning which were formerly provided only in those classrooms where a dedicated teacher gathered an abundance of varied materials and exhibited her confidence in the multimedia approach. To assure optimum learning outcomes, today's classrooms must also be so equipped and managed as to permit the reading of books, the use of projected and recorded materials, of radio, television, and programmed materials — in short, the use of the whole spectrum of traditional as well as newer aids to learning.

4. Finally, some IMC's are being constructed with a kind of permanency and finality which would suggest that the millenium has been reached

Since we have actually just crossed the threshold of a new era of mediated instruction, the planning of an IMC must include long-range considerations for possible expansion as new learning resources are developed.

A disquieting observation about IMC's has been made by James Finn, professor of education at the University of Southern California. Finn for many years has been considered one of the country's prime movers of audio-visual instruction. At a national conference on instructional materials in Austin, Texas last year he said, "The IMC concept to which this conference is addressing itself is outmoded."

Finn points to rapidly emerging technological developments such as remote access facilities, computer assisted instruction and television and claims that current conceptions of learning resource centers are fast becoming obsolete. His remarks only tend to emphasize the unavoidable conclusion that once set in motion, the application of modern technology to instruction results in dramatic and continuing change.

More Media, Services Found In Modern Resource Centers

Philip Lewis

When the traditional school library started to add record players, filmstrip iewers, and other equipment and facilities to its book, periodical and vertical ile collections, the metamorphosis from plain library to learning resource center egan. As emphasis moved toward more extensive use of media and associated oftware, learning packages and integrated media equipment developed. The esult was the evolution of a broader and more flexible concept for organizing naterials, equipment and services: the instructional materials center.

Recently, these centers have taken another step by including an even wider ariety of materials and providing "experience" facilities. For example, lab tations provide students with the opportunity to work with simulators or other elf-directed learning devices. This follows the trend toward self-directed ndividual study and flexible or modular scheduling.

Today, they are aptly called learning resource centers and are not only the eographic center of schools now, but have tended to become the focal point of lifferent kinds of educational activity.

The challenge to educators will continue to be how to best serve student nd teacher users of materials in terms of collecting, processing, retrieving and ataloging the devices and software available. Use can also spread to the ommunity at large, utilizing sophisticated electronic equipment.

Here are a few of the interesting approaches currently in operation:

- A loan selection of books, filmstrips, 8 mm film loops, records, tapes, overhead transparencies, models, study prints, and kits is offered by the Hampton, N.H., instructional materials center serving 12 schools. Each school has a complete card catalog of materials. Teachers fill out request forms and drop them in the delivery box at each school, where they are picked up three times a week.
- Separate resource centers for Portland, Ore., public schools are organized on a subject-matter basis, with materials restricted to a single subject or core of related subjects. All types of media are available in the resource centers. Departmental offices are also frequently included, providing facilities for student-teacher conferences.
- All ordering, processing, distribution and cataloging of books and A-V materials for elementary and junior high schools in the district is done at one school — McDonald — in Warminster, Pa. A file of annotations for all materials — paperbacks, films, filmstrips and other visual aids —

is also maintained here. Plans include duplication of heavily used titles and expansion to include tape cassettes.

- Library-media centers are found at both the elementary and intermediate school levels in Temple City, Calif. At Longdon Elementary, four classrooms of the same grade are arranged around a resource center. Classrooms have movable partitions which provide access to the center. The center has 55 carrels for viewing and listening.

- The entire Piney Woods School in Chattanooga, Tenn., is a research and demonstration center consisting of three basic organizational structures: self-contained, multigrade and team teaching in learning centers. The materials are located in centers grouped by three subject areas: language-social science, math-science-cultural arts, and family living-industrial arts. Students, under teacher guidance, decide how many 30 minute periods they will spend in a given center. Teachers review to see that certain objectives are realized, and there is a period at the end of each day when students return to their homerooms for a review of accomplishments.

The organization and operation of learning resource centers has not been standardized, nor is it apt to be. Concepts must remain varied and flexible so they can be tailored to differing needs of educational programs.

Independent Study Centers: Their Relation to the Central Library

J. Lloyd Trump

Is the school library obsolete? The study hall has disappeared in many schools because it was not a good place to study. How much better is the library as a locale for inquiry? Not much, I fear. Is it because of people — librarians, teachers, or administrators? Or is it because of things — the schedule or the physical facilities? Should we abolish the library as the next move to improve schools? Certainly not. But some basic changes are needed.

The heart of the school program is what is called independent study or learning. Here is where students "cover the subject" as determined by their teachers, go beyond the minimum essentials to inquire and to create as their individual interests and talents dictate; they learn how to learn, and develop more responsibility for their own learning. Today's teaching methods and school organization frequently get in the way of those pupil goals.

Reprinted from *NASSP Bulletin*, January 1966, by permission of the National Association of Secondary School Principals. Copyright, 1966, by the National Association of Secondary School Principals.

The typical classroom lacks adequate materials, and the rigid schedule pre-vents effective independent study. This same schedule, plus the usual teaching methods in self-contained or self-sufficient classrooms, also keep most students from effective independent study in the traditionally organized library. It is difficult to get to the library; it is even more difficult to stay there very long.

The typical library is frustrating to students for other reasons. They cannot find quickly what they want. The materials largely are documents to be read; other visual and audio materials are scarce or nonexistent. Students cannot talk and work together as needed because "Silence" is the key word. Record keeping makes it difficult to get materials out of the library to use elsewhere. Although librarians are sympathetic and want to help students, they lack sometimes the specialized knowledge in the subject that is needed.

Solving the foregoing problems requires basic alterations in our concepts of classroom instruction. Teaching roles and organizational patterns need changing. So do the roles of libraries and librarians. The changes involve team teaching, varying the size of pupil groups, flexible scheduling, using teacher aides and technical devices, improving evaluation, and altering educational facilities and finances.

Education has three dimensions. First, *large-group instruction* aims to moti-vate students, to give students information not readily available to them else-where, and to give assignments. Second, *small-group discussion* teaches oral and aural communication skills and better interpersonal relations. This article con-centrates on the third phase of the proposed changes: *independent study*.

Five kinds of facilities are needed for comprehensive independent study. How separate these facilities become depends on the size of the school, but one fact is certain — successful independent study requires more than the library, and more than an added room with audio-visual aids. The five facilities are: (1) the learning resources center, hereafter called LRC, (2) the library, (3) the conference area, (4) the relaxation space, and (5) the formal study room. Each facility is described in subsequent divisions of this article.

THE LEARNING RESOURCES CENTER

The LRC has two parts: the area for study and the area for more active work. The study area is where students read, listen, view, think, write, and converse informally — with frequently used materials at hand. The work area is where the specialized "tools of the trade" are available. Because the noise and activity levels vary between the two areas, they should be separate although close to each other in location. Certainly in all but the smaller schools, separate LRC areas are needed for each of the different areas of human knowledge that are called school subjects.

The science LRC, for example, in the study part of the facility, needs pupil carrels where students can work with quasi-privacy. A broad collection of science magazines, paperback books, textbooks, and references are at their fingertips in the room. Tape recorders, audio and video, are available with earphones so students can see and/or hear large group presentations, specially prepared materials for students of varied abilities or talents, and commercial materials. Some science programmed books or machines also are located here. The room's viewing area includes filmstrip, slide, and motion picture projectors, and other viewers. Dialing equipment, photographic and electronic copiers, microfilm readers, and similar items increasingly will be available.

The *workroom* of the science LRC is similar to today's laboratories in many respects. Although separate areas for botany, zoology, physics, and chemistry are identifiable , much more equipment than now is portable so that combination experiments can be conducted easier. Moreover, areas are provided where individual experiments lasting over a period of time can be protected.

The physical education LRC also provides a place where students can read, view, listen, think, and write with health, physical fitness, safety, and recreation materials readily at hand. The collection of audio and visual materials is more extensive than most schools possess today. The other part of the physical education LRC, namely, the gymnasium-fitness-practice room, is designed for students to learn and practice skills that can add to their health, fitness, and recreation, realizing that most students live in apartments, in houses on 50-foot lots, in urban, suburban, or rural settings, as the case may be. The LRC also provides facilities to teach basketball, swimming, golf, dancing, and the like — skills that are a part of general education for some students and vocational education for the specially talented and interested.

These two divisions of the LRC are needed in *every* subject area. Fine and practical arts students need to read, see, view, think, and write — and they also need the "tools of the trade" room. So do social studies, mathematics, and all other students. Some pupils need to work in reading laboratories — a part of the LRC in English.

These LRC rooms are supervised by instruction assistants — advanced undergraduate college students, housewives, retired teachers — carefully selected adults who are knowledgeable in the subject area to the degree of having completed at least two years of college work in it. Instruction assistants are used not only to save teacher time and energy, and costs, but also to keep teachers from supervising students too much. These assistants can answer most student questions, keep equipment in order, check on supplies, refer students to their teachers when necessary, assist in evaluation, and so on. The assistants are different in these respects from the librarian because they are specialized in the respective subject fields.

The LRC has the atmosphere of an office and workroom. Students move about and talk to each other on occasion. This is not a recreation room, or a "talking" room; neither is it a quiet room. As indicated later in the article, students can be removed from the privileges of working in the LRC when necessary.

Supervision of the LRC's is shared by the various teaching team or departmental leaders and the librarian. The librarian teaches the instruction assistants the techniques for managing, circulating, and storing materials. Also, the librarian assists in locating, ordering, and maintaining inventories. The team leaders evaluate the use of materials and take ameliorative actions after team or departmental discussions. The instruction assistants carry out the program. All of these persons are on guard to keep the LRC's from becoming miniature libraries of the conventional type. The LRC emphasis is on use rather than on storage.

THE LIBRARY

Some independent study occurs in the library. Two kinds of students use the library. There are those with advanced or unusual projects who find specialized resources located there. For example, less frequently used and specially valuable printed, audio, and visual references are kept there for safeguarding. Other students come to the library because it is a quiet place. They frequently bring most of their study materials with them. Strict silence is the rule.

No longer are students brought in class groups "to learn to use the library." In contrast, the librarian participates in large-group instruction in the different subject fields to help motivate the use of learning resource centers and the library. Instruction assistants in the LRC's and the library assistant complete the instruction as students "learn by doing" in those facilities. This whole process puts the librarian more in the center of the school's instruction program, meeting regularly with teaching teams, helping to evaluate the quality and quantity of independent study.

The library on this basis can be a smaller space than present standards specify. Also, it does not require tall ceilings, chandeliers, and other expensive artistic features that do not contribute to the foregoing stated purposes. More emphasis on function, however, does not necessarily produce ugliness; it redistributes expenditures in order to emphasize utility and productivity.

CONFERENCE AREAS

Just as adult workers gather to discuss their projects in order to solicit help and criticism from each other, so do students need to confer. Although some of these conferences of two, three, and four students may occur in the LRC, mostly they will take place elsewhere. These conferences in older buildings typically may be around tables in the cafeteria — apart from the lunch periods. New buildings can provide special conference rooms. However, in either case, provision for supervision is essential.

The conference area is not subject oriented. Thus students from various subject fields gather in the same area. The noise level in this room is quite high because many persons are talking at once. The instruction assistant(s) in charge maintain reasonable control. Of course, teachers frequently join students in these conferences.

Some conferences are teacher initiated. A selected group of students may need remedial or supplemental instruction to enable them to improve their independent study. Or a teacher may wish to talk with a particularly high-level group. These teacher-oriented conferences should be held in separate rooms.

THE RELAXATION SPACE

Students, like all of us, need a change of pace. The conventional school tends to deny students that privilege except for intermissions between classes — and even then teachers are stationed as policemen in the corridors to keep the students from relaxing too much. Teachers can visit the faculty lounge. The principal can leave his desk to go on an errand. But the students are in class or study hall all day — they are not supposed to relax!

A student lounge with an open snack bar is an essential ingredient of independent study. A general aide supervises the room to maintain reasonable order and to check the use of the room by various students. Of course, if certain students "goof off" too much, the privilege of using the room will be denied to them. However, until that happens, all students regardless of the level of their achievement need this space.

Some schools use a section of the cafeteria for the student lounge. Whatever the room, its location needs to be somewhat isolated so the natural noise of the room is sufficiently contained.

FORMAL STUDY ROOM

A few pupils — their number is smaller than most persons realize — cannot at the moment assume responsibility for their own learning. They need close supervision in a formal room similar to the old-fashioned study hall. A teacher is in charge who is successful in controlling students. However, the teacher needs also to possess competence and interest in helping students to solve the problems that resulted in their being there.

Pupils are assigned to the formal study room by instruction assistants or teachers. Some reasons for their being assigned are: causing disturbances in a LRC, library, conference room, or recreation space; spending too much time in the conference room or recreation space, needing more direction than the LRC and library provide; showing obvious need of constant supervision. Students are *not assigned* to the formal study room because their work is unsatisfactory in relation to their estimated potential. That problem is handled by counselors and teachers elsewhere.

The goal is to reduce to zero the number of students in the formal study room. Realistically, not more than one or two per cent of the students should be there.

SUMMARY

We suggest here a school quite different than the conventional school today. Independent study or learning occupies at least 40 per cent of the students' weekly schedule. The balance of the time is spent in large-group instruction and small-group discussion in spaces especially designed for those purposes. The conventional, multi-purpose classroom is not right for any of these teaching-learning activities — too small for instruction and unnecessarily large for discussion, and inadequately equipped for independent study. So the conventional classroom has to go, too!

The library changes with the classrooms. Along with the other four spaces described in this article, the library and the library staff are more in the mainstream of education than now and less a sideshow. Together, these five spaces used properly can change education in ways that for years have been sought after goals, namely, to individualize learning for students and to professionalize teaching for teachers. Working toward these kinds of arrangements challenges the courage and imagination of teachers, librarians, and school administrators.

Individualized Instruction

Dwight W. Allen

Achievement, not *time spent in class* should be the criterion for educational progress. Emphasis should be on the continuous development of responsibility rather than on a demanded metamorphosis at the time of college entrance or vocational employment. The only way educators can achieve continuous development of responsibility among their students is to provide for new levels of individualization within the school program.

Appropriate steps toward effective individualized instruction may include: Particularize opportunities for mastery of common material. Allow opportunity for more extensive practice or experience. Allow alternative topics to be considered. Differentiate levels of responsibility and control. Provide for more immediate information of accomplishments and difficulties. Increase the efficient use of staff, facilities, and time. Provide schedule flexibility.

Individualizing the design for a common goal is a matter of pacing, intensity and repetition of common materials. The rate and timing of achievement will vary from student to student. Too often we neglect to identify a definable standard of achievement which students are expected to master; we rely too often upon intuition and pious hopes. Without definable and precise standards of achievement, there is no way to diagnose student differences or to develop individualized instruction. Evaluation tends to be time oriented; we ask students to confront a body of general instructional materials in a "reasonable time," hoping that such exposure will in some way be equated with learning.

Individualization will occur as one decides which of several alternatives is appropriate for any one student on the basis of interest and ability. The same level of performance definition is necessary, however, if the alternatives are to have significance.

When the goal itself is a matter of individual determination, the selection of material is uniquely determined for each situation. The student and his teacher must decide the means of attack, the depth of investigation, the appropriate extent of study, the elements contributing a reasonable expectation for mastery of material, and finally a specific program designed to cover the agreed-upon performances. This does not mean that all learning must be deductive. Often the performance definitions will be open-ended. The student may be asked to develop alternatives, to go beyond the materials he has studied, to make new syntheses. Precise definitions of the outcomes of learning are entirely compatible with learning, variously described as inductive, discovery, or inquiry.

Individualization is a type of instruction in which the student engages in activities uniquely appropriate to his learning. This type of instruction promotes independence, provides opportunities for study beyond the regular curriculum, and permits maximum use of instructional resources.

The concept of individual instruction does *not* necessarily mean the teacher must deal with students one at a time; it means that presentation and choice of materials for the individual student should be appropriate for him at that time. The goal of individualization is not a tutorial situation, but an appropriate instructional content for each student. If a basic and common presentation is given to all students, some are immediately ready for the next presentation, some need additional presentations, some need individual and independent study, and some need discussion of the material in a group situation. The problem here is to identify groups ready for a series of alternatives and to provide that series of alternatives. Some might be repetition, some elaboration, some a presentation of the same material from a different point of view or perspective.

The unfortunate organizational constraints of the present program have prevented us from gaining any real perspective on individualized instruction, except as a strictly tutorial situation. Providing more varied instructional group-ings — larger and smaller classes, longer and shorter classes, meetings of varied frequency — suggest wider ranges of alternatives for individualized instruction. Individualization can be stimulated within the formal classroom or it may take place as one phase of laboratory instruction. It can be developed by efficient grouping practices for either short or long term. Class facilities can be utilized on an individual basis with the requisition of unused classroom seats or unused laboratory stations; auxiliary spaces may serve the purpose in the library, in vacant classrooms, or in supplementary facilities such as the cafeteria; specifi-cally designed spaces for individual and independent study or for formal or informal small groups are also particularly adaptable to this type of instruction. Resource centers may be planned specifically for individual study in a given subject with individual carrels and technical centers for such activities as pro-grammed learning or linguistic practice. The emphasis on individualization of materials, and independent study as a basic type of instruction, assumes facili-ties and organizational alternatives not commonly provided at present. There is a need to develop new concepts.

The *resource center* is an integral part of the instructional program. It is a site for personal, individual study. It is a center for supervised practice and remediation. It equalizes study conditions and reduces mislearning.

Each resource center serves a precisely defined group of courses and subject areas. A resource center typically would be established within a department, as distinguished from the general purpose area of the library. The resource center is program oriented; the library is materials oriented. The resource center may have library books assigned to it, usually on a temporary basis. The maintenance of a resource center, including the ordering of materials, is properly under the control of teachers, not the librarian.

Resource centers are typically available to students at their discretion, although formal assignment is possible. The center is not a departmentalized library, but is designed for the particular program it serves. It is the administrative center for individual courses or subject areas and it is used for the distribution and collection of materials. Teachers should not have to spend instructional time passing out materials. Student records and historical records of assignments, tests, and evaluations may be maintained in the resource center.

The resource center may be a diagnostic center for initial placement, reassignment, and remediation. It may function as an information center for courses; teachers may file assignments and requirements in the center. Students may come to the center for make-up work after absence, freeing teachers from another bothersome administrative detail. It may be used for information on advance assignments for those students who wish to work ahead, thereby providing an impetus for student responsibility. It may function for guidance purposes so that teachers can easily find students' records and progress reports. It may be useful for teachers in other subject areas and courses for immediate information regarding coordination of requirements, cutting down student work-load, and cutting over-lapping in scheduled assignments. It functions as a center for specialized individual instruction, providing for programmed learning, a viewing area for audio-visual materials, and for specialized individual projects.

The potential value of a resource center is realized only when school programs provide substantial time for individual study. Practice and study under supervision reduces mislearning. Remedial help is provided as needed by professional staff. Individual help is available within the school day. Experiments have indicated that a better atmosphere is created when students have the choice of when they will use the center. Marshall High School in Portland, Oregon, has no discipline problems in the centers because students go there only if they want to study.

With resource centers available, students can be released to independent study time if a teacher is absent. The need for short-term substitutes is eliminated. The resource center is better than a baby sitter.

Such centers require coordination of multiple staff. Teachers must anticipate program needs in advance, and goals must be clearly defined. Teachers must accept responsibility for directing the study of students they are not teaching in their own classrooms. Non-professional staff must be added to assume the burdens of non-professional or administrative trivia.

At Marshall High School, formal instructional responsibilities average between 45-50 per cent of a teacher's day. Working in the resource centers becomes a planned part of teacher work-load.

Provision must be made for professional staff (the senior teacher, staff teachers, first-year teachers, and intern teachers), and for supporting staff (teaching assistants, technical assistants, clerical assistants, and specialists from the community).

Lack of facilities need not prevent any school from developing a resource center individual study program, but planning for efficient use of facilities is essential. Resource centers require provision for storage, retrieval and display of materials. Study carrels are necessary for individual study as are small-group spaces with acoustical separation. Media facilities for audio-visual display are needed, as well as acoustical treatment of walls, floors and ceilings. If the centers are to function smoothly, conveniently located teacher offices are required.

With the establishment of resource centers, the point of psychological identification for students may occur as association between teachers and students in resource centers, rather than in formal classrooms. Teachers and students might be matched by mutual compatibility for academic advisement instead of typical guidance procedures where one counsellor may be assigned as many as 350 students. Identification of mutual compatibility is feasible in an environment designed to maximize individual instruction.

The *open laboratory* is appropriately used in the instructional program when instruction requiring special facilities can be individualized and if specific performance criteria can be defined. Whereas in the resource center the concept could be used with or without pre-scheduling, in the open laboratory the essential idea is that students are free to schedule their time as necessary to complete specific performance goals, within certain time restrictions.

The open laboratory is an impetus to the careful definition of performance objectives. In one high school using an open laboratory, the teacher found that several students had finished the first year of drafting by November. They were allowed to start the second year of drafting, and by the end of June, a few students had finished three years of drafting. Other students had not finished performance criteria for the first year. Remedial students in this subject could be given an incomplete in June and complete requirements the following autumn. Grades can be determined by the quality of performance in meeting each objective. Eventually the criteria of grades may be bypassed if performance criteria are successfully met; a student's education can be described in terms of the performance criteria he has mastered.

When open laboratories are maintained, students can anticipate their own requirements, allowing more or less than average time as they deem appropriate. Limited laboratory experiences may be introduced as necessary in traditionally non-laboratory courses. Students may be easily scheduled to use more than one laboratory facility for a single course. A wider range of alternatives may be routinely accommodated in open laboratories than in laboratory experiences tied to a fixed time schedule. Re-grouping and re-assignment of students can be accomplished whenever achievement warrants a change. A flexible rotation system is possible with adaptation of the open laboratory and student responsibility is increased.

A diversified range of offerings is possible within staff and facility limitations, giving leeway for special tasks. Staff time and facilities can be used more effectively and efficiently.

Certain disadvantages must also be considered. Logistics are complex. Supplies can offer difficulties, especially perishables such as those needed for a homemaking class. Difficulties can arise over the set-up of equipment unless students are trained to set up and replace equipment themselves. Under the traditional schedule of 50-minute periods, no time is available for experimentation if students are responsible for the equipment they use; flexible scheduling is essential. Storage and availability of equipment may be chaotic if students are working with several types of equipment simultaneously. There is increased opportunity for supply and equipment loss because it is harder to maintain consistent control. Student training is essential in the use of the open laboratory as a preventive of such problems. Requirements for multiple-class teaching and recording student progress offer difficulties. The open laboratory could be expensive in terms of staff time and requirements in areas of small enrollment. There may be an uneven demand on facilities so that a set of priorities must be established.

Considerations regarding staff and facilities are necessary in planning for open laboratories. There must be proximity between teacher offices and the open laboratories for effective utilization of this type of instruction. Facilities must be designed for students to be responsible for the equipment they are using, with additional provision for multiple-session projects.

If the school maintains classes of approximately 30 students for a significant part of the program, then the problem arises as to where to find time for students to individualize the time they study in the open laboratory. The total school program must be opened up so that the individualization of the open laboratory is real rather than imaginary.

The assignment of staff to the open laboratory is another important factor for consideration. Who gets the job of supervising in the laboratory — and when? What kind of administrative constraints are necessary to insure some minimal level in monitoring and recording student progress? What remedial procedures will be utilized for unsuccessful students? What procedures will be developed for keeping track of supplies and equipment? One solution for combating the overflow of demands on facilities is the establishment of priority requests. The laboratory must be coordinated with other phases of specific courses and administrators must decide how to make the laboratory a part of the total program.

Currently many activities which are actually independent study activities have to be planned only within the context of the classroom because of the demands of equipment. Substantial allowance for individual study within the framework of the school day, however, makes it possible for the student to have facilities available beyond these limitations. Study-skill sessions beyond scheduled class time may be assigned in the laboratory or resource center.

New concepts of indpendent study introduce a flexibility within the school day which gives the student a new range of learning situations. This makes possible different kinds of demands on his performance and suggests a re-definition of what he can or should learn.

More on Learning Resource Centers

Doris W. Like

Education is not a process of memorizing facts and dates, nor is it merely the ability to recall the facts and dates as needed. Education is learning where to seek the information that is required and knowing how to use that information once it is found. In a nation of television viewers who placidly lounge in front of the screen, too often believing everything they see and hear, children must be taught to think for themselves, using more than one source for information and analyzing what they have seen or heard.

New directions in the traditional elementary library have been brought about by the happy marriage of human resources and multimedia resources (printed and audio-visual forms of communication and accompanying technology). Today's library facility recognizes the individual student by establishing centers of learning that seek to fit the curriculum to the child rather than the child to the curriculum. Resource centers help students become independent, self-directed learners by providing normal library content plus audio tapes, filmstrips, records, film loops, slides, picture files, charts, maps, vertical files, tape recorders, filmstrip projectors and viewers, record players, 16 mm projectors, models, and listening centers — all designed for student users.

Reprinted from *Childhood Education*, January 1970, by permission of Doris W. Like and the Association for Childhood Education International, Washington, D.C. Copyright © 1970 by the Association.

The American Library Association and the National Education Association recently established significant new standards for school media programs:

> The pupil will not only need to learn skills of reading but those of observa tion, listening, and social interaction. He will need to develop a spirit o inquiry, self-motivation, self-discipline, and self-evaluation . . . Media are in the format most appropriate for the learning task. The emphasis is alway: upon the learner and upon the function of the media staff as a supportive arm to the teacher in achieving the goals of the instructional program . . The media program is indispensable in the educational programs that now stress individualization, inquiry, and independent learning for students . . The move away from textbook-dominated teaching has made the schoo media center a primary instructional center that supports, complements and expands the work of the classroom.*

Neither the establishment of standards, however, nor the availability o funds to purchase a melange of materials and equipment will ensure success of a resource center. These are only preliminary steps. The attitude of the teacher and students toward use of such a center is what ultimately contributes to achievement of the goal of individualizing for each student.

Greater effectiveness accrues when the contents of a resource center are listed in card files by subject, giving the student a list of all information on hi particular subject. Wider student utilization comes about when the materials are also shelved by major subject areas; e.g., science and social studies. Perhaps the easiest way to begin a resource center is to begin with the vertical file by subscribing to the *Educator's Guide to Free Materials*. For the cost of a postage stamp, free materials can be received from almost every major industry, many U.S. government services, city chambers of commerce, state capitols, etc. Many booklets are sent in classroom quantities and include teaching guides. Student add to the vertical file by including units or reports they have developed. The latter may include overhead transparencies, stories, drawings, and the like.

Audio tapes not only complement the curriculum but help children who have reading difficulties or who, because of limited cultural background, would be unable to understand more advanced material. Teachers and parents car record their own tapes; professional announcers are not needed. A child whose assignment leads him to a science chapter that he cannot understand would normally be discouraged; not so the child whose teacher knows his students reading abilities and records the chapter for those students to hear as they follow in the book. Many students are capable of more extensive research than they are able to read and, by means of tapes, are able to progress beyond their "reading ability." More advanced students, on the other hand, can use tapes for enrich- ment. Professional tapes for math, history, science and language arts are already

---

*American Library Association and National Education Association, *Standards for School Media Programs*, 1969 edition. Reprinted by permission.

n the market. Some state education agencies and regional service centers urnish free tape duplicating service to school districts.

Usage of the tape library is limited only by teachers' imaginations. Taping pelling tests, sentence dictation, etc., frees the teacher to work with individual tudents and allows the student to progress through spelling assignments as apidly or slowly as meets his needs. The student learns to use the equipment roperly and assumes the responsibility of helping to plan his own spelling rogram.

Many so-called discipline problems in the classroom are manifestations of eading problems, non-English-speaking backgrounds, or boredom. A resource enter is no panacea for such problems. But if its uses are clearly understood by eachers and students and it carries a minimum of rules and regulations, it can be major factor in helping children develop self-discipline, self-motivation, interest nd leadership while improving their ability to think critically through research nd acquire skills — instruction not normally available in a self-contained class-oom. The student who is confident that he can find success in his assignment or dvance beyond the minimum requirements is a student who is happily produc-ive.

When studying about life in a particular country, the student who has easy ccess to filmstrips, pictures, magazines, records and tapes in addition to his extbooks does indeed receive a broader background in understanding other eople and how they live in relation to his own life. Often a filmstrip or film hat is shown once to a large group of students is then used many times by ndividual students seeking specific information or having special interests. Math nd science filmstrips reinforce concepts presented by the teacher in class. Avail-bility of filmstrips for individual use by a student, whether researching a given ssignment or seeking information of personal interest, has a tremendous effect n the independence of the child. The attitude of the learner toward himself — is own feeling of self-worth — is improved when he is capable of using equip-ment and materials as he is ready for them, desires to use them, and knows how o use the information he finds.

Every area of the curriculum can be improved by using multimedia. nclusion of a closed circuit television system in the schools serves a very impor-ant auxiliary purpose when the videotaping of a class presentation, whether by tudent or teacher, allows the opportunity to view oneself "in action."

The equipping and managing of a resource center varies from school to chool. Whether a multimedia specialist, a paraprofessional, parents, teachers, or combination of these persons directs the center, it must be equipped and built with the user in mind — recognizing that he is the one who must be taught to use nd operate the equipment and materials; that he is as responsible for them as ny adult; that he is considered a contributing member of the teaching-learning rocess; and that above all he is free to regard it as a place for him to continue his education in a relaxed, informal atmosphere with a minimum of rules and regulations. Such a center will meet the needs of the individual learner.

We all *know* the necessary ingredients to help a child develop as an individual but sometimes find it difficult to consider individual abilities, achievements, strengths and weaknesses when we must work with groups of children of varying degrees of each. The resource center can help in this all-important task.

Creative teacher, begin a resource center for your self-contained classroom. The odds are your neighbor will ask to use it and contribute his ideas, and the materials stored in a cardboard box will turn into a beehive of activity where children learn by living! All *really* need are a couple of cardboard boxes, imagination, students eager to research; and you are on the way!

REFERENCES

Allen, R. Van. "Grouping Through Learning Centers." *Childhood Education* 45,4 (December 1968) : 200-203.
Childhood Education 43,2 (October 1966). "The Modern Library."
Davis, Sara. "A Teaching and Learning Environment." *Childhood Education* 43,5 (January 1967) : 271-75.
Veatch, Jeannette. "Improving Independent Study." *Childhood Education* 43,5 (January 1967) : 284-88.

Basic Education Resource Centers for Adults

Leo J. Cantelope

New Jersey's adult population is such that an acute need for basic education exists throughout the state. Vast areas in South Jersey are devoted to vegetable farming, and hundreds of migrant workers have flocked there from other states and Puerto Rico. Not all of them are seasonal visitors, many have established permanent homes. Likewise, the congested industrial communities of the north, particularly Jersey City and Newark, have attracted large numbers of Puerto Ricans and Cubans. Situated as it is, adjacent to New York State, New Jersey has always received a large percentage of "fall-out" from the huge incoming quota of immigrants that poured into New York City's port of entry. And, of course, the state has its usual share of dropouts and natives who have successfully evaded

Reprinted from *The Clearing House*, October 1968, by permission of the publisher.

the compulsory school law. In all, the 1960 census revealed that New Jersey had 740,000 adults, 25 years of age and over, lacking the equivalent of an eighth grade schooling. Thus, the Adult Basic Education Program was welcomed in the Garden State as the answer to an educational need of significant magnitude.

In the early days of the Economic Opportunity Act's operation, it was recognized by the adult education leadership of the state that some meaningful marriage was necessary between the colleges and the public schools if the adult basic education program was to achieve its desired potential. Although an excellent program of this nature has been carried on for years under the public schools of the state, they simply did not possess the funds and resources necessary to accommodate the numbers envisioned under the expanded adult basic education operation of Title II-B. More teachers needed to be trained, materials needed to be produced, and local directors of adult education needed to be advised with respect to program planning.

Accordingly, four state colleges — Glassboro, Newark, Jersey City, and Montclair — were approached by representatives of the State Education Department and the Office of Economic Opportunity. These discussions resulted in a cooperative plan under which the colleges agreed to set up resource centers designed to serve the adult basic education programs of the public schools in their respective geographical areas.

The understanding reached by the architects of the plan provided for the initial costs of the centers — and the first year's operation — to be financed by funds from Title II-B. These funds were to continue to support the undertaking in each college until such time as the college budget enabled it to absorb the cost of the center's operation through its own sources of revenue. It was also envisioned by those who participated in the original planning that although the center's initial activities would be limited to serving the adult basic education program future development should entail the expansion of the program to serve the total field of adult education.

These centers have now been in operation three years. All parties concerned are highly pleased with their progress. Dr. Clyde Weinhold, Director of Adult Education with the State Education Department, under whose guiding hand the venture has developed, is convinced the adult basic education program in New Jersey owes much of its success to the help that has been given by the colleges in this cooperative undertaking.

One factor contributing to the professional quality of their service has been the caliber of their leadership. Ray Ast, Director of the Montclair Center, has long been recognized as a national leader in adult education, with involvement in many AEA and NAPSAE activities. Dr. Livingston Cross, Director of the Glassboro Center, is a veteran of many years dedicated service in the field of migrant education. Joseph Tiscornia and Mrs. Dorothy Minkoff, Directors of the Centers at Jersey City and Newark, respectively are, likewise, leaders of highest stature in New Jersey educational circles.

These resource centers were charged with the responsibility of providing a menu of comprehensive service to the adult basic education programs in their areas. The following types of activities were envisioned by the authors of the program:

1. The creation of pre-service and in-service training programs for the teachers on the Adult Basic Education programs.
2. The provision for consultative services in adult education to the school districts and community groups in their regions.
3. The establishment of libraries and information centers containing both curricular and professional materials in adult education.
4. The review and evaluation of curricular materials in adult basic education.
5. The initiation of adult education courses, at both undergraduate and graduate levels, in the curriculum of the college.

Abundant evidence that these responsibilities were carried out in richest measure is found in the reports from the centers covering this first year of operation. In spite of the time lost and problems encountered in getting a new program underway, a great deal was accomplished. Over 800 teachers of adult basic education received some form of specialized training. Eighty-seven school districts were contacted with some form of aid. Many non-school community organizations were given assistance. A total of 43 programs and activities were held "off campus," indicating the willingness of the center leadership to take the service out into the community where the problems exist.

In addition to these major accomplishments, countless other special forms of assistance were extended by the four centers. Designed to enhance and enrich the cause of adult education in New Jersey, they included: a pilot project consisting of the introduction of concepts from Structural and Transformational Linguistics into the teaching of adult functional illiterates, production of a training film depicting the nature and psychology of the adult learner and its relationship to effective teaching, the development of a manual of teaching units and lesson plans, librarian workshops, and the development of guidance, counseling and testing procedures.

This project was conceived and launched as a part of a total effort which is now underway in behalf of adult education in the Garden State. The first legislation providing state financial aid for adult education under the public schools was passed only two years ago. This law provides for the state to pay two-thirds the salary of the local director of adult education up to a limit of $12,000 on the state's share. Governor Richard Hughes, acknowledged as one of the staunchest friends of adult education in the nation, recently created a Literacy Task Force composed of some of the state's leaders of adult education. Rutgers, the

State University, has been providing courses in adult education under the leadership of Dr. Ernest McMahon for some time. All of these factors contribute to a climate of high promise for the future of adult education in New Jersey.

One of the frustrating deterrents to the progress of adult education in this country has been the problems of professional training of its personnel, both teachers and administrators. For most people, adult education is still a moonlighting business. This is particularly true of the adult education teacher. Few have the opportunity for full-time employment in this field. We cannot expect them, therefore, to spend the time necessary for adequate training in our teacher-training institutions if it takes them away from their regular jobs. Their training must be acquired while they are on the job. Furthermore, it must be available in some place that does not require them to travel far from home.

Then, too, there has been another roadblock to the adequate training of adult education personnel. This is the simple fact that not many institutions of higher education in this country have the faculty and the resources necessary for the job that needs to be done. This is particularly true of the training needed by teachers in the specific field of adult basic education.

Against the background of these factors, the college resource center concept, as conceived and implemented in New Jersey, seems to provide a satisfactory answer to the problem. Federal funds were used to establish the program and sustain it until such time as the college can take over their responsibility. Parenthetically, it should be mentioned at this point that discussions with the presidents of all the colleges mentioned here seem to indicate that this can and will be done, if and when federal funds are withdrawn. With the college situated within close geographical proximity to the teachers who need the training, it is easy for them to acquire it while on the job.

Perhaps the most important aspect of this innovation is the fact that it is consonant with traditional American educational philosophy. The public schools have always looked to the colleges and universities for the education of their professional leadership. At the moment, the institutions of higher education are handicapped by a lack of funds and resources. This project points the way for this difficulty to be overcome with a mutual advantage accruing to all parties concerned. Inasmuch as the new title relating to adult education under the Elementary and Secondary Act provides for a percentage of its funds to be spent for training, the initiation of similar activities in the future may be a possibility. If so, other states may wish to consider the New Jersey innovation of college resource centers as a model to be followed in the development of their adult education program.

SECTION TWO / LEARNING RESOURCE CENTERS IN THE ELEMENTARY SCHOOL

Educational Center Provides Variety

Richard E. Tenhaken

"An Educational Center to incorporate the best present educational thinking with sufficient flexibility to be adaptable for future changes, built at a reasonable cost," was the challenge presented to the architect by Ticonderoga Central School District officials. The design and plan which evolved out of many discussions and trials is exciting, extremely functional, meets the needs and expectations of the locality, and captured the imagination of the many persons who participated in planning the Chet F. Harritt School.

The educational program was to provide for the many varied and changing interests and needs of the students as well as their difference in maturation. This necessitated areas and resources not usually found in a typical school or in a classroom-oriented situation. It required specialized areas, a comprehensive resource center, and facilities for small and large group instruction. It also required a setting to provide for individual development and a place to pursue individual interest. This necessitated "opening up" the school in order to create a total educational area in which the students could move easily and purposefully in order to take advantage of these resources.

The Educational Center complex for 1,100 students provides an elementary section, grades 1-5 with a separate Kindergarten facility and a middle school, grades 6-8, surrounding a shared cafetorium and a three-station gymnasium.

An "open" concept was utilized in the design. An attempt was made to integrate all aspects and areas of the complex. The whole educational area is to be available or open to the student in his educational pursuits. Walls which formerly separated the classrooms from the corridor have been eliminated; cabinets, seven feet high, are used as a partial divider. These cabinets are used for the students' coats and for storage of instructional materials. Two openings, each four feet wide, enhance the "open" concept. Only a relatively few doors have been used in the total educational complex.

The Resource Center, located in the center of each facility, elementary and middle, becomes the focal point in the Educational Center. Thus, the Resource Center becomes, in effect, an extension of the learning areas. Each student and teacher has greater access to educational opportunities because of the integration of resource and learning areas.

General construction costs in the 105,712-sq. ft. structure amounted to $1,099,600. Heating and ventilating costs totalled $247,608; plumbing cost

$159,400, and electrical work cost $217,000. Total construction costs amounted to $1,723,608, or $16.57 per sq. ft.

The Harritt Educational Center design *received a special citation from the School Building Architectural Exhibit Jury of the American Association of School Administrators* when the group met in Washington, D.C., and the plan was on exhibit at the Atlantic City meeting of the AASA.

The Kindergarten unit is separate to provide for an easy transition from home to school. The multi-colored, carpeted structure provides a warm environment in which the child may become accustomed and adjusted to his peers and further develop the necessary social skills. Readiness for learning is achieved by means of flexible arrangements permitting individual, small and larger group participation.

ELEMENTARY SCHOOL FACILITY

The Kindergarten pupils have their own entrance and play area. Early and easy identification with their environment in a relatively small setting increases their feeling of security and enables further educational progress to develop.

The Resource Center, comprising library and audio-visual materials and equipment, a science room and an art room, is designed to provide appropriately for the changing needs, interests, and abilities of the students as they mature. The library area for the primary children includes a tiered, carpeted storytelling and instruction center, complete with floor-level tables and cushions. The more mature, intermediate-aged children are provided with appropriate-sized furniture and materials.

Books, paperbacks, records, tapes, and magazines are readily available to students and teachers. Provision has been made for a future sound console and listening stations.

The 42-in. high book stacks and a generous use of colored tackboard provide a setting conducive to extensive utilization by students.

With only the book stacks separating the library from the classrooms, plus wide carpeted openings, students will be able to move easily in and out of this area. Psychological and physical barriers separating the student from this center where individual interests and abilities can be explored and developed are at a minimum.

SCIENCE AND ART AREAS

A science area and a separate art area combine to provide further educational opportunities for the student. Provisions have been made for regular class instruction in these areas. They also serve as a resource area for students and teachers at other times. Science materials, exhibits and displays and art materials such as paintings, statues, and other items are arranged to be accessible and visible to all other children in the learning areas.

A tiered, carpeted learning area for approximately 75 students completes this center. No seats are provided, allowing maximum flexibility, utilizing the natural tendency for children of this age to sit on the floor. Students sit and stand directly on the carpeted tiers. *This will be used for large group instruction, movies, plays, and whatever else imaginative teachers and students feel is appropriate.*

MIDDLE EDUCATIONAL UNIT

Each learning area has a work area, sink and water supplemented by movable storage and work-area cabinets. Direct exit to the outside from each learning area is provided by means of sliding glass doors. Individual and small group instruction is easily accomplished by the arrangement of the area. The Special Education Room is spacious, flexible, and a delightful "room within a room."

The Library in the center of the area is the focal point of this facility and truly is a learning center. The inclusion of a listening room, a lounge with appropriate furniture, a reference area, and spaces for books, paperbooks, tapes, magazines, records, and other audio-visual supplies and equipment, as well as provision for micro-films make this a very functional, flexible, and inviting area.

The two science areas, one with physical emphasis and the other with a biological emphasis, with the student laboratory tables, chalkscreen rear projection unit, and other appropriate equipment, enable students to obtain a strong science background.

The Art, Home Economics, and Industrial Arts areas all contribute markedly to the educational opportunities available to the students in grades six, seven, and eight.

A large, tiered learning area in which approximately 80 students can gather provides additional flexibility and strengthening of the educational program.

Movable partitions in each learning facility enhance the flexibility and enable the faculty to provide a wider range of activities. *Conference areas provide a suitable location for student-teacher, parent-teacher, and teacher-teacher meetings as well as small groups of students.*

EACH UNIT HAS GYM AREA

The gymnasium and locker rooms are designed to separate the elementary from the middle facility students for instruction and while taking showers. Each unit has its own gym area. However, the movable partitions may be opened to provide 6,990 square feet of gym space, if desired.

Ticonderoga's Educational Center provides its students and community with what we believe is one of the finest educational facilities in the country. This provides each child an opportunity to develop his abilities to an extent never before possible in our area. It incorporates many things which have been shown to be beneficial in the learning process. With proper utilization by talented and able educators, great achievements can be accomplished.

Science Resource Center

Earl Brakken

Are you interested in the new science curriculum? Do you find yourself wondering how it could be introduced in your school?

Today many teachers are becoming excited about new science materials. They want to implement a new science curriculum with student-use materials, but budget limitations stand in their way. The science resource center offers a solution to this problem which can be justified in terms of both program and cost.

Let's assume that there are three sections of each grade level within a building. Under a traditional arrangement, there might be $50 to $100 per classroom available for science-related equipment. There would be a textbook for each child, and perhaps some supplementary printed materials stored in the room, with more science materials housed in the library. Each teacher would spend a portion of the teaching week on science, but lack of equipment would likely prevent individual student activity, and lack of science background could possibly hinder teacher demonstrations.

In contrast, suppose that one area, possibly a regular classroom, could be designated exclusively as a science center. An equipment budget of $900 to $1800 would immediately become available. Rather than individual texts, there would be one set per grade level, plus some spares to be checked out for individual work outside of class. The school would be able to provide multiple texts or a broader range of supplementary materials in place of the extra sets of a

Reprinted from *Instructor*, April 1969, by permission from Instructor, © Instructor Publications, Inc.

single text, and far more materials could be provided for individualized instruction.

Establishment of such a center could also make possible the adoption of one of the new curricular approaches entailing use of rather sophisticated and often expensive teaching kits. Such kits, which frequently are not practical for individual classrooms, become feasible on a shared basis. This is even more true in projects which have extensive audio-visual materials and other supplements associated with them.

The setting for a resource center obviously varies depending on the school. Ideally, facilities are included in the initial school plan and specifically tailored, but such possibilities are rare. In converting a classroom, one with an outside wall should be selected if possible, so that it can have exhaust venting, an important consideration. There should be installation of many multiple electrical outlets. Running water and several sinks for washing glassware and disposing of waste chemicals are desirable and may involve special plumbing installations.

Desks and other fixed furniture should be removed in favor of tables and adequate shelving. Science tables which fold up into the wall are specially practical. Tables located around the perimeter of the room are useful for project work and those along the window wall especially provide for plant study. A guideline to keep in mind is the prime need for both storage and work area.

Small adjacent project rooms are valuable additions to a science center. They allow for individual work and temporary storage of it without interfering with a total class activity. They are almost a requisite where flexible scheduling is employed. Some schools have used vacant hallway space, former coatrooms, or storage areas for such project areas.

If your school is to have a science center, how is it to be manned? One answer is to have one teacher who has a particular science emphasis to direct the center, but for all teachers to use it with their classes on a scheduled basis. The science specialist holds workshops to orient the classroom teachers. He also works especially with new teachers. Overall, he assumes leadership in the total science program of the school and teachers turn to him for help at any time.

In a large school, the science specialist might be a full-time job. However, in many schools, curriculum emphasis is assigned to regular classroom teachers who are relieved of other duties to compensate.

A second answer, and one I favor, is specialization of instruction — that is, having children go to the science center to be taught by the science teacher. Specialization is, of course, an answer to the problem of adequate teacher preparation in science, and in the other curriculum areas as well. Assigning a teacher with a particular interest and facility in science to teach science works well in elementary schools in urban areas, and in consolidated districts where multiple sections of a grade make departmentalization administratively simple.

Such a specialist can be expected, as part of his assignment, to keep up-to-date on significant curriculum developments and new materials. The typical classroom teacher or administrator, in my opinion, can hardly be expected to do an adequate job of this on a total subject-area basis.

Adjustments in school organization are, of course, necessary. One approach is to totally departmentalize for certain subjects so that each teacher involved has an area of specialization. Children move from one teacher to another as they will later do in the junior and senior high school.

In systems with several elementary schools in near proximity and where most of the children are transported, it would be possible to set up K-4 and 5-8 schools or some other arrangement that would allow more sections of one grade level within a building. Then the center and a specialized teacher can work even more effectively.

A third scheduling technique is flexible or modular scheduling, which would allow more and smaller groups to use the center. This system would also provide free time in the schedule so that those who wished to work on individual assignments, or those with special science interests, could utilize the center beyond the normal periods.

The resource center is useful at all elementary grade levels. With new science curriculum available as early as kindergarten, it should be used at every grade level, whatever the organizational technique.

When discussing whether such a plan should be implemented in your school, you should not consider it from the angle of whether you should make such a radical change. Instead, you might see if there is any defense for not having a science resource center. It is a must for bringing together today's children and today's learning materials in a rich program.

Instructional Materials Centers

Nina J. Mahaffey

Children, bless them! They ask questions. More than ever now because they have more things to wonder about. And the more answers they find, the more questions they ask. Isn't this what we want? Children who keep their natural curiosity and continue questioning throughout their entire lives? Questioners are thinkers and these we need. It is when we stop questioning that we become prey

Reprinted by permission from *Arizona Teacher*, volume 55, May 1967. Copyright 1967 Arizona Education Association.

to any idea put before us as truth. Our problem is simply to keep questions coming.

If answers are great question stimulators (and who having known children can doubt it) we must make answers available. This means giving children respectful answers always but it also means teaching them how to find their own answers and thus encouraging them to pursue learning by their own initiative. With direction and guidance certainly, but primarily under their own steam.

To provide answers, our schools must have an abundance of instructional materials and these materials must be available and accessible to all children. A fourth grader must be able to use seventh grade or second grade material if he needs it. If we think of the span of different abilities and interests represented in a single classroom, the material needed for question answering is mountainous indeed. Even homogeneous grouping doesn't take care of differing interests and the ability range is narrowed but not closed. No classroom is large enough to hold everything needed nor do we have money to provide all the unnecessary duplication this system entails.

Nearly all educators are agreed that a better way to provide the abundance needed is to centralize materials in one or more places in a school and permit individual children and teachers to borrow whatever is needed at the appropriate time. This not only makes a wider selection available to all children at less cost, it also relieves teachers of added routines.

Now that we are on the far side of the bush, it is time to call a spade a spade. The only trouble is, this spade has many handles. Long ago, when all supplementary materials were printed, the more forward looking schools gathered them together and called the place a library. Then someone took Confucius seriously, added the sound concept, and informational material began taking on many forms. Most of us lost sight of content, saw only the variations in form and developed separate centralized collections of non-print materials into audio-visual departments. Some libraries absorbed the new types of materials and we have been thinking up new names for the libraries ever since.

We are not concerned here with either the names by which all these collections are known or whether the administrative organization is single or dual. We are concerned with the importance of making an abundance of all kinds of materials freely and easily accessible for use by children and teachers. The single or dual type of organization can do this and do it well, but for the sake of brevity we will refer to all organizational patterns as Instructional Materials Centers (IMC's).

Yes, our schools need IMC's with ample resources and facilities because our children need answers. But let's remember to put the emphasis where it belongs, on the importance of children, not materials. The most extensive collection is worthless if it is unavailable or inaccessible when a child needs an answer. The rigidly scheduled weekly "library class" doesn't meet the child's needs. His questions simply do not come at evenly spaced intervals. This brings up all kinds of administrative problems but solutions should be sought, always with the child's best interest in mind.

Finally, but really first instead of last in importance to the IMC, is its professional and clerical staff. The professionals are teachers first and IMC'ers second. They know children, they know instructional methods and they know materials. Their job is to make children welcome and comfortable and to help them find answers. This involves teaching them where and how to look and letting them alone when they are finding what they need, even if they are a little noisy doing it. It also involves promoting appreciation for the aesthetic value of materials whether or not they are curriculum orientated.

The IMC'er also has a responsibility to assist classroom teachers in the area of materials, especially new materials with which the teacher may not yet be acquainted. Schedules should allow time for cooperative planning of units and the selection of useful materials to be purchased. The IMC staff should be represented on curriculum committees not only because broad knowledge of available materials is advantageous but also to make sure that the materials collection is prepared for coming changes. In addition to professionals, an adequate clerical staff is needed to carry out the myriad routine details.

How many materials and how much staff is provided in any given school is really a local decision. Administrators, school boards and taxpayers must determine the importance of answers for children and in so doing they determine the level of educational opportunity their children are worth. Happily, Arizona believes in answers and loves its children.

Many of our schools have long provided IMC services and have strong programs in operation. Others have only recently been able to begin and a few have not yet started. Now we know there are no Arizonians who remember the word "can't" but for any newcomers who still use this archaic expression occasionally, we cite an example.

Flagstaff District developed ten elementary IMC's from scratch in a period of six months. While this is somewhat spectacular, it is their method of procedure which is worth noting. Mr. Sturgeon Cromer, Supt. of Schools, gave support to the plan and in March of last year hired Mrs. Evelyn Fambrough, a professional IMC'er, as district director. She was given complete responsibility for developing collections and supervising services. This is unusual and important because it insured planned growth. Too often professional personnel are the last to be provided in individual schools and almost never first at the district level.

Furniture and equipment were purchased and a classroom in each school was set aside for the IMC. Then came probably the biggest problem: the pulling together and organizing of existing classroom collections. This was done as tactfully as possible and teachers soon learned they hadn't really lost all the materials they had been able to accumulate. In reality, they now had access to a far greater selection than ever before. All they lost was the chore of storing and caring for materials between times of use. In the meantime these resources could be answering questions for other children.

Flagstaff elementary schools opened last fall with each IMC having the services of at least one half time IMC'er. Emphasis this year has been on establishing services, planning programs and strengthening collections. While their work has really only begun, they have made an excellent start.

This is but one Arizona example of demonstrated belief in the value of abundant instructional materials in educational programs. It is good to know of the tremendous numbers of resources which have gone into other schools during the past two years. These resources will provide many answers *if* they are made available and accessible to children who are welcomed and wanted.

The Instructional Program and the Library

Robert S. Gilchrist and Willard G. Jones

Changing concepts in education dictate a drastic change in the role of the elementary school library and librarian. This change results from an onslaught of knowledge in communications and technology which has greatly influenced the curriculum content. As a result, the library must now serve as an information center for storage of teaching aids and materials and a depository for learning devices. In essence, the library must become the nerve center of the school. This calls for a special relationship between the elementary school library and two major dimensions of curriculum development — a curriculum that is (1) idea centered, with greater emphasis on (2) independent learning.

THE IDEA-CENTERED CURRICULUM

Acceleration in the growth of knowledge makes apparent the inadequacy of the approach of memorization of facts as a basic for lifelong learning. This approach can hardly be considered an adequate basis for farsighted curriculum planning. It is obviously impossible for one man in his lifetime to absorb all knowledge in a single traditional discipline. Consequently, visionaries are making monumental efforts to mechanically record new knowledge as rapidly as it is

Reprinted from *Theory Into Practice*, February, 1967, by permission of the publisher.

generated. These efforts, however, only scratch the surface of this problem. Mitchell recently pointed out that today's researchers find it more efficient and economical, in some instances, to repeat an entire research project than to gather the existing diverse knowledge from its scattered locations.* This is an indicator of present progress toward keeping up-to-date with the knowledge explosion. Thus, it follows that curriculum content and organization must be something other than fact centered.

The recent impetus toward the search for the basic structure of subject matter provides focus and indices for learning and curriculum planning. The search for the central ideas of each subject matter area has been a vital part of nearly every serious curriculum endeavor in the past few years.

Procedures of the idea-centered curriculum development seem to follow a sequence. At the onset, a thorough examination is made of how a particular subject matter area may contribute to the learners' development. Areas judged significant are analyzed for their critical and consistent academic ideas. Both scholars and educators cooperate in this task.

The ideas of primary concern are those which make a significant difference in a learner's behavior and/or decision-making. These key ideas become the framework for curriculum development. They are subdivided into their functional elements and, finally, various particular learning experiences are suggested to provide the activity necessary for the learner to understand central ideas. These are not presented for memorization; pupils will be involved in experiences which, when understood, will lead them to understand key ideas. Sequenced learning experiences of increasing complexity enable the learner to be re-exposed to key ideas at spaced intervals in his school experience and provide opportunity for rediscovery and use of the key ideas leading to a fuller and deeper understanding of them.

The key-idea approach stresses the use of facts and information to provide a better frame of reference for further study and exploration and development of an awareness of the interrelationships between information and central ideas. In brief, these key ideas are "what is left over after the facts are forgotten," which to some is the definition of education.

One result of the idea-centered approach is a trend toward fewer units to be taught per year, however, with a greater in-depth approach. This stems from the realization that not all countries or periods of history need to be taught to establish the central ideas of the social studies. There has also been a rediscovery that each child need not have an identical experience to understand key ideas. This notion has been incorporated in recently developed curriculum materials allowing for much greater flexibility in planning specific learning activities.

*Mitchell, Maurice B. Speech given at Kansas Elementary School Principals Meeting, Emporia, Kansas, October 1966.

The idea-centered curriculum structure determines certain imperatives for the library. Most obvious is the necessary provision for the selection, acquisition, and organization of a broad, diverse collection of book and nonbook media. Therefore, the librarian becomes a critical member of the instructional team and, consequently, all faculty members, as well as expert consultants, must be involved in materials selection. Obviously, the classroom teachers must be informed of the wealth of materials to aid instruction.

The library collection must be diverse to accommodate the needs and interests of children seeking information relative to classroom activities. It has been observed that through the central idea curriculum approach, children develop a wide variety of interests not formerly regarded as part of the curriculum. Given greater latitude, creative teachers and pupils may approach a topic in all kinds of unusual ways. This often results in an intense questioning attitude in pupils which may be squelched if they often have difficulty finding answers in the library. Children, with competent guidance, can discover key ideas and their relationships through exposure to a wide variety of experiences. A fringe benefit is the potential for lively discussion, since children are able for the first time to acquire information from a variety of sources.

It is apparent that the library must be a place of activity — a place to be sought rather than avoided. The library should be one of the most attractive rooms in the building. It should be spacious with enough room to accommodate twenty per cent of the student body at any given time.* Certainly, the library must be open to any child or teacher whenever he seeks an answer. Natural outgrowths of the concept-centered curriculum are its allowance for individual differences and teaching children to become independent learners.

INDIVIDUALIZED AND INDEPENDENT LEARNING

Accommodating of the individual needs and abilities and nurturing the interests of pupils has long been a professed goal of education. Many agree with Suppes that this goal is ". . . the most important principle of learning as yet unaccepted in the working practice of the classroom and subject-matter teaching."**

Educators have previously paid very little attention to the child who is either above or below normal grade expectancy. Teachers are often provided with a single textbook as the source of all information — there are those who call

---

*Brown, B. Frank. *The Appropriate Placement School: A Sophisticated Nongraded School Curriculum.* West Nyack, N.Y., Parker Publishing Co., Inc., 1965.
**Suppes, Patrick as quoted in Charles E. Silberman, "Technology Is Knocking at the Schoolhouse Door," *Fortune*, August 1966, 74, 125.

this curriculum planning. "Read pages fourteen to twenty-five and answer the questions at the end" still occurs in too many classrooms.

A six-year spelling study using a single graded spelling text indicated that, at best, only one in five children is being instructed at an appropriate level. This conclusion makes one wonder about the disparity in achievement among children in broad fields of study, such as science or mathematics. It would appear that at least part of a child's learning should proceed at his own pace.

Not only do children differ in their learning levels, but also in learning styles. For example, some children grasp ideas more readily when presented orally rather than visually, even though research shows the opposite more often to be true. It has, however, been well established that learning and retention can be enhanced when more than one sense is involved in information acquisition. Teachers have often become eclectic in approach, with the naive hope that they will miss no one. It seems plausible to hope that soon it will be possible to assess appropriate learning styles more adequately and, therefore, adjust individual learning activities.

The library can provide needed assistance. It can, in reading, become a storehouse of directed and extended reading materials enabling the teacher to select and try various techniques. In content, the library can contain basic information related to key curricular ideas and subject matter. Materials selected would accommodate reading competence and related areas. Curriculum guides are being developed with complete bibliographies related to the basic unit ideas and selected to accommodate all children. Since reading is not the only means of acquiring information, and often not the best, the library must develop adequate collections of all types of media and equipment.

Such a collection will include: trade books, textbooks, single concept loop films, filmstrips, pamphlets, pictures, newspapers, transparencies, records, tapes, 16 mm films, programmed instruction, manipulative devices, and other equipment. This will allow the teacher to become an organizer of learning activities, not an information disseminator, and will facilitate the meeting of individual needs, interests, and capabilities. With these materials and proper encouragement, each child might pursue learning independently.

Development of skills, capacities, and the desire to pursue independent learning is of prime importance. Greater attention is being paid to this goal in curriculum development. Some programs are now being developed with inquiry training as the central goal. Taba substantiates that this task has not been well conceived or attacked in the past.* She found that children responded quite well

---

*Taba, Hilda. "Thinking in Elementary School Children" (USOE Project No. 1574) San Francisco State College, April 1964.

to fact and information questions but poorly to questions regarding relationships, interpretations, and conclusions.* To develop proficiency in independent study requires a sensitivity to relationships, an ability to draw conclusions and make interpretations and to plan for organization of work in a series of meaningful steps to arrive at the goal.

The library provides the natural setting for development of these capabilties. Our observations in libraries in Shaker Heights, Ohio, and Prairie District, Kansas, have shown that nearly all sixth-grade pupils are capable of using the library for independent and class-related projects with an efficiency admirable for college freshmen. This results from teacher-librarian cooperation and instruction in problem-solving and library skills throughout the elementary school experience. A capacity for lifelong learning is necessary to cope with change. It would thus be hypocrisy not to move rapidly toward preparing high school graduates who are independent learners. They will not want to forget their school experiences. The elementary school is challenged, as never before, to provide a balanced and sequential K-6 program allowing for pupil development as far as maturity permits and as actively and independently as possible. If individual, active, independent learning is the goal, then all available media should be utilized.

The library is not exempt from the onrush of knowledge and technology. As libraries strive to make basic improvements in quality and standards, they must prepare to accommodate new devices for collection, storage, and retrieval of information that are rapidly being developed.

We must not react as Socrates did to an alphabet inventor in Phaedrus: "This discovery of yours will create forgetfulness in the learners' souls, because they will not use their memories, they will trust to the external written characters and not remember themselves. . . They will appear to be omniscient and will generally know nothing."

Since the library has, in fact, become the central information center of the school, it is necessary and vital to consider the idea that the computer will increase by millions a man's capacity to handle information. Electronics manufacturers, publishers of educational materials, and mass communication companies are looking at the computer and at technology as a means of revolutionizing education.** These developments will not come at some distant point of time. They are here; educators must use them now.

Ibid.
**Silberman, Charles E. "Technology Is Knocking at the Schoolhouse Door," *Fortune,* August 1966, 74, 120-25, 198, 203-205.

Mediating the Elementary Social Science Curriculum

Joseph M. Conte and Jane Meyer

Which comes first — the chicken or the egg? — the technology or the curriculum? — the hardware or the software? The sterility of the one-textbook curriculum is no sadder than the most modern audio-visual equipment hidden in a cupboard for lack of a vital course of study to put it to use.

Temple City Unified School District, a residential community of 32,000 people living within commuting distance of Los Angeles, is currently developing a model of mediated instruction for the social sciences at the fifth grade level and, concurrently, a model elementary media resource center including a library and learning laboratory equipped with the finest audio-visual facilites. Both the laboratory and the curriculum are prototypes for other systems to be installed in elementary schools throughout the district.

Studies of the needs of Temple City students posed problems with a familiar ring to educators everywhere. Just how can a public school meet individual student needs? What can be done to maximize education for *all* children? How can schools cope with individual learning rates and levels? How can the emphasis be shifted from Quincy box rote learning to the development of the ability to make abstract generalizations? How can schools make education relevant and prepare students for tomorrow's world?

One of Temple City's tentative solutions to these problems was grounded in the development of a performance curriculum encompassing baseline instruction, enrichment experiences, and remediation. The instructional strategy adopted was heavily dependent upon a multisensory approach. Essential to this strategy is the use of *all* media — books and the total spectrum of non-book materials.

Innovative staff members were facing the realization that the lag between the writing of textbooks and their use by students can be as much as eight years. In terms of relevancy in the contemporary world, the textbook thus becomes one of the least effective teaching tools in the field of social science.

What, then, can complement the textbook? Modern technology provides an answer through multimedia which not only has the advantage of shortening the lag but can be designed for individual use which is learner-controlled; is amenable to programming, utilizing branching techniques; and may provide for immediate reinforcement as well as student-material interaction.

Of grave importance is the unavoidable change in the role of the teacher. No

Reprinted from *Educational Screen and Audiovisual Guide*, September 1967, by permission of the publisher.

longer may we expect the teacher to carry the responsibilities of presenting data. The emerging role of the "new" teacher demands that he be a manager of learning. His primary responsibility is that of managing the learning of individual students. As the pivot of the instructional system, he must assess the individual needs of his students, prescribe strategies which satisfy those needs, and administer treatment in accordance with the diagnosis. Continuous evaluation throughout assessment, prescription, and treatment of student progress (as well as of the program itself) is the integral factor for success.

Temple City's Board of Education, administration, and most staff members wholeheartedly embraced the concepts of the value of mediated instruction and the changing role of the teacher. In the fall of 1964 a supportive citizenry approved a five-million-dollar bond issue which provided funds for new school buildings and extensive renovations. At Longden Elementary School, the site chosen for the prototype Media Resource Center, a new building was constructed which offered the necessary physical setting in which to launch a multimedia instructional program. Beyond that, the District (which is of moderate wealth) found itself unable to support the developmental program. It was necessary to seek "outside" funds, and an E.S.E.A. Title III Planning Grant was the answer.

Provision was made in the Planning Grant for the services of a Project Director, an instructional technologist, special consultants in the fields of curriculum content and educational systems, and the teaching team which is doing continuing work on curriculum development. The many universities and colleges within driving distance of Temple City made it possible to obtain outstanding consultants for the Project.

If the teacher is truly a manager of learning, calling upon all resources at his command to meet student needs, then it follows that he must design a curriculum which will exploit the tremendous opportunities offered by technology.

Temple City chose to begin the design of mediated instruction with the crucial fifth grade social science curriculum. For more than a year the groundwork for the project was laid through probe and survey. During the summer of 1966 a team of eight teachers was employed to develop model lessons, with the professional guidance of special consultants and the project director. Stringent requirements for a conceptual framework for lesson development were set up:

- The curricula must be amenable to programmed instruction and educational technology.
- The curricula must be stated in terms of observable learner behaviors so that they may be measured.
- Evaluation must be an integral part of the curricula.

With these requirements in mind, the following outline was developed for he curricular aspects of the project:

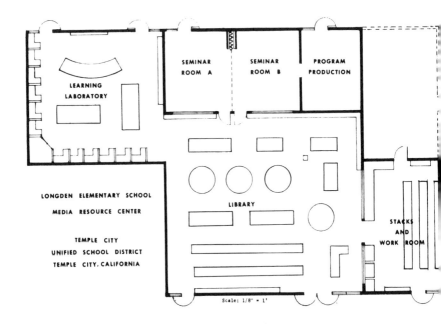

1. Unit parameter objective(s)
2. Discipline objective(s)
3. The parameter objective(s) stated as an hypothesis
4. Establishment of pupil set
5. Pre-test (learner entrance performances)
   a. Knowledge as measured by test behavior
   b. Skills as measured by activities or products of learner behavior
6. Reinforcement/interaction (teacher-learners) for motivation
7. Sequence (learner enroute performances)
   a. In terms of teacher-directed presentations with media
   b. In terms of learner-oriented behaviors as stated in the parameter objectives
8. Post-test (measurement of parameter performances)
9. Reinforcement/interaction
10. Re-cycling (the re-sequencing of production of presentation)
11. Post-test of re-sequencing (measurement of parameter performance)
12. Reinforcement/interaction
13. Unit evaluation of learner parameter performances as stated in original parameter objectives

Now we have the chicken, what about the egg? The new building at Longden Elementary School offered the rare opportunity for design of a technologically oriented media resource center adjoining the school library — a perfect wedding of the book-non-book environment. Thought was also given to the future with provisions for powerful electrical conduits.

A variety of instructional techniques is possible in the Media Resource Center: individual listening and viewing, small group listening and viewing, and small group discussion.

For individual instruction there are fourteen study carrels, each equipped with a tape-audio system having a six-channel capability. The broadcast source is a six-unit playback machine. Each channel is cartridge load with foil-controlled stop. Viewing equipment in the carrels includes: 35 mm filmstrip projectors with three-inch lenses; 2" x 2" slide projectors with three-inch lenses; 8mm and super 8 mm loop projectors; and 9-inch portable sets.

Group activities take place near the center of the laboratory at two specially-designed tables, one rectangular and one semicircular.

The rectangular table accommodates one group of ten students for viewing, listening, and discussion. Collapsible dividers can modify the tables to handle three separate groups of students.

The semicircular table was designed to make full use of the overhead projector as a learning device. A graphic artist is employed to help students prepare materials for the projector.

Two adjoining seminar rooms, glassed-in and noise-proof, offer flexibility to teachers scheduling use of the Media Resource Center. These rooms are also used for noon-hour activities such as music appreciation classes and story-telling.

An intensive student-training program in use of the Center's equipment has been carried out during the past school year and will, of necessity, be a continuing activity. The program has resulted in proper use of materials and equipment and reduced damage to a minimum.

Although it is too early to assess the total value of the initial curriculum, there is no question about student response to mediated instruction and the Longden Media Resource Center, as the combined learning laboratory and library are known. After-school use of the learning laboratory is gratifying, and increased usage of the library has been little short of phenomenal.

Future plans in the District include construction of learning laboratories in all elementary schools.

During Phase II, the fifth grade social sciences curriculum is to be developed in accordance with the model. One profitable result will be a teacher guide and curriculum manual complete with overhead transparencies, pre- and post-tests, enroute tests, and a bibliography of instructional materials and aids essential to the program.

A Mathematics Laboratory — From Dream to Reality

Patricia S. Davidson and Arlene W. Fair

Just a year ago last September, the mathematics laboratory program at the Oak Hill Elementary School was still a dream. A few plans had been made during the previous spring for an initial purchase of materials, and the first job in the fall was to find "the place." It was decided to convert a small storage room on the basement floor into a mathematics laboratory. By the end of the year, the dream had become a reality — the laboratory approach to learning mathematics had become a vital part of the mathematics program in the whole school.

Since visitors to the lab ask so many of the same questions — "How did you organize the room?" "Just how did you begin?" "What is the purpose of a math lab?" "How do you organize the children?" "Are the classroom teachers involved?" "How does the lab program relate to the class work?" "What materials are needed?" — we should like to share some of our experiences with those of you who may wish to develop a laboratory program.

GETTING STARTED

First of all, we were going to have to wait several months to have the room painted (Does this sound familiar?) — so with the help of the children, we cleaned, washed, and made the room colorful and attractive in other ways. Some sixth-grade boys, who enjoy this type of work and are particularly adept at it, took great pride in repairing and painting — in bright colors — some discarded tables and chairs, which were then decorated by the art teacher. (We have been asked several times where to obtain such delightful furniture!)

Along one of the long walls we hung a piece of fabric on which we had sewn pockets to hold individual problem cards and booklets.

PROJECTS IN MATH

Reprinted from *The Arithmetic Teacher*, February 1970 (vol. 17, 2, pp. 105-110), © 1970 by the National Council of Teachers of Mathematics. Used by permission.

Such a rack can be made any height or length. To be most serviceable, the background should be of a dark color with bright colored pockets adding to the decor. The pockets can be made in different sizes to accommodate various-sized cards, booklets, or project sheets, and they can be labeled if they are to be used for the same thing all the time. We never have labeled ours because we are constantly evaluating the written materials that we are developing, and with the help of the children we are always adding new ideas.

The other long wall had shelving from floor to ceiling which we used for storing the concrete materials. We organized and labeled the shelves in categories so that each item could be found easily and the children could learn to put away their own things. Since our particular shelves had six major sections, we used six main headings:* *Blocks* (with subheadings such as Attribute Blocks, Geo-Blocks, Poleidoblocs, Logical Blocks, Discovery Blocks, . . .); *Geometric Materials* (with subheadings such as Models, Mirror Cards, Geoboards, . . .); *Measuring Devices* (which included drawing tools and all kinds of balances); *Numerical Games* (with subheadings such as Calculators, Chips, Abaci, Kalah, Oh-Wah-Ree, Tuf, Imout, Heads Up, Card Games, Slide Rules, Cuisenaire Rods, . . .); *Strategy Games* (with subheadings such as Tower Puzzle, Qubic, Twixt, Jumpin, . . .); and *Shapes and Tiles* (with subheadings such as Tangram Puzzles, Pattern Blocks,** Mosaic Shapes, Linjo, Three-D-Dominoes, . . .).

In addition, the room had some book display racks to hold other kinds of student instructional materials and cupboards that contained labeled boxes of miscellaneous items like paper, pencils, oak tag, construction paper, scissors, string, rubber bands, needles, thread, buttons, tongue depressors, egg cartons, beans, sticks, and so forth.

A large sheet of brown paper helped to cover one cracked wall while serving also as a useful backing for hanging students' work − for example, various geometric designs, curve stitching, and graphing projects. Also early in the fall, some students made coat-hanger mobiles with colorful three-dimensional models cut from contact paper to hang from the ceiling.

We placed a bulletin board on the fourth wall with pictures from magazines headed with the caption "Guess How Many." Underneath was a small table with jars of peas, beans, macaroni, rice, etc., for the "Peas and Particles" unit. A few study carrels made by students out of Tri-Wall† cardboard and a portable blackboard completed that side of the room.

*For a detailed listing and ordering information for most of the materials mentioned here, see P. Davidson, "An Annotated Bibliography of Suggested Manipulative Devices," *The Arithmetic Teacher*, October 1968. These six categories were a consolidation of the fifteen used in this article.

**Not available at the time of the bibliography, Pattern Blocks were developed recently by Elementary Science Study. The materials and Teacher's Guide are available from Webster Division, McGraw-Hill.

†For information on Cardboard Carpentry write to Education Development Center, Inc., 55 Chapel Street, Newton, Massachusetts 02160.

We started out with one small patch of rug so that children could work on the floor, and since that time parents have donated enough scraps to "cover" the floor patchwork style. Pupils enjoy working with materials on the floor. The rugs help to cut down the noise level and also the amount of furniture necessary.

Several teachers who have visited the lab have used many of these ideas to convert a corner of their own classrooms into a math lab area.

WORKING WITH CHILDREN

Although we were able to have some small groups of children working with materials during September – as they helped us get the room ready – the lab really opened in October.

During the month of October, our aim was to have every student come to the lab for at least one 1/2–1 hour session. In order to make it possible for each teacher to come to the lab along with her students, we worked with whole classes, which often meant that there were too many children for the small room. But the orientation for a teacher with her own students is very necessary. In these first sessions, we tried to set a tone –

1. that you can learn math not only with paper and pencil, but also through the use of manipulative materials.
2. that the math lab approach involves active investigating, exploring, hypothesizing, looking for patterns, and "doing" rather than being told or shown.
3. that mathematics is many things; that there are often many right answers to a problem; and that usually you can check your hunches yourself by means of the materials.
4. that although much of the work will seem like fun and games, all of the lab experiences can be related to specific math concepts, to problem-solving techniques, or to modes of mathematical thinking.
5. that at the beginning, the lab teacher will choose what activity you embark on, but once you have pursued enough of the materials to know what some of the possibilities are, you will be given some choice.
6. that care of the materials is the responsibility of each student; that the loss of one piece may mean that the entire set of materials is unusable; and that you are responsible for putting the materials you have used in their proper place.
7. that often projects will be started or materials introduced in the lab that will be followed up in your classroom or at home.

TRAINING OF TEACHERS

Simultaneously, the classroom teachers were trained. We tried to do different things with each class during that first month, in order to get most of the materials in use. Also within each class, groups of children worked with several different things. For example, in one third-grade class, a little group worked with Pattern Blocks; another little group with balances; another little group with geoboards; while a fourth group did chip trading activities,* two students worked with Tangram Puzzles, and two explored Geo-Blocks. When each class left the lab after their initial session, the students took one or two things — for example, chips and geoboards — back with them. The teacher was responsible for reading manuals and getting help from us to be able to continue the work. Those children who had used these particular materials also helped the other children get started.

There were also workshops for all or some of the teachers on Tuesday or Thursday afternoons throughout the year. (We are fortunate in Newton in that elementary teachers have released time every Tuesday and Thursday afternoon.) Also several members of the faculty attended citywide math workshops, and needless to say, there were many informal discussions in the teachers' room. Within the building, as well as citywide, there was a constant sharing of ideas and of written sheets or math lab cards.

EXPANDING THE PROGRAM

After that first month, the lab really "exploded" to permeate the whole school. As much as possible, a lab schedule was built around the math periods of the entire school, so that each class including kindergarten and special classes could have 1/2–1 hour each week. A copy of the schedule was given to each teacher who was responsible for sending her children to the lab on time.

How many children came at once? Occasionally, the children still came *by classes* with the teacher so that a unit with such materials as geoboards, rods, balances, or various measuring devices could be introduced by the math lab teacher (Mrs. Fair, who had some time released from other teaching duties) with the help of the classroom teacher, and then taken back to the classroom.

---

*See P. Davidson, "Chip Trading — a Strategy for Teaching Place Value," *Professional Growth for Teachers*, Third Quarter Issue 1968-69, and "Exchanges with Chips Teach 'Borrowing' and 'Carrying,'" *Professional Growth for Teachers*, First Quarter Issue, 1969-70. Croft Educational Services, Inc., 100 Garfield Avenue, New London, Connecticut 06320.

More often a teacher would send *one of the arithmetic groups*, say 10-12 children, for special help in some area. These children were taught by the math lab teacher or by a capable college student teacher. Sometimes, the classroom teacher arranged for coverage of the rest of the class in order to come too.

Very often, *small groups* of students worked in the lab on anything that the math lab teacher, or a college student teacher, or a high school student teacher, or a parent volunteer* wished to introduce or that they might choose. The games became very popular, as we constantly changed the rules to make them more mathematical and more challenging.

Nongraded sessions, with 4-6 children from three grades at once or with three children from each grade, proved very fruitful. Sometimes many units of work were introduced; while at other times, the students of various ages worked on the same thing, going as far as ability will allow. (Most of the materials are so open-ended that they are appropriate for students, kindergarten-grade 6 and higher.) We were in for many surprises as to what children can do when given concrete situations – it became clear that many of the common conceptions about age and ability grouping need to be challenged seriously.

After the program got started, the children often acted as *lab assistants.* Children from all grades acted as teachers in an area for which they had been checked as being well versed. Eventually, we accumulated enough materials in the lab to start a loan service to each classroom. Many of the teachers established a math lab day once or twice a week in their classrooms and used children to help.

THE BUDDY SYSTEM

Another aspect of the program was the buddy system, in which sixth-grade students volunteered to work in math with first graders. A workshop (four sessions) was given to these sixth graders in the use of materials, with the stress on the meaning of number and number relationships. The first-grade teachers identified those children who needed help or enrichment, as the case might be. Each sixth grader was assigned one of these first graders with whom to work throughout the year. They worked for about one-half hour at a time, usually three afternoons a week. The improvement in attitude of all of the children was remarkable. A couple of youngsters who no longer needed help did not want to give up their "buddies," and every first grader wanted to be included. We were never lacking in teachers (sixth graders); students kept volunteering as those involved shared their experiences. The comments of the sixth graders were interesting: "I didn't realize teaching was so difficult." "It is such fun to see him

---

*Through math lab sessions with parents and invitations for them to visit the math lab in session with children, several parents became interested in helping in various ways.

)egin to understand it." "I didn't think I could find so many ways to show 3 + 4 = 7." "It is like having a real sister," (said an only child).

The buddy system gave the sixth graders a real purpose, a feeling of impor-ance, and a sense of responsibility. The children initiated the system that if a ixth grader was to be absent, he would call a friend on the phone to arrange for substitute who was to report to the lab teacher in the morning. In handling all of the materials and games, the sixth graders really improved their own back-rounds — "to teach is to really know it."

THE MATHEMATICS LAB FAIR

The year culminated in a Math Lab Fair at which more than 350 children in he school were at work with materials at the same time in nine classrooms, the orridors, the gym, and the math lab. In one evening, over 500 parents came to observe and to work with the children. The Fair was also held on a Thursday fternoon for teachers from the other 22 elementary schools in the city and for isitors from other communities. During another morning, the Oak Hill children helped groups of children from other schools in the city which were planning for math lab program.

HOW TO MAKE A START

Starting a math lab program in a school is no easy adventure. The success of he program at Oak Hill is highly dependent on the cooperation and support of he principal, Mr. Samuel Turner, and the hard work and enthusiasm of the ntire staff. From a small beginning, the program is now growing and expanding n ways that could not possibly have been anticipated. You must begin at what-ver stage is appropriate to your present mathematics program.

In deciding what to purchase initially, consider each large category of manipulative materials and get some from each, as much as money allows. The materials specifically mentioned in this article have been particularly useful for our program. Materials like geoboards, Cuisenaire Rods, balances, chips, etc., hould be bought in small quantities, but there is no need to start with more han one each of numerical games, strategy games, and puzzles. See which ones he children like before ordering more, and also use your own ingenuity in making materials. Once you start, you will find that through improvising, you often can add many improvements that "hand tailor" the materials to the needs of your particular students. The children can make a great many things and will njoy creating some of their own games and problems. A must is adequate space or proper care of the materials.

But most of all you need one large bottle of vitamin pills, unlimited vitality and enthusiasm, and the patience of Job, for you will not only be the mathematics coordinator for your building and the resource person for every teacher in the school, but you will be expected to know: every game and how to "win"; the answer to every puzzle presented to you by kindergarteners through sixth graders; where all the missing pieces are; and how to mend every broken game.

But when you sense the enthusiasm and see the growth in your students, you no doubt will share the feelings of the teachers at Oak Hill — that the laboratory approach to teaching mathematics is exciting and rewarding.

What Do You Have That a Kid Can Use?

Doris W. Like

New student to school librarian. I'd like to look at your filmstrip card file, please.

Librarian. My what?

Student. A filmstrip card file. I need some information.

Librarian. *You* need a filmstrip? Which teacher sent you here? Do you have a pass? Your teacher has a list of my filmstrips.

Student. I need a filmstrip about life in early Texas. No teacher sent me, but I have a pass to come to the library.

Librarian. Your Social Studies teacher will show you a filmstrip about Texas if he wants you to see it. Students are not allowed to use filmstrips.

Student. Oh. Well, maybe there's something in the vertical file I can use for my project. Where will I find that?

Librarian. The vertical file has professional reading materials for teachers only!

Student. Oh. Maybe I could order a film?

Librarian. Students are not allowed to order films!

Student. Oh, Do you have any audio tapes about Texas?

Librarian. No, we have no tapes for student use.

Student. What do you have that a *kid* can use?

What *do* you have in your library that a kid can use? Today's innovative instructional programs have brought an acknowledged change in the roles of the student and the teacher, but what about the new concept of library usage and library personnel? More and more schools across Texas are fitting the curriculum

Reprinted from *Texas School Business*, October 1969, by permission of the publisher.

o the child rather than fitting the child to the curriculum as we have been attempting to do for 100 years in our graded system.

We have recognized the need to develop independent and responsible students who will become self-directed learners. These concepts in basic philosophy have caused us to focus our attention on providing for greater individualization of instruction to realize our goals. Greater individualization calls for a variety of approaches to learning as well as a variety of teaching methods and techniques. Regardless of the operational structure — whether it be non-grading, team-teaching, departmentalization, turn teaching, or cooperative teaching — the basic concept is the same. A child is recognized for what he is — a unique individual who progresses according to his own rate, acquiring academic and social skills as he is ready for them.

As we concentrate on development of these programs, one of the first considerations should be the development of a resource center. Today's library can easily become a resource center which is the heart of an innovative program and library personnel become vital contributing members of the teaching-learning process.

What better way to provide a variety of learning materials, develop student responsibility, and help students become proficient in research skills and learn to think critically than through a resource center? In addition to normal library contents, a resource center provides audio tapes, filmstrips, records, films, a variety of reference materials, newspapers, magazines, film loops, slides, picture file, charts, maps, vertical file, tape recorders, filmstrip projectors, filmstrip previewers, record players, 16 mm projectors, and listening areas complete with headsets — all designed for the student to use, himself.

Unlike most traditional libraries a resource center is located within a few steps of every child who uses it. The quick accessibility of materials and equipment enables the student to pursue his research independently, allows him to move freely without asking teacher permission to leave a teaching area, and provides him with many more audio and visual aids than can be provided in a traditional library. It is advisable to provide a resource center for each module, pod, cluster, grade level or similar organizational plan within each school. It is possible for the library to become one resource center and others established in unused classrooms. Perhaps a wall between two classrooms needs to be removed to create a spacious, functional resource center.

The resource center is as valuable a tool to the teacher as it is to the student. How many times has a teacher had to postpone a question that has arisen in the self-contained classroom because he had to wait until he could check out the necessary materials from the library? With the availability of equipment and materials in a resource center, student interest can be pursued immediately. A case in point: a student brings an aquarium with frog eggs to school. Present science plans are set aside and a microscrope set up. The microscope and aquarium are placed in the resource center which every child uses daily. An immediate interest, increased and satisfied by inquiry, filmstrips, observation, films, science and reference books brings a living science lesson to 230 children.

How is a resource center used by students? It is not uncommon to see one child stretched out on the floor previewing a filmstrip while a few feet away a small group is watching a 16 mm film, receiving the audio portion via headsets, still other students are engaged in quiet research in study carrels, others are browsing through the book section, some students are searching the picture file for pictures of life in Africa, a few more may be using the controlled reader to brush up on math facts, a group may be listening to audio tape, and others may be assisting a para-professional check equipment, file materials, etc. Its uses are limited only by the imagination! The resource center is as flexible as the program itself.

This brings us to a very important point . . . flexibility. This seems to be the magic key that unlocks the door to an innovative program whose very nature is flexible scheduling, grouping, and planning to provide for each child. We expect our teachers to be flexible, we go to great lengths to take them visiting to such programs, and we provide in-service training on "how to be," but what about library personnel and their roles?

It is of vital importance that a librarian becomes an integral part of the planning for a resource center, that she be able to accept the philosophy on which it is based and be able to function as part of the program. The librarian needs to reach a point in professional growth which accepts the fact that equipment and materials provided in centers are primarily for *student users*. Students can easily be taught the proper use and care of materials and equipment. Librarians, teachers and administrators have too long expected only teachers to use the precious few filmstrips and transparencies housed in a library. Now that we furnish as many as 200 filmstrips in one center, our thinking has expanded along with our acquisitions. A book or piece of equipment that shows wear from continuous use is a much more valuable learning tool than one sitting on the shelf gathering dust.

Technical skill of librarians in the use of multi-media is called for. The librarian, in the past, had only to concern herself with a few pieces of equipment but today's technology presents quite a challenge. Now the librarian must be familiar with the operation of fifteen or so different pieces of equipment, she must be knowledgeable about their proper maintenance, see that they are repaired as needed, keep abreast of new equipment on the market, and be able to determine those suitable for her school's needs.

As we recognize the need for teacher aides, so must the librarian have assistance. Her duties multiply as she becomes responsible for the resource centers in a school. Aside from routine duties she is expected to assist students in conducting research, preparing reports, taping, instructing in the use of equipment, order materials, and a melange of other services.

No matter how innovative the program, flexible the building, or creative the teacher, without new directions in the use of a library and library personnel we may as well remain in our present egg crates rather than move ahead in education by individualizing instruction. Mister Administrator, what *do* you have in your libraries that *kids* can use?

SECTION THREE / SECONDARY-SCHOOL LEARNING RESOURCE CENTERS

Pseudopodial High School Can Shrink or Spread Its Learning Center
Robert S. Brady

Hub of the Instructional Program
Rena Clay

Hagerman Finds an Answer

George M. Carnie

Magic Valley cuts deeply into the sagebrush plateau of south central Idaho. Springs, believed to be the outlets of Idaho's famed Lost River, gush from the valley walls. The spring water is captured not only for the generation of power, but as a media for the world's largest trout farm whose product appears on the menus of many of the most fashionable restaurants. The Snake River, tamed by dams, flows placidly through the valley. On the northern horizon are the Sawtooth Mountains and Sun Valley.

The fertile valley soil produces watermelons and vegetables. Cattle and sheep graze the plateau. The mild year-round climate is attracting retired couples who yearn for the wide open spaces and excellent fishing and hunting.

Across Highway 30 which cuts through the valley is Hagerman, population 480. The four-lane main street is not much longer than it is broad. Two markets, a like number of cafes, gasoline stations and bars are crowded into a couple of blocks. At one end of main street is a grey stuccoed building, distinguished by a 40-foot television antenna on the roof, and identified by orange letters under the front eave as the "Hagerman High School."

The antenna proclaims that progress has not bypassed Hagerman. But, not even the antenna prepares one for the exciting atmosphere within those walls and under that roof.

The 180 students who attend the 7th through 12th grades in that building, and the faculty of 11, are continuing an experiment which educators believe will have a great impact on rural education.

"This school," says Dr. Homer Johnson of Utah State University, who has been associated with the Center since its inception, "belongs not just to Hagerman, but to all the small schools of Idaho, and hopefully to all other states. It is an exciting school because it has demonstrated to all small schools the potential which is available to them for the education of the rural child." Some two million students attend small secondary schools across the nation.

Excitement is aroused as one enters the building. The hallways are carpeted and the walls and lockers are an attractive pastel. Art, the product of local amateurs of talent, decorates the walls. Up a few steps at the end of one hallway are glass doors which swing into Hagerman's "Individualized Learning Center," which is an attempt to "break the lock-step on rural education."

A little over three years ago, it was a typical study hall, occupied by restless

Reprinted from *Educational Screen and Audiovisual Guide,* February 1970, by permission of the publisher.

teenagers seated at Panama ink-well desks marred with the initials of students who long ago left Magic Valley.

Seated on a raised platform was a teacher, usually irked by the assignment of trying to inspire one student while watching others squirm in their boredom. Off in one corner, partitioned from the study hall, was a small library where books were guarded and were wearing out from age — not use.

The new Learning Center is an educator-planned and architect-designed, comfortably furnished, carpeted and sound-deadened room. It is crowded with intent, well-behaved youngsters who are finding that learning can be stimulating and fun.

The staff spent considerable time developing educational specifications which described, in detail, the environment and space relationship necessary for providing individualized learning.

The project was approached with the idea that educators are competent to plan education and that architects are competent to design buildings. The two competencies were welded together through the careful writing of educational specifications. These specifications spelled out the objectives of the program, the sizes and kinds of spaces necessary for student and teacher activities and the support activities. The relationship of one space to another was diagramed with circles for spaces and arrows for traffic flows.

This material became the document which was translated by the architect into a functional space for learning.

The goal of the Learning Center is to cater to the individual interests and needs of the rural student so that he will not be left untouched by the knowledge explosion.

Traffic flows easily through the airy, bright Learning Center. Study carrels are grouped to one side of the check-out counter and the electronic audio-visual control center.

The white vinyl-padded carrels may be occupied simultaneously by students listening to language tapes, viewing a video science lesson, running through a filmstrip, viewing an overhead projection, inspecting a geometric model, using a speed-reading machine, or reading the *Wall Street Journal.*

Lounge chairs are clustered in front of a wide window overlooking the Snake River Valley. A television receiver can be swiveled for viewing by the occupants. Earphone plug-ins are conveniently nearby so that the television sound will not disturb others in the Center. Also, a choice of five taped or recorded programs are available for student listening in the lounge area.

A door leads from the lounge into a small seminar room. A magazine and newspaper file separates the lounge from a study table and the instructional materials storage area.

The instructional materials storage area includes audio and video tapes, books, films (motion, slide and strip), microscope slides, programmed material in all subject areas, models, charts and globes, language tapes, programmed remedial reading material, reference and other books, and equipment including film and slide projectors, tape recorders, and portable TV receivers. Behind the electronic control center is a video tape recorder.

"Although most people seem to think that television is only for enjoyment," a junior student said, "they just don't realize the many benefits that can be derived from the video recorder." She explained for example, that in speech class, speeches are video taped, giving the speaker a "chance to watch and hear his speech on replay and correct his own faults." "It is far easier to correct your own faults," she added, "if you can see what you are doing wrong. A recorder can work on a similar basis in other classes."

A discovery that Hagerman students were being bypassed by the knowledge explosion led to the conception of the Individualized Learning Center. It came about when the custodian of the few books stacked in one corner of the study hall, Mrs. Patricia Strawser, complained that the library contained only two references to atomic energy.

Spurred by Mrs. Strawser's complaint, the administration went into action. At their request, she wrote a six-page report in red ink.

With the assistance of the Utah State University faculty, Idaho State Department of Education consultants, the Hagerman teaching staff and school board members, the report grew into a proposal for federal funds to establish an Exemplary Individualized Learning Center.

The application developed the rationale that

- growth and child development are continuous, but occur at different speeds.
- individuals usually learn serveral things simultaneously.
- each individual is unique in his ability to learn.
- self-motivated learning is the most effective type of learning.
- in order to keep pace with today's fast changing world, students must be instilled with a desire for life-long learning.
- learning is more effective when a feeling of self-accomplishment results from the activity.

Federal funding posed a problem, because it was not wholly welcomed by the conservative citizens of the Hagerman community. Nevertheless, the farmers and ranchers looked upon the experiment in rural education akin to the agricultural experiment stations with which they are familiar.

Although Hagerman had federal funds with which to work, it has developed a program which smaller schools can afford. The school has kept accurate and detailed cost figures, so that any school can be informed of what it would cost to duplicate the program in whole or in part.

Approximately $73,000 was spent in remodeling the old study hall and purchasing educational materials and equipment for the new Center. The school board and superintendent are continuing the Learning Center with the addition of only one para-professional staff member even though the three-year grant ran out in August of 1969.

Of the 180 students in the school, fewer than 10 did not accomplish more than previously. Many students complained that they could not spend enough time in the Learning Center. Although Spanish is the only foreign language formally offered in class, several students are studying German and French under the direction of the Spanish teacher. A consultant brought in to the school tested the self-taught German students at the end of the 1969 school year. Her evaluation showed that 8 students had completed a year's course work with "A" quality while the ninth student had completed the course with below average work.

Over 90 of the 125 students in the top four grades are serving as volunteer aides, working in the audio-visual production room, serving as electronic equipment engineers, and otherwise freeing the teachers of noninstructional duties so that they can concentrate on making full use of the Center and expanding its opportunities. The aides are responding to the challenge of responsibility, acquiring a more positive attitude toward school, and learning to cooperate with their fellow workers.

The job of updating instruction can be done with local money in small school districts if the board, staff and administrators work together to adopt those things they find at Hagerman that fit their local needs. Many small school personnel throughout the nation have visited Hagerman for ideas and assistance.

Many schools in Idaho have made significant changes: Grandview High School, Grandview, Ida., organized and developed a very attractive learning center including closed circuit TV, carrels, small group space and a production room. Elk River High School, Elk River, Ida., has remodeled two dreary old study halls into one large modern center. They have carpeted the area, panelled the walls, added closed circuit TV, study carrels, tape recorders, small group space, and a lounge area. They have 410 students in grades 1 through 12. Midvale High School, Midvale, Ida., is in the process of remodeling, organizing and equipping a learning center. The school hired a student teacher who was trained at the Hagerman Learning Center, as their librarian, to organize their center. The staff is equipping the center with TV, tape recorders and many other audio-visual components of an up-to-date learning center. Wendell High School, Wendell, Ida., has removed walls, lowered ceilings, and added audio-visual equipment to up-date their library into a modern facility. Marsing High School, Marsing, Ida., has developed an excellent learning center in both their grade school and high school. Cascade School District, Cascade, Ida., spent last summer tearing out walls and converting two old study halls into a much expanded and up-dated learning center.

At Hagerman the individualized program has been expanded with district money to include grades 1 through 6 to make the opportunities available for grade school students as well. Concentration in the lower grades is primarily on individualized instruction in reading and mathematics.

Also initiated this past year, was a new series of seminar classes in which students enrolled for a two-week period of time. Instructors for the class changed quite often with the topics being planned by the students. Considerable use was made of outside resource personnel to supplement the instructional program.

Probably one of the best programs to be implemented the last year of the project operation was one of individualized inservice training for staff members. Instead of providing each teacher the same instruction in group faculty meetings, inservice education was individualized and designed around each teacher's specific educational needs.

For example, to insure each staff member's competency in using AV equipment, 40 behavioral objectives describing operations involving tape recorders, video equipment, various types of projectors and production room equipment were written and handed to teachers. The Learning Center was chosen as the setting for most of the faculty inservice activity. Equipment was set up at various stations allowing for individual or small group work. Five minutes of large group instruction was adequate to orient teachers to the format of the inservice training. Staff members worked independently or with a partner to attain satisfactory performance of the 40 objectives. A few staff members completed every objective within 20 minutes while others took 10 to 12 hours.

After three years of successful operation what will happen now that Title III funds have been exhausted? Will the school revert back to the old way? The teachers say never. Roy Strawser was hired as principal a year before the end of the project and has since been appointed as school superintendent. The temporary positions held by George Carnie as part-time project director and Gerald Prince, learning director, have been phased out as planned. They have moved to Denver, Colorado, to develop, with the assistance of an educational foundation, CFK, Ltd., a new prototype school, building on their experience at Hagerman.

Yes, Hagerman will continue!

High School Library Plus

Michael Printz

"If you can carry it out the door, you can check it out. We'll check out

Reprinted from *NEA Journal*, February 1963, by permission of the publisher.

everything but the card catalog and the librarians."

That's what students at Highland Park High School, Topeka, Kansas, hear when they are introduced to the school library and its services. While no one has tried to check out the furniture, students and teachers are using library materials more and more and relying less and less on textbooks. Quality films, books, recordings, periodicals, study and art prints, and educational games fitting the school's wide range of educational needs are available in quantity.

Creative imagination and money are requisites for a curriculum-oriented library program of this type. At Highland Park, much imagination and creativity come from Principal Erle Volkland, the administrative staff, faculty members, and the library staff. The federal government is furnishing the money — $53,000 from Titles I and II of the Elementary and Secondary Education Act of 1965.

Highland Park was one of two senior high school libraries selected as demonstration centers in Kansas in 1965. The demonstration centers are full of the things of which good libraries are made — adequate staff, microfilm, recordings, films, art prints, transparencies, a stereo system, books, and more books — to say nothing of air conditioning and wall-to-wall carpeting.

In the demonstration center at Highland Park, students have freedom to do almost anything as long as they are working. For example, one corner of the library is a lounge with comfortable chairs, where students can read magazines and books without having to sit behind a library table. They don't even have to use the chairs in this corner; if they prefer, they can sit on pillows on the floor or lie propped up on an elbow.

This area contains about a hundred current magazines and 20 newspapers from Kansas and other states as well as English editions of several foreign papers. (The school has such a good collection because one of Highland Park's 50 student librarians collects the papers which the Topeka Public Library discards as the new issues arrive.)

Guests often show surprise as they approach the lounge area. The stereo provides soft background music. At an antique drugstore table, students seated in bentwood chairs roll dice and shuffle cards as they play curriculum-oriented games. These academic games simulate real-life situations and play a great role in social studies, language arts, business education, mathematics, and science. Some of the instructors feel the games offer opportunities to act out lifelike, decision-making roles in realistic settings.

One of the library's few rules is that talking above a whisper is taboo. Students know that the library is one place where it is always quiet. By the time students are juniors, the rule doesn't require much reenforcement, and seniors have been known to ask the younger ones to "keep it down." It's obvious the Highland Park students have a healthy respect for their library. They enter quietly and in a minute or two are hard at work.

The students know how to use the library's facilities or they know where to get help. My desk and that of the assistant librarian are in the reference and reading rooms "where the action is." Our feeling is that for too long a time librarians have been shut back in offices with uncataloged books and unfiled cards. Students and teachers like their librarians to be at hand when they need their services.

Such equipment as tape recorders and phonographs with headsets, microfilm readers, filmstrip viewers and loop projectors are available for the students and faculty to check out. Since school started last fall, 1,300 students and approximately 70 staff members have checked out between 70 and 90 films and records daily, and 5,500 books a month.

Even reference books may be checked out overnight. Several years ago, the school had trouble with stolen reference books — not because students were malicious but because they were desperate for books they couldn't take home overnight. Now that trouble has vanished.

The center has a collection of 350 large art prints. A local art shop has mounted the prints on mat board, sprayed them with a washable, invisible coating, and put hooks on the back. Students can check out these prints to hang for a month in their homes.

Generally, students come to the library in class groups to complement and supplement their classroom experiences. Teachers do not need to schedule their classes ahead of time. At the beginning of the year, the librarians tell the teachers, "If the chairs are filled and the students don't mind sitting on the carpeting, come on in." As a result, an average of 150 students use the facility every hour, even though it has only 95 chairs.

More and more faculty members are using the library facilities as part of their regular teaching programs. Instruction comes from a wide variety of sources at this school, and teaching from a single textbook is considered old hat.

Teachers find direction for incorporating the varied learning materials in a practical professional library located in a former office of the librarian. Library-use guides prepared by the library staff and free coffee are also available here.

Because of crowded conditions, the library will open its first branch — a social studies center — in September 1968 as Phase Two of the demonstration project. This facility, to be located in the library wing, will be staffed with a social studies specialist. Plans for the future call for an expanded reference room and a science center.

Although the 17,000 volume library usually is crammed with students, visitors are always welcome. Since the new program began in September 1966, more than 3,500 educators have visited the demonstration center.*

*This article was planned with the cooperation of the American Association of School Librarians, an NEA department.

Inquiry Laboratory: Environment for Independent Study

James A. Jacobson

An inquiry lab? Sound exciting? It is at the William E. Orr Junior High where a steady stream of students come to carry on individual or small group learning activities involving primarily nonbook materials. It is unique in its construction, yet is so simple a plan any school could have one of its own.

LAB FACILITIES

The inquiry lab is located adjacent to the library which is the center of the curvilinear school. Cupboards, less than ceiling height, separate the lab from the commons area. "Packets" are classified, put in tote trays, and stored on the cupboard shelves. The ceiling and part of the floor are acoustically treated. One professional person with responsibility for lab development is assisted by one full-time aide for the management aspects. Teachers help provide materials and act as resource people. Student lab assistants aid in retrieving and cataloging materials as well as operating audio-visual equipment, and assisting other students.

Students are given approximately three hours per week for independent study. They make their own decisions about what they will study but they are accountable for their time and location during the independent study period. They may arrange to use either the inquiry lab or the library as a home base, and can change their plan if they do desire.

LAB ACTIVITIES

The activities in the lab are in four classifications: inquiry, audio-visual, manipulative, and games. A pupil may choose any category.

The inquiry "packets," stored in tote trays, vary in time required to complete them as well as in sophistication and interest. One of the more sophisticated options is a three-phase inquiry packet in music which centers around the concepts of rhythm, harmony, and melody and includes such things as tone bells, claves, a metronome, test tubes, tuning forks, string, paper cups, and so on. A coded tape based on the binary system which requires a response; a boiled

Reprinted from *Instructor*, April 1968, by permission from Instructor, © Instructor Publications, Inc.

turkey skeleton; modeling clay; paper sculpture; and a packet to test the strength of plywood versus unlaminated wood, are some of the interesting examples of inquiry packets.

If a pupil opts to work with audio-visual materials, a media catalog of various materials housed at the central office lets him order whatever 16 mm film, filmstrip, tape, or model he is interested in. Teachers also place various audio-visual materials for student review and enrichment. Single-concept film projectors, phonographs, and filmstrip viewers are in packet form for students to check out.

The manipulative packets consist of basic woodworking hand tools; tools for metal working, carving, block printing, linear measurement, weight measurement; and drafting tools.

Games such as chess, checkers, Scrabble, and Space Tic-Tac-Toe are provided to help students build vocabulary and develop their ability in problem solving and critical thinking. Some of the options are for small groups rather than individuals.

LAB OBJECTIVES

Specific objectives of the lab include:

- To give the student a wide variety of materials, light tools, machines, and equipment which he may utilize.
- To provide a pleasant laboratory facility conducive to experimentation and other activity-oriented methods of inquiry.
- To provide many opportunities for manipulative activities.
- To give the student an opportunity for the pursuit of self-initiated and self-motivated learning activities.
- To provide an environment which reflects the interrelatedness of all subject matter, and helps a student integrate his knowledge with all the disciplines.
- To provide an open laboratory for all disciplines to utilize.

LAB RESULTS

Student interest in and exposure to a wide variety of experiences and varying disciplines have been one of the most beneficial results of the inquiry lab. An area for divergence as well as enrichment has been beneficial to students as they work in small groups as well as on an individual basis.

The most critical problem in such a program is an adequate number of options for students, both commercial and teacher-generated. The amount of money available is a direct limiting factor on the number of commercially developed materials. Developing teacher-generated packets is also a problem, as teachers, at best, have inadequate preparation time. A released-time program for teachers during in-service days or a stipend for a summer workshop to develop packets would be a definite benefit to both teachers and students.

Staffing an inquiry lab might be a problem in some schools. William E. Orr School was fortunate in finding a person who conceptualized the purposes of the inquiry lab and developed excellent rapport with students. The success of such a program depends a great deal on well-chosen staff members.

Future plans for the inquiry lab at William E. Orr call for increase in the variety and number of options as well as the use of community resource people. These people will be asked to demonstrate and relate a skill, or provide information relating to occupations, banking, education, or any other topics of interest to students.

The inquiry lab has continued to grow in interest to both staff and students, and has been an effective new dimension to independent study.

Minnesota's Science Center: An Auto-tutorial Laboratory

Barbara Gross

A self-instructional method of learning to operate instruments and handle laboratory techniques essential to new science curricula is being tested at the University of Minnesota High School. Under the supervision of the method's originators, Clarence Boeck, professor of secondary education, and Eugene Gennaro, assistant professor of secondary education and science area head at the high school,* a Self-Instructional Demonstration Science Center has been opened to secondary education majors and teachers. The Center, consisting of 19 carrels, each containing equipment and mimeographed, step-by-step instructions for using the instruments, operates in one room of the high school's science suite.

Although the Center did not open until January, 1967, it was devised in 1965, after "the need for such a program had become increasingly apparent to us," Boeck explained. "Every methods teacher has been concerned over the fact that students in college lab courses are not at all prepared in advance to demonstrate and operate instruments and to teach the new techniques. We also noticed that much of the new equipment made available by scientific companies and

Reprinted from *The Science Teacher*, September 1967, by permission of the publisher

*Information for this article was obtained chiefly through interviews with Clarence Boeck and Eugene Gennaro. Both have approved the manuscript.

through Title III of the National Defense Education Act was never used because the teachers lacked the knowledge."

Two surveys bore out these observations. One, part of a University of Minnesota master's degree study by Paul Chalmers Beisenherz, indicated that in 1963 most Minneapolis and St. Paul high school teachers were unfamiliar with newer experimental procedures; if they wanted to learn the skills, they attended summer or in-service institutes. The other study, done by Gennaro in the 1965-66 school year, revealed that future teachers were not learning the laboratory techniques they would need to know when teaching, and that other University of Minnesota professors considered a revision of lab technique methods courses imperative.

The self-instructional method subsequently decided upon was suggested by a course called Demonstration in Physics which was offered at the University in the 1930's and by school programs, such as the one at Florida State University that incorporates physics lab techniques into methods courses, and another at Purdue University that employs a self-instructional method of learning botany lab techniques. Gennaro and Boeck obtained a grant from the Upper Midwest Regional Education Laboratory, stating as their objective the establishment of an auto-tutorial laboratory to serve as a model for other midwestern schools.

They assembled displays in the booths with the help of teaching assistants, selecting equipment that suited University High School's science curriculum and represented the new programs with which most present and future teachers would be working. Programs represented include BSCS, CHEM Study, CBA, ESCP, PSSC, and IPS. Carrel material varies in difficulty from contour mapping to operating the stroboscope and pH meter. The $3,000 laboratory is open Monday through Friday, from 9 AM to NOON and from 1 to 6 PM with teaching assistants on duty to offer help and to make changes in the instruction sheets. Teachers, student teachers, University High School students in advanced science courses or in the school's science club, and visitors wishing to use the equipment sign in and work at projects at their own speed. The teaching assistants have already noticed one advantage of the self-instructional method: "A project that takes one student a half hour may take another several hours," one commented. "Here students can work at their own speeds."

Although laboratory work in the carrels is not yet mandatory for student teachers, many have taken advantage of the Center, and Gennaro and Boeck hope eventually to integrate laboratory work in the carrels with the lab work already included in the curriculum.

"Another aspect of the program that is worth noting is the enthusiastic use of the carrels by the high school students," Gennaro said. "They are perhaps more enthusiastic than the student teachers and come in during the science club activity hour and with the advanced science class. The students are learning the techniques and then using them to further explore some area of science."

Scheduled improvements in the Center will include the use of demonstration films and tape-recorded directions to supplement the mimeographed instruction sheets. Two- to three-day institutes are planned for Twin City teachers. These institutes will include lectures exploring problems encountered when teaching with the new programs, as well as instruction in practical skills.

In its second year, the Center will offer statewide assistance and eventually will serve as a model laboratory for high schools and colleges throughout the Midwest. "We have already had people come in from around the state to check on the program, and had some out-of-state inquiries," Boeck said. "As a pilot project, we would hope other states would take the program and suit it to their own needs, as we suited it to ours. Although it's difficult to tell, since the program just started, the lab appears to be a success. Certainly everyone who uses it or sees it is enthusiastic. It will be interesting to see what happens."

Individualized Instruction in a Learning Laboratory Setting

Lola May

In this period of education it would seem the pressure is on to cram more and more into heads in a mad race to produce more and more right answers in shorter and shorter periods of time. It was decided in Winnetka, Illinois, to produce a laboratory setting of learning, a place where children could have searching experiences that would challenge them to use their thinking power, a place where children could make mistakes, learn from them, and thereby build more adequate comprehensive thinking power.

The learning laboratory in Winnetka is housed in the junior high school. The junior high school consists of 750 students in sixth, seventh, and eighth grades. The lab itself is a large L-shaped room that has carpeting on the floor, drapes on the windows, individual mobile carrels, tape booths, lots of supplies in all subject areas, and the usual variety of visual aid materials. It is not the material setting that really makes the difference, although one cannot but admit it does help. The thing that makes the difference is that there is a place where children can come to work where there is no *outside* pressure of learning, just the *inward* pressure of wanting to work on something that will satisfy them. They can go at their own rate and follow their own route.

Of the 750 students in the junior high school, over 200 are presently involved in the learning laboratory situation. Some children are studying a

Reprinted from *The Arithmetic Teacher,* February 1966 (vol. 13, pp. 110-112), © 1966 by the National Council of Teachers of Mathematics. Used by permission.

second language on the Army language tapes; others are improving their reading skills; some are working on social studies projects; and there is a group of ninety students who are working on mathematics projects. It is this group that I am going to describe in this article. During the course of an entire school year, there will be about 150-175 students who have worked on some mathematics project.

Mr. Joe Richardson is the director of the learning laboratory. His position is one of "jack-of-all-trades." He has a high regard for the student who wants to explore, question, and investigate. Mr. Richardson believes that making mistakes and questioning is the true discovery approach. He believes also that a mistake is one's own evaluation or assessment of one's own effort and with the help of an understanding adult who can ask the right questions, the significance of the mistake can be realized. There is no failure in the lab, for Mr. Richardson believes failure is a judgment of another and carries the irrevocable quality of finality. If mistakes do not take place, then there is no learning taking place. The individuals are helped to make the effort to see where their plans have gone wrong.

Of the ninety students presently in the lab working on mathematics projects, most of them have been referred by their classroom teacher. Some of the students are ahead of their class and can be released from class a few periods a week. A few of the students are so advanced that they are not enrolled in any class but do all of their work in mathematics in the lab. There are some average learners who come to the lab during study periods to work on something that is of interest to them. This gives them more incentive to do their regular work in the mathematics class. Last, there is the slow learner who comes to the lab to get help in some area so he can gather enough strength to continue his work in the regular classroom.

The students interested in mathematics are under the guidance of the author, who is mathematics consultant in Winnetka. Each student is on his own individual program planned by the consultant after conferring with the student. Much of the beginning material used by the student is material written by the consultant. There are units on Geometric Construction, Probability, Introduction to Algebra, and Graphing. The units are written so that the student can work independently. If he needs help, his questions are answered. After a student gets a start on a subject with the units he is then referred to other materials in the lab that will allow him to go into greater depth.

There are several students who have gotten so excited in the area of geometric construction that they have constructed very complex polyhedrons out of plastic materials. Renee and Lisa look at pictures of models and then figure out the basic patterns with their compasses, rulers, and pencils. Both of these girls gave up the opportunity to take ninth-grade algebra in the eighth grade. Renee decided she would rather have a year of working on projects in mathematics she would enjoy, and this way be able to explore many different areas; Lisa followed her example. Neither of the girls regrets her decision.

There are some slow learners who have never succeeded in the classroom in the area of numbers, but find great satisfaction in learning how to construct tetrahedrons, octahedrons, bisect line segments, etc. The glow in their faces as they hold up their geometric models that they have constructed by following the simple instructions, is worth a great deal. Then they advance to the solid lab kit where they learn about the relationship of faces, vertices, and edges of polyhedrons.

Several seventh-grade boys started out on Suppes' *Elementary Logic* book and from this have started to play the Wff'n Proof game. They are now in the advanced stages of this game; they have found the study of logic a fascinating project and cannot get enough of it.

Some students are studying probability. They all started out on the unit written by the consultant and then went to the probability kit that takes them into permutations, combinations, and binomial theorem. Many of them end up by creating their own studies of chance.

Two sixth-grade boys became interested in number patterns and puzzles. They worked together to find their own patterns and after many weeks printed their own book of mathematics puzzles and patterns.

Topology has become an area of interest of several students. One can find them sitting together with their rubber sheet and flow pens, discussing variant transformations. One day they figured out a formula for cutting a möbius strip into many parts. Their source of information is a pamphlet on topology and then a book on experiments in topology.

As one watches the students at work in the lab, he sees some students working alone and others working in small groups. If someone is having difficulty, another student who is beyond that stage often will help him figure out the trouble spot. Many students take great pride in their work and, as they become excited, will go over and share their excitement with other students. This type of learning can happen only in a setting that is flexible.

On the other end of the spectrum are the students who come because they need help in a specific spot, such as the the multiplication tables. They are given programmed material, filmstrips, and work on a machine that will help increase their speed after they have an understanding of the facts. The joy they receive when they find they can develop speed and accuracy with a little outside work away from the pressure of a classroom situation, is most gratifying.

The closed-circuit television is connected with the learning laboratory. The mathematics consultant can teach all nine sixth grades at one time. On the average of twice a month, a mathematics program is developed. This is timed so that the material given over television coincides with the work that most of the students are doing in the class. The objective is for the consultant to present material that will give background for the units to be covered in the classroom.

The classrooms have telephones, enabling students to call in questions at the end of the presentation that can be answered immediately. Usually during every broadcast there are work sheets distributed that the students work during the television period. Sometimes the program is just an enrichment program to get students interested in various aspects of mathematics that are not covered in their daily work. The teachers find that the television program is a good change of pace, and the students enjoy watching someone they know on the screen.

The two art teachers in the junior high school spend half of their day making projectuals, charts, slides, and models for the teachers. This is a great assistance to the teacher who does not have the ability or the time to make the visuals that she needs to make her work in the classroom or on television more meaningful.

For years Winnetka has been known for individualized learning. What is meant by this is that a child can progress at his own rate in any subject while the classroom teacher tries to extend herself to help all the children. In theory this is fine, but in practice it is almost impossible in the upper grades. The learning laboratory is making this myth come true in the upper grades. Students can really progress at their own speed along the lines of their greatest interest. The people connected with the lab are the consultants in various fields who know their subject matter. These people can help a student extend himself in any direction his interest dictates.

The enthusiasm of the consultant for his own subject soon rubs off on the student and the joy they share together cannot be measured.

We believe in grouping in Winnetka, but it is not the grouping that is meant by placing all the bright together, the average in another group, and the slow learners in a group. In the lab the children are grouped according to their ability, enthusiasm, and interest. The grouping is an individual grouping, and competition is within the individual. The slow learner does not feel he is slow because he is working in the same room with all types of children. His work is not compared to someone else's work because each is on an individual program.

The days of one teacher facing twenty-five children in a small rectangular room, trying to care for all their needs within that small area, are over in Winnetka. We still need the classroom teacher, but he needs the extension of his classroom into the learning laboratory to care for the individual needs of his children.

We have not done any research with data and statistics to prove any hypotheses. This will come in a year or two, when we finally settle down to prove some small area of our work. What we have found is that children can learn a great deal on their own without the lock step of the classroom situation. To really individualize instruction you have to stop talking about it and start putting it into practice.

There are children in Winnetka today who really see the beauty of mathematics because they have the opportunity to explore. They are learning how to educate themselves. The only reward they receive is the satisfaction of producing a piece of work that they are proud of and then, if they wish, they can share it with others. Motivation is transmitted only through human beings, not through written pages; these children motivate each other. In the words of Andy, who last year was an average eighth-grade math student: "If mathematics had been like this before, just think of the things I would know today!"

Effective Use of the Resources Center

Charles F. Cardinelli

In his historic book *Focus on Change — Guide to Better Schools* and in the January, 1966 Bulletin, J. Lloyd Trump calls for a student study area radically different from the traditional. He calls for a *learning resources center*. This would not be an expansion of the library along old lines. It would be, instead, the heart of the school. Such a center would include a variety of spaces for students' individual or group reading, viewing, and listening, and for various kinds of laboratory work in all subject areas.

Is such a practice feasible in today's high school? Experimentation along the lines of Trump's proposal has shown that such learning centers can help children learn to work independently. The establishment of learning centers in various curriculum areas will give students opportunities to develop an awareness of the need to make intelligent choices concerning the most effective use of their time. This seldom results consistently from the traditional study hall-library assignment.

This suggests that the child, given the opportunity for unstructured inquiry and the pursuit of intellectual ends important to himself, will gain an added dimension of scholarly satisfaction. For a particular child with an intellectual task of his own making and of appropriate high order, study and investigation time spent in a learning resources center will be profitable and will carry over affirmatively into the more conventional classroom.*

· Reprinted by permission of the National Association of Secondary School Principals from *NASSP Bulletin,* September 1966. Copyright 1966 by the National Association of Secondary School Principals.

*Marland, Sidney P., Jr. "Winnetka's Learning Laboratory." *Educational Leadership* 20: 459; April, 1963.

The Portland Public Schools have recognized that one of the important goals of education is to develop a person who can be self-sufficient. To accomplish this, the student must be given opportunity for such independent study and research. The Portland schools recognize that not all students can develop the same degree of independence. Realizing this, they are striving to provide each student an optimum amount of independent study.**

Learning resources centers have been established in five Portland high schools, and a high school under construction is being designed around this philosophy. Learning resources centers are being established in other high schools as rapidly as funds and facilities allow.

FACILITIES, EQUIPMENT, AND MATERIALS

The facilities that are to be available in a learning resources center depend on the unique activities of the particular area. What is provided depends basically on what the school is trying to provide for its students. The design of a social studies learning resources center is used here to illustrate the kinds of equipment that should be included in most learning centers.

In one subject area, the social studies, the purposes are three: (1) to prepare youth to become participating citizens in our democratic form of government; (2) to transmit our cultural heritage; (3) to give students a mastery of the skills of the social studies.†

The environment of a learning resources center must be conducive to study and to use of varied media. Examination of the following list which was drawn up for social studies resources centers will reveal that nearly all of the facilities would be common to centers in other academic areas. In fact, several Portland resources centers are shared by social studies and modern languages. The facilities and equipment are used interchangeably by students of both areas.

    chalkboard
    tackboard
    map rails
    closed circuit television facilities
    radio and television antenna lead-ins
    heat, light, and ventilation equal to regular classroom standards
    acoustical treatment on ceiling, walls, floors
    floor space equal to 30 square feet per child

**Portland Public Schools. *Educational Guidelines for Southwest High School*. Portland, Oreg., 1964. p. 13

†For a complete statement of the system's educational goals, see p. 8 of *Principles of Education*, published by the Superintendent's Curriculum Advisory Council, Portland (Oregon) Public Schools, 1961.

sink
adjacent room for meetings, rehearsals, etc.
adjacent room for arts, crafts, activities
adjacent room for librarian work
display area, both shelves and glass cases
storage for: artifacts, realia, models, maps, charts, posters, arts and crafts
    materials, films, filmstrips, recordings, library materials, back issues of
    periodicals
desk for staff
staff coat and hat storage
library counter and charging area
power facilities for an increased concentration of audio-visual equipment
display and easy-to-use racks for newspapers and magazines
book shelving

As yet, no one resources center in the Portland schools has been able to incorporate all these facilities. The list was intended as a goal for schools to strive for and was used as a basis for establishing new resources centers.

In selecting storage facilities, shelving and student study stations, it would be wise to choose semiportable, modular-designed units that may be arranged as desired within the resources center. This design feature will be of particular use in the open central cores of classroom buildings now being constructed. It is envisioned that within these core areas, such modular furnishings as bookcases, storage units, carrels and wall partitions could be combined and recombined as need arises into the type of resources centers desired.

Children studying independently in the learning resources center need to use a variety of materials and equipment that formerly were reserved for large group activities. Children in the resources centers are encouraged to make use of films, filmstrips, recordings, wall maps and the like on their own as they need them.

Equipment needed in social studies learning resources centers include:

tape recorder and disc record players equipped with headphones for quiet,
    individual listening
motion picture, slide, and filmstrip projectors usable on table top
maps
globes
magazine display rack
flag holders
study tables with chairs
flannel board and materials
sand table for terrain studies
filing cabinet for clippings, pictures, pamphlet files
library card catalog of materials in the center
raised relief maps of locality, nation, world
typewriters
chairs, upholstered, for reading

study carrels
portable microfilm readers
reading accelerators
intercom between resources center and central library

Selection of books and other materials is dependent on the study area. General recommendations for a social studies learning resources center include:
approximately 100-200 reference books
encyclopedias
comprehensive world atlas
6-10 magazines espousing different points of view
dictionaries
pamphlet and clipping files
facsimiles of famous documents
pictures of historical nature
portraits of national and world leaders
supplementary texts
biographical titles to supplement and enrich the subject
fiction titles related to the study area to motivate students to independent reading
library catalog of materials in resources center
catalog of visual aids available from a central depository
films, filmstrips, and slides relating to the study area
recordings, tape and disc
Readers' Guide
selection of materials to fit needs of children of various abilities

Resources centers draw from the central library in the building. Funds are provided for purchase of multiple copies of basic reference materials so that there can be copies in both central library and resources centers. Materials are changed frequently as needs arise. A subject catalog will show the books in each resources center, while the central library has a union catalog showing the location of all books to be found in the high school.

In addition, Portland high school resources centers borrow specialized books from other libraries such as the Library Association of Portland and the Oregon State Library. Such interlibrary loans are essential to students carrying on independent research.

Visual aids, microfilms, tapes, and recordings are available from ever-growing building collections. Extra materials of this nature are available from the Portland schools' central repository for use in the resources centers.

UTILIZATION AND ADMINISTRATION

Schools with learning resources centers allow children to come to the centers in lieu of assigned study halls. Children who want to study in a particular area go to the appropriate resources center. Students desiring to study in depth will sometimes turn to the central library for its greater resources.

While it was originally expected that resources centers would relieve the load on the central libraries, Portland high schools have found that there is increasing interest in using library facilities. Standing-room-only situations prevail, forcing children to decide whether to go to the more spacious central library in the hope of finding similar materials or to go to another study area. While frustrating, having to choose between these alternatives is an acceptable part of the Trump philosophy. It in itself is a valuable educational experience and well within the goals and objectives of a good high school program.

Supervision of resources centers has been satisfactorily handled by library aides. Generally they are noncertificated personnel drawing less salary than teachers or librarians. They have training to help students use effectively the resource materials in the centers. Material selection, policy making, and student disciplining are left to professional members of the staff.

Increasingly, schools have an associate librarian to coordinate the various resources centers within each high school and direct the efforts of the aides. To test out the idea of the superiority of professional librarians over aides in resources centers a notable study was undertaken in one Portland school.

During the school year 1965-66, Portland's Roosevelt High School received a grant from the Knapp School Library Project. Funds were provided for establishment of three new resources centers and hiring of professional librarians to staff them. While a professional librarian was in each center nearly all the time, they were rotated to insure that all centers operated in the same manner and to allow particular librarians with special talents to be in the various centers when their talents could be capitalized upon.

In addition, library aides and library assistants were assigned to center staffs. Lines of communication were established between the teachers and the library and resources center staffs for reporting pertinent information about interests, needs, abilities, attitudes, achievements, and performances of students.

The professional librarians undertook an intensive in-service training program for library aides, library assistants, and the teacher aides in the building. Frequent orientation tours were given the faculty during the year to keep them aware of new facilities and services being added by the library and resources centers.

COOPERATIVE EFFORT

As in other Portland high schools, maintaining the centers' selections of materials and upkeep of bulletin boards is a cooperative effort between teachers and library staff. Teachers come to the resources center librarians with the general outline of their curricula. The librarians then assemble suitable collections for the centers from various sources available. Displays of books are made that will interest students of all abilities. The team approach between classroom teacher and librarian results in a use of library resources seldom possible before. Roosevelt High School reports that student demand for all library services has tripled in the first year of the Knapp Library Project.

While high schools report increased numbers of students using resources centers there are, generally speaking, few discipline problems. One possible explanation might be that only the highly motiviated students choose to use the facilities. Practice has shown, however, that where special centers or collections are established for slower learners, these children use them with the same high purpose and seriousness as do the more able.

Other than reminding children to converse in library tones, the aides do no disciplining. Referral to a teacher for possible deprivation of resources center privileges is usually the necessary deterrent. Most high schools require students to remain the full period in the resources center.

Successful resources centers in a variety of subject matter areas have been established in Portland high schools. The most numerous centers are those with specialized materials for the ninth grade combined English and social studies classes. Separate resources centers for advanced English and social studies are also in operation. Foreign language centers are often provided. One school combined the materials for fine arts, industrial arts, and homemaking into a novel and effective resource center. Science and mathematics were combined in another school. No set pattern prevails at the present time in all Portland schools.

In summary, for effective utilization of resources centers, a school must make the following commitments:

1. Teachers will place curriculum emphasis on exploration of materials and inquiry rather than having children routinely answer pedestrian study questions. By the school's placing a high value on the inquiry approach to learning, children will in turn become highly motivated to use materials in the centers.

2. The school, preferably with student interaction, will set up policies that will eliminate the possibility of discipline problems in the resources centers. Supervised study areas are necessary for those students not yet able to work independently. (Several Portland high schools have special rooms for such upperclassmen. In addition, as part of the team teaching schedule at the ninth grade, medium-sized groups either study under supervision, learning to work independently, or are taught independent study skills by teachers trained and assigned for this.)

3. Resources centers will be staffed by professional librarians or highly trained library aides who maintain the resources of the centers and who help students with research rather than merely dispensing books on required reading lists.

4. Teachers will work cooperatively with the librarians in revising and obtaining new materials for the resources centers. Teachers, and students for that matter, should take part in keeping the center an alive, stimulating place to study by means of bulletin boards, displays of pictures, murals, and artifacts.

EVALUATION

The key to effective learning resources centers lies in a total school commitment to a program of independent study. Such commitment includes adequate facilities, equipment, and resource materials. The faculty and library staff must cooperate to make sure the materials available are appropriate and that the resources centers are exciting places to study. Constant evaluation of the resources centers will make them effective in furthering children's ability to study independently.

Evaluation must be in terms of the desired educational goals of the school in general and of the special subject matter area in particular. The following criteria are submitted to help schools evaluate social studies learning resources centers. All activities undertaken in the social studies resources center should be evaluated by one or more of these criteria. The specific facilities and materials in other resources centers can be similarly evaluated.

1. Is the resources center used by students independently in pursuing intellectual ends through unstructured inquiry?
2. Is the student developing an awareness of the need to choose intelligently in using his time?
3. Are materials available for the student to add to his study a dimension of scholarly satisfaction?
4. Is the student gaining the skills to use reference materials independently and effectively?
5. Are materials available that interpret the contemporary natural and social environment of the student?
6   Are the materials available such that will kindle interest for further study and leisure-time activity in the social sciences?
7. Are the skills that the students are learning those that will be used further in education, work, or citizenship?
8. Are materials available that will encourage the student to appreciate his cultural heritage?
9. Do the resources center and its materials have an aesthetic appeal to kindle interest and participation in the fine arts?
10. Are the materials available that can be used by students of all interests and abilities?

The Student Resource Center

Jack Tanzman

I've spent many hours discussing "student resource centers" with school administrators. They all tell me that, "No school should ever be without one." And in the next breath they hasten to explain that their reason for not having one is because it is "far too expensive."

This is nonsense. What they're really saying is that they don't know how to install a resource center without spending thousands of dollars and utilizing an ultramodern facility. And this shows that they don't really know what a resource center is.

Despite the fancy name, the resource center is nothing more than the old study hall, outfitted with some new equipment and materials.

TAKE THREE CLASSROOMS . . .

You don't have to build a replica of the New York Public Library. Students simply need a place where they can study independently using materials *other* than library books. It can be part of the library or even a little-used office area. The trick is to locate it where students can reach it easily — and use it.

Let's look at the Garden City, N.Y., high school center. David V. Guerin, coordinator of instructional materials, claims he got the center through a lucky break. I think he got it because he wanted it badly enough. Guerin asked for — and got — three classrooms in a new wing of the school. The classrooms ran adjacent to the library. He knocked down a few partitions, took over a very small portion of the library, and divided the entire area into space for (1) 24 individual carrels, (2) a "vision panel," utilizing a rear-screen projection system and, (3) a production and equipment center for developing, producing and storing AV aids.

The carrels are built in six clusters. Each cluster contains four carrels, radiating out from a common central leg. Each is a "wet" carrel, electrically geared and wired for listening. If a student wants to listen to records or tapes, he simply gets a headset from the nearby issue counter. A librarian "plugs him in" by putting on the record or tape *at the issue center*, and the student is all set. Each carrel can receive a different recording, or the same material can be piped out to many carrels simultaneously.

. . . AND ADD A VISION PANEL

The "vision panel" is a pane of ground glass — a strip, 14 feet wide and one foot high — set into a floor-to-ceiling partition. Students sit on one side of the partition to view films; projection equipment is set up on the other side, about eight feet out from one of the center's permanent walls. Two more partitions run at right angles from the vision panel to box off the chamber from the rest of the center. A built-in door is the only means of access.

The "vision room" is lined with shelves which house a series of rear-screen projectors. When a student wishes to view a film he simply submits his request to an aide at the issue counter. He is furnished with a headset and given a seat facing the glass panel. The aide then sets up the projector behind the panel. The opaque glass strip becomes the viewing screen, the headset transmits sound, blocks out extraneous noise. When the student is through, he returns the headset to the issue counter. The aide then returns to shut off the projector but no one has to be in the vision room while the film is being viewed.

The vision panel provides many of the advantages of a movie theater, yet retains the privacy of television. As many as six or seven students can view different films simultaneously, with no cross-over of sight or sound. And, several students can view the same film together by plugging their headsets into the same sound track.

The center is staffed as simply as it is designed. One librarian operates the resource center's issue counter. The school's AV coordinator is in charge of producing AV materials and keeps an eye on equipment in the center. And 25 to 30 students work part-time distributing AV equipment and materials in the center.

Now, this may not be the type of "student resource center" that you've been dreaming about for your school. But it's practical. It's inexpensive. And most important, students use it.

Study Centers for the Underachiever

Al G. Langford

What are the public high schools of Texas doing to help the underachiever? A few schools have added to the curriculum vocational and nongraded courses,

Reprinted from *Texas Outlook*, December 1968, by permission of The Texas State Teachers Association.

ut the mass of underachievers receive little additional help. For more than three years, Lamesa High administrators have been seeking an efficient means of tutoring these students.

In the 1964-65 school year, the growing list of failing or unsatisfactory students caused the high school counselor to become alarmed. After several weeks of studying this situation, Lamesa High began its first supervised study hall, meeting from 8 a.m. until 8:45 a.m., when the first bell rang. All students failing one or more subjects were urged to attend. Outstanding students were selected to serve as tutors in certain academic areas, with the counselor serving as coordinator.

From the beginning, the underachievers evidenced a desire for additional help. They turned out in great numbers for the respective study halls. Before long, however, the attendance declined considerably.

The student tutors, even though they enjoyed their roles as tutors, were lacking in skills, knowledge, and experience to do a satisfactory job of supervising the study halls. After four weeks, the experiment was abandoned.

In the fall of 1965, Title I of the Elementary and Secondary Education Act became a reality. We immediately sought ways to aid the educationally deprived child in Lamesa High. After numerous faculty meetings and department conferences, it was decided to begin night study halls, with teachers serving as tutors in their fields. The library also became an after-school study center.

The following objectives were established: (a) To improve performance as measured by standardized achievement tests; (b) To improve classroom performance in all skill areas; (c) To improve student attitude toward self and school; (d) To improve the holding power of the school; and (e) To provide a suitable place in which to study and read.

With these objectives in mind, we organized the study center according to the following plan: The library was opened from 6 p.m. until 9 p.m. on Mondays, Tuesdays, and Thursdays for use by all students (plans are now being formulated to open the library six days a week after school hours).

The school employed a library clerk to work part-time during the regular school day and supervise the library at night. Students in English, math, and science were in the greatest need of help. The study hall rooms for each of these subjects were open to students from 7 p.m. until 8 p.m. on Monday, Tuesday, and Thursday each week.

Teachers volunteered for work as supervisors and received pay for one and one-fourth hours according to their individual salary scale per hour during the day. Teachers might supervise only in their area of certification.

The assistant principal and the counselor supervised the study center on an alternating basis, since someone needed to be responsible for the overall operation of the study center. Few discipline problems occurred, because the students were in attendance for a definite purpose.

School buses transported students from the economically deprived areas of the school district to the after-school study center and back home again after it was over.

Students signed in and out in each study hall and in the library. This record aided in evaluating the program.

After the program was started, business, foreign language, and remedial reading were added to the supervised study hall areas. Reading was abandoned after a short trial run because of the lack of student interest. Business is now offered on Tuesday nights, and foreign language is offered on Thursday nights.

Large attendance in some areas has at times necessitated two supervising teachers. The program plan calls for a supervising teacher to work with not more than 12 students each night. Underachievers need individual instruction, and a limited number of students makes possible such instruction.

The study center began operation at midterm of the 1965-66 school year. It has been a highly successful program for Lamesa High, and attendance has grown considerably from the beginning. The circulation of library books has nearly doubled, and adults have used our library at nights on numerous occasions.

A comparison of students on the unsatisfactory report at midterm 1965-66 with the students on the unsatisfactory report at midterm 1966-67 revealed the following results:

- Of 848 students in school during 1965-66, 241 were on report, or 28.52 percent of the total.
- Of 815 students in school during 1966-67, 203 students were on report, or 24.90 percent of the total. This is a 3.62 percent decrease from the year before.
- Breaking the students on report down by ethnic groups, 21.16 percent of the Anglo students were on report in 1965-66 as opposed to 19.57 percent in 1966-67. This is a decrease of 1.59 percent.
- A decrease of 7.46 percent was noted among Mexican American students in 1966-67, as the percentage of students on report dropped from 47.46 in 1965-66 to 40.00.
- Among Negro students, the percentage of those on report fell from 73.16 percent in 1965-66 to 50.00 in 1966-67, or a decrease by 23.16 percent.

A degree of the program's success may be found in the significant decrease of 23 percent of Negro students and 7.5 percent of Mexican American students on the unsatisfactory report after one year in the program, and in the rise in attendance. During the first year, an average of 49.5 students were in attendance per night. This year more than 100 students have been present on several occasions.

The tutoring after-school study center is not the only answer to solving all of the problems of the underachiever. However, it can be a method to provide needed help for these students.

The Instructional Materials Center

Bruce R. Purrington

In public school education where an emphasis on quality is stressed, authorities and organizations promote the use of instructional materials as a means of revitalizing and strengthening the curriculum.

In a 1959 report on quality in education, the Educational Policies Commission of the National Education Association describes teaching as being more than the use of textbooks and workbooks. The Commission envisions present-day teaching as utilizing multiple texts for students with differing vocabularies and reading abilities. In addition, teaching at present must necessarily deal with magazines, newspapers, films, filmstrips, television, pictures, maps, globes, models, museum materials and recordings.*

Likewise, music education must use similar materials in addition to musical instruments, radio, tapes and video tapes, resource people, and live performances to realize its potential in a quality education program.

What is the instructional materials center? It has been called a variety of names, such as a library, a resource center, a materials center, and an audio-visual center. Perhaps this center can best be understood by relating it to that of a university. What is a university? It is a collection of several schools or colleges. The instructional materials center is very much like a university, with a collection of several libraries or resource units containing libraries of printed materials, projected materials, transmitted materials, and recorded materials. When centrally organized, an instructional materials center evolves.

INSTRUCTIONAL MATERIALS CENTER

In a published article concerning school library service, the author selected

---

Reprinted from *Music Journal*, March 1968, by permission of the publisher.

*National Education Association, Educational Policies Commission, *An Essay on Quality in Public Education*, Washington, D.C., The Association, 1959, p. 10.

four areas in which the functions of the center may be divided, and he entitled them in the following manner: (1) a service agency, the function being to advance the objectives of the educational unit, (2) a teaching agency, the objective being to stimulate interest and to supply a vast variety of materials, (3) a materials center, the purpose being to house a variety of materials, and (4) a reading-viewing-listening center, the concern being the guidance, selection, and the furnishing of a room for these activities.**

PROGRAM

How does the music program fit in with the instructional materials center and its services? An example of each of the functions provided by the center as it applies to music education will illustrate avenues to quality music education.

I. The first function of the instructional materials center is *service*. A typical service for the music program might be materials selection for classroom use.

Instructional materials find many avenues of approach to the classroom, often passing through the skillful, selective hands of the director of the center, the classroom teacher, by way of the specialist, and with the student himself. Books and audio-visual aids offer boys and girls sources of inspiration, enjoyment, and information for general and special topics through reading, viewing and listening. Such materials are considered a basic part of any classroom activity.

But what books and audio-visual aids are best suited for any particular classroom or grouping of students? The classroom teacher, music educator, and students should consider whether the materials available cover the topics that are needed for the classroom projects, whether there is an adequate variety of materials, and whether the reading and interest level is appropriate for the individuals that constitute the class.

To illustrate, a music teacher is considering a unit on "The Instruments of the Orchestra." Within the limits of this subject, the music teacher and students, with the aid of the professional personnel, can select appropriate resources from a wide variety of materials which are located in the center.

> Books:
> The Heart of the Orchestra (Craig)
> Shining Brasses (Tetzlaff)
> Science and Music (Berger)
> The Story Behind Musical Instruments (Montgomery)
> What Makes an Orchestra (Balet)
> All About the Symphony and What It Plays (Commins)
> Horns (Kettelkamp)

**"Philosophy of School Library Service," *School Library Bulletin* 43:2 April, 1950.

Drums, Rattles, and Bells (Kettelkamp)
Flutes, Whistles, and Reeds (Kettelkamp)
Shining Strings (Kettelkamp)

Films:
Development of Musical Instruments (NET)
Instruments of the Band and Orchestra (Coronet)
Instruments of the Orchestra (Contemporary)

Filmstrips:
Instruments of the Symphony Orchestra (Handy)

Pictures:
Meet the Instruments (Bowmar)

Recordings:
Hunter's Horn (Y.P.R. Series)
Instruments of the Orchestra (Walton)
Young Person's Guide to the Orchestra (Britten)

Slides:
European Musical Instruments (Crosby Brown)

Tapes:
Musical Treasure Series (WBUR)

II. The second function of the instructional materials center is *teaching* the uses of the materials therein. An example: teaching the use of the music dictionary-encyclopedia *Oxford Junior Companion to Music*.

Within this single volume for children are found articles, definitions, composer backgrounds, musicians, instruments, various forms and styles of music, musical terms and expressions, church music, and a vast variety of musical information.

For students to locate needed musical materials and information as well as to gain a better understanding of many music topics, the staff in the center teaches the efficient use and content of such a music tool.

III. The third function of the instructional materials center is the housing and distribution of *many types of materials*. One such project which calls upon the extensive resources of the center is the preparation of a debate on a music topic.

Developing a music debate for older students can be one of the most rewarding projects that a music teacher can inspire. The opportunity to get extensive use of instructional tools, exercises in thinking in both the preparation and presentation, profound understanding of some aspects of music, development of confidence in oral presentation, and ability to prepare, write, and organize materials for debate – all these are worthy outcomes from initiating an activity of this nature.

How might a music teacher and his class go about developing such a unit?

The ideas may give the teacher some direction as to how to proceed.

1. Selection of a music problem that is pertinent and worth investigating, as "Should the United States Government Subsidize the Arts?"
2. Study of the music problem that the class has selected from resources, many originating in the instructional materials center. Part of this step should include a working bibliography of materials in the center, containing references to books, pamphlets, newspapers, instructional tools, vertical file, list of the people in the community appropriate for resource information, agencies which are connected with this type of problem, periodicals, documents, reports, and audio-visual materials.
3. Record evidence in support of the debate argument.
4. Conduct the debate.

IV. The fourth function of the instructional materials center is a reading-listening-viewing center. For most students, performance and musical composition terminate with the formal education experience. But the role of the adult as a listener (especially in music) never ceases. The individual who studies one concerto or one ballad will benefit immeasurably in his future listening habits since all concertos and all ballads have similarities.

Perhaps the most important single aspect to music education is teaching students how to listen and gain knowledge, understanding and appreciation. The variety of activities in this area offered by the center will serve the future adult with a tremendous background of musical knowledge. Such a program may include innumerable approaches and possibilities for listening experiences through recordings.

1. Listening to recordings either as individuals or in small groups through earphones at a listening table or in a soundproof cubicle.
2. Developing organized and theme-centered musical programs to be given in the listening area of the instructional materials center. Various music students may be in charge each week and have typed-out programs with program notes they wrote from the resources found in the center.
3. Reading the musical score along with the recording to get an intelligent insight into the music.
4. "Browsing by ear" so that an intelligent selection of recordings may be made for borrowing and buying purposes.
5. Making comparisons of musical interpretations for critical analysis of music.

Many of these activities should be augmented with further investigation into the study of music through the other musical resources that are located in the center.

Since musical recordings are playing an important part in the lives of people today, these activities should be carefully and fully developed, for they will determine the musical knowledge and taste of tomorrow.

CONCLUSION

A number of important indicators seem to assure a strong future for a music education program with instructional materials: (1) there is a number of rapidly expanding sources of quality musical knowledge for children, located in printed, graphic, projected, and transmitted materials, (2) there is an increase of audio-visual departments in public school situations which are combining with library facilities, creating instructional materials centers, (3) there is a variety of functional facilities that are now being included within the center, such as extra rooms and electrical equipment, (4) there are a few centers which are beginning to employ subject matter specialists rather than general librarians, and (5) there are educational institutions which are presently placing an emphasis upon the instructional materials center as the hub of the curriculum.

Music education is reorganizing and broadening its scope of studies and activities so that its focal point is now on scholarship and musicianship. These two curriculum aspects are becoming the backbone to a solid foundation in public school music education.

Information Retrieval for Teachers

F. Curtis May

Are teachers aware of the advances in pedagogy? Are they keeping up with changes and advances within their own subject fields in any manner other than by taking miscellaneous courses from time to time? The Boulder Valley School District, Boulder, Colorado, feels that while most teachers read some professional literature, the coverage is limited. The costs of maintaining a personal library of sufficient depth and breadth is beyond most teachers; the amount of writing to be culled is enough to discourage even those with the best intentions; worthwhile information is frequently available in forms and from sources which are not readily accessible to an individual. This is where the library can be useful.

The complexity of the problem is beyond most school librarians. Busy as they are with students in a school situation or, in a professional library, with so many teachers with such varying needs and interests to serve, they attempt to provide a greater or lesser amount of data. Is it possible to provide for teachers information in sufficient quantity and adequate specificity which will at the

Reprinted from *California School Libraries,* November 1968 by permission of the publisher.

same time not overwhelm them with unwanted data? Can this be done within a reasonable cost?

Mr. Leonard Freiser of the Toronto Schools attacked the problem by photoduplicating the tables of contents of professional journals and then sending them to teachers who were interested in specific subject fields. Consequently teachers could request the original journal or a copy of the specific article from the central library. This solution has its drawbacks, however, when any depth of coverage is attempted. It requires that the teacher plow through a great amount of extraneous material. An article of interest to a mathematics teacher might be in a general interest periodical or even a journal of another related field. Titles are not always indicative of the contents of the article, and frequently do not indicate grade level or bias. While periodicals cover a wide range of data, other information, which may be specifically wanted, is available only in other forms.

Many librarians have sent out short abstracts of articles, but usually because of limitation in time or space, these have been limited to items of general interest. If the listing is expanded to any great extent, the teacher is burdened with a quantity of materials which are not pertinent to his interests. If special subject lists are produced the amount of labor involved is often too great for the librarian and the lists are still too general for most teachers to pay attention to them.

Under the leadership of Mrs. Violet Wagener, the Boulder Valley School District presented to the U.S. Office of Education an application for an Elementary and Secondary Education Act Title III grant to demonstrate an answer to the problem. A Cooperative Community Educational Resources Center was established to keep teachers, administrators, and the community aware of developments in the educational field and of the resources available within the community.

Information from all possible sources has been used in the system. A major new source of information is ERIC, *Research in Education.* These monthly catalogs index and abstract numerous articles, reports, pamphlets, and other documents. The originals are available on Microfische, so the entire library of ERIC materials is being purchased. The ERIC catalogs are also indexing some four hundred periodicals. Since the Microfische does not contain the periodicals, subscriptions to all of these journals have been added to the library. New books purchased by the professional library, whether pedagogy or student texts, are analyzed and abstracted. The University of Colorado cooperates by abstracting some of their new purchases which are thought to be of interest. Speeches are recorded on tape and listed for future use. Conference proceedings are not neglected, whether in print or non-print form. Films, slidetapes, videotape presentations, curriculum guides, unpublished papers, and even community resources including both people and places are included in the data bank.

As these materials are gathered, the original is abstracted as is necessary (this has already been done for ERIC materials), a list of subject headings or descriptions for each item is decided upon, and, with an identifying accession number, the package is fed into a computer for later retrieval.

Teachers and administrators are queried about their interests. The individuals specify what subjects or what portions of subjects they are interested in and the center staff translates these requests into subject descriptors which match the machine input. These requests may be as general as a request for all materials on mathematics or as specific as teaching chemistry to blind students.

Once a month each teacher receives a computer print-out tailored specifically to his requests. The print-out contains only those items whose descriptors match those which he has requested. Each item contains the full bibliographic data and the abstract. It has been found that in 75% of the cases the abstract contains sufficient information for the user, but in the other 25% of the cases the original item can easily and rapidly be sent to the individual. Special requests can be answered at any time. When a teacher develops a new interest or is about to teach a new class, the computer can be queried to retrieve all old information in the data bank; when a community problem arises, the background of research and articles can be culled for appropriate materials.

Thus it is hoped that the teacher will obtain only those items in which he has a potential interest; that the list will be long enough to give him a sufficient coverage of the field and at the same time not overwhelm him with unwanted information. The usual problems of inadequate descriptors (frequently lack of specificity) have arisen, but they are being constantly lessened by constructive criticism from the patrons and the library staff. At the present time the program has the capacity of retrieving in two ways: (1) when the subject is listed and (2) when two subjects or descriptors are listed jointly (e.g., remedial reading, but only if at the secondary level). It is planned to add the capacity of retrieval in a third manner: one subject but only when a second is not listed (e.g., algebra, but not if also described as new mathematics).

The cost of the operation during the 1967 planning period when the system was first set up and when the first materials were purchased was $27,000. The current year's budget is $50,000, which includes all costs for the indexing, the abstracting, the input to the computer, the computer costs themselves, the print-outs, the purchasing of materials, and the management of the project. It has been estimated by Mrs. Wagener, project director, that as a long term operation, it would cost $15 per teacher if there were one thousand persons served, but that the cost per person would decrease considerably as the number of patrons increased.

Pseudopodial High School Can Shrink or Spread Its Learning Center

Robert S. Brady

When educators and architects get together to plan new schools, their working sessions are filled with talk of flexibility and advanced teaching technics. Unfortunately, these two ideas have a disturbing habit of getting in each other's way.

Spaces designed for team teaching, electronic teaching aids, or large group instruction tend to develop distinctive characteristics which inhibit subsequent flexibility. The attempt in the initial design to make them convertible to something else in the future tends to limit their ability to serve their initial purposes. And, while the basic aim of flexibility is the most efficient use of the dollar in the long run, none of it reduces initial cost. Often, what's left after all the compromising gets done is a few folding partitions and combinable classrooms which serve chiefly to remind the planners that modern flexible teaching space is a great deal easier to talk about than build.

In planning a new high school in Briarcliff Manor, N.Y., school officials and their architects and consultants have established a design that tries to make flexibility meaningful. It does so by starting out with space that can be reshaped right now but building in a specialized physical adaptability to the unknown curriculums and teaching technologies of the future.

The scheme has a central library with carrels wired for electronic teaching aids, certainly desirable by today's educational standards. What's so unusual — and flexible — in this school is the way this library is intended to work. The district's educational consultant, Stanton Leggett, calls it pseudopodial. For those of us who can't remember much about biology, pseudopodia are temporary extensions of the protoplasm of unicellular organisms used for getting them around and for gathering food. Therefore, somewhat similarly, a pseudopodial library is one that creeps. It expands and contracts somewhat the way an amoeba does. Indications are that in the future, students will spend more of their time in individually monitored study using electronic teaching aids — and less of their time in classroom lectures.

As this trend proceeds, the second floor of the central library can expand, by stages, into the second floor of the academic houses to absorb some or all of the standard recitation rooms in the building. Note that this provision is intended not to reflect changes in student population, but rather the type of instruction given. Perhaps most important, the school never becomes irrevocably

EXPANSION

The library-classroom areas are designed to accommodate changes in the curriculum. Increases in student population will be handled as follows:

1 MOST SCHOOL BUILDINGS TRY TO LOOK COMPLETE BEFORE ADDITIONS ARE MADE TO THEM. BRIARCLIFF WILL HOUSE ITS INITIAL POPULATION BY BUILDING SIX OF ITS NINE BASIC PARTS.

2 THE REMAINING PARTS WILL BE BUILT IN THE FUTURE. THE CONSTRUCTION OF HOUSE "B" WILL DOUBLE THE ORIGINAL STUDENT CAPACITY. FURTHER NEEDS CAN BE MET BY ADDING TO THE HOUSES.

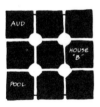

3 WE ARE NOT ATTEMPTING TO PRODUCE GEOMETRICALLY "PURE" RESULTS AT ANY STAGE. WE INTEND THAT THE AUDITORIUM, THE HOUSES AND ALL OTHER UNITS WILL REMAIN AS FREE AS THE LIBRARY IS TO TAKE WHATEVER SHAPE THE FUTURE DICTATES.

PSEUDOPODIALITY

The relationship between library and classroom areas is intended to work like this (upper floor plan):

1 THE LIBRARY, INITIALLY LOCATED IN THE CENTER,

2 CAN EXPAND TO ABSORB THE CORES OF THE CLASSROOM AREAS,

3 OR, IF NEEDED, THE ENTIRE FLOOR

4 THE PROCESS IS REVERSIBLE, AND THE LIBRARY CAN ALSO REVERT TO ITS ORIGINAL SIZE.

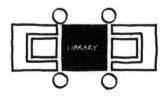

BASIC DIAGRAM

The program breaks down into nine parts which assemble themselves into three groups:

1 TWO-STORY ACADEMIC "HOUSES" LINKED BY A TWO-STORY LIBRARY.

2 AUDITORIUM AND CAFETERIA LINKED BY COMMON SERVICED FACILITIES.

3 GYMNASIUM AND POOL LINKED BY COMMON LOCKER FACILITIES.

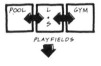

4 WE HAVE ASSEMBLED THESE GROUPS INTO A DIAGRAM ROUGHLY SQUARE, WITH THE LIBRARY AT ITS CENTER.

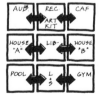

CIRCULATION

A central library isn't much good if i be easily reached:

1 THE SPACES BETWEEN THE SQUARES CAN BE MADE INTO CORRIDORS WITH STAIRS AT THE END OF THEM. TH RESULTS IN A LOT OF STAIRS BUT MINIMAL EASE OF ACCESS.

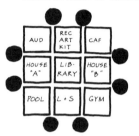

2 WHAT SEEMS TO BE NEEDED INST ARE CONVENIENCE STAIRS AT THE CORNERS OF THE LIBRARY.

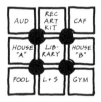

3 SO THAT THEY MAY DOUBLE AS LEG EXIT STAIRS, WE HAVE TURNED FOU OF THE CORRIDORS BETWEEN THEM THE PERIMETER INTO EXTERIOR "ST.

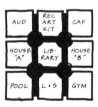

committed to electronic instruction. If experience should show that enthusiasm for it has been excessive or premature, the classrooms can be restored and the library reduced to its earlier size.

The building is designed for an initial population of 600, which can double by the addition of a second academic house and can be ultimately expanded through add-ons to hold 1,500 students.

The sketches on the previous pages show how Briarcliff Manor's new school will look and work.

Hub of the Instructional Program

Rena Clay

At Sheffield High School in Memphis, Tennessee, one far-thinking administrator has devised a unique arrangement of library materials that has taken much of the "search before research" out of using the library. Corbet R. Washington, principal, saw an opportunity to implement this departure from the traditional library arrangement as he prepared to open a new high school in the Memphis City System.

Located between the second and third floors of the main building, the Multimedia Center is unique. Brightly decorated in gold, orange, and buff, this spacious area provides a most inviting work and study space for Sheffield students and faculty. Four doors open into the center, one at each point of the compass, which places the facilities within one-half flight of stairs of 85 percent of the classroom areas. Bulletin boards display information about school and community activities. Student assistants are responsible for these and other attractive displays.

Shelving is installed around the perimeter of the reading room with ranges of counter height shelving radiating from the walls toward the circular circulation desk. Individual study carrels, tables for four, and informal furniture in the periodicals area provide ample seating space. A large conference room with operable walls accommodates large or small groups. A semienclosed area houses the listening center. Individuals or small groups may use the three remaining areas for working with audio-visual materials or study. The periodicals storage space is adequate for a three- to five-year holding. Audio-visual equipment for use in the center and for classroom use is housed in this storage area. A well-equipped work room and office provide ample space for the technical work,

Reprinted from *American Libraries*, February 1970, by permission of the publisher.

such as ordering, repairing books, and processing materials. The audio-visual materials are shelved in this work area.

The capital outlay for equipping the center was provided entirely from local funds and is currently in excess of $30,000. An annual materials and equipment budget makes possible the continuous updating and enlarging of the collection.

Now in its third year of operation, the center has become the hub of the instructional program as well as the school plant. The media center is used for many purposes and activities. Teachers bring groups for reading, research, and visual reports; students come individually, in small groups, and committees. There is every indication that the library is an integral part of the school program and is a unified media center in its services to the development of the school's educational program. Students may tape their role-playing performances for self-evaluation or to share with others. Members of the swimming team may be using a film loop on diving or a stroke, while others may be viewing a film on the techniques of dissecting a frog. A sound filmstrip projector, a tape recorder, filmstrip previewers, a 16mm projector, a listening center, television sets, film loop projector, overhead projectors, and a copying machine are set up for immediate use. Additional pieces of equipment are also available for classroom use.

Central cataloging leaves time for the two professional librarians and one full-time clerk to work with students and teachers to make maximum use of materials. Students and teachers have access to all materials, both print and nonprint. Materials for inclusion in the collection are recommended by teachers and students to meet curriculum and recreational needs and standards for variety, breadth, and scope.

Administrators, supervisors, principals, and teachers feel that a good media program must be a cooperative effort as far as planning, selecting materials, and evaluating services are concerned. Out of such an effort evolves a team of teachers and media specialists who work closely in implementing the teaching-learning process.

The media specialists serve as resource persons with the teachers and students in building a flexible program. The stage is set in the classroom where students are motivated to come to the center for individual or group research. The media specialists seek to correlate book and non-book materials with the curriculum and recreational interests of students.

An expanded, adequate, supportive staff including trained technicians is necessary to insure continuous service. Increased staff would free the librarians from technical work, enabling them to spend more time in planning with teachers and guiding students in research projects.

The purpose of the media center is to support the instructional program of the school, as well as to meet the needs of the individual students. The center seeks to give each pupil a unified program to improve all the approaches to learning. Learning is a personal, individual process, and the center provides effective tools toward this end. Thus, the Sheffield High School Media Center serves as a resource for learning and inquiry which cuts across grade levels in concepts and ideas.

E.C. Stimbert, superintendent of schools in Memphis, has this to say about the media center at Sheffield High School:

> Recognizing the media center as the very heart of the educational program, the Board of Education of the Memphis City Schools has provided an adequate facility with trained personnel to delve deeper into the teaching and learning process. The media center staff is in the mainstream of the educational program at Sheffield High School. The librarians are the teachers whose special competencies are professional knowledge about all materials of instruction. In Sheffield High School the librarians spearhead the search for better services to students and teachers through the media center. As we move ahead in our media center program in the Memphis City Schools, more exciting and more meaningful programs of service will be provided. We feel it is worth every effort to bring quality education and media service and resources to the boys and girls of the Memphis City Schools.

SECTION FOUR / HIGHER EDUCATION AND THE LEARNING RESOURCE CENTER

A Fresh Look at Scheduling, Teaching, Learning

(Total!!) Independent Study at Oakland
John E. Tirrell

Resource Centers for Teacher Education
Gayle Rahmes

Mt. San Jacinto Multi-Media Instructional System
Joseph L. Bishop, Jr.

Motivating the ABE Student
Ruth Goodman

At Lansing Community College: Audio-visual-Tutorial Instruction in Business
Ronald K. Edwards

Multicampus Instructional Resources Services
Robert C. Jones

Electronic Learning Center
R. Stafford North

Learning Resources Approach to College and University Library Development
Fred F. Harcleroad

CMSC's Self-Instruction Center

Self-Instruction Lab Teaches Communication Skills
Lucius A. Butler

A Fresh New Look at Scheduling, Teaching, Learning

You're probably familiar with James A. Garfield's bromide, "Give me a log hut, with only a simple bench, Mark Hopkins on one end and I on the other, and you may have all the buildings, apparatus and libraries without him." This paean to individualized instruction may well have given you a good belly-laugh, since truly individualized instruction is about as easy to come by as a student who'll learn on a log.

But don't laugh too hard. For all intents and purposes, Oakland Community College, Oakland County, Mich., is doing "the impossible." It is allowing each student to work at his own pace, in his own time, on a one-to-one basis, with a professor of his own choosing. The Oakland system amounts to even more than putting a student on a log: It puts him on a well-equipped bench, complete with tapes, films, books and exhibits — as well as a teacher.

How is this possible? Is Oakland resorting to technological hocus-pocus in lieu of an education? On the contrary, Oakland's system is based on the fullest knowledge of learning procedures and is built around the theory that, if a student knows where he's going and how to get there, he *will* get there if he wants to. Oakland sees its role as giving help and motivation. When a student registers for a course at the college, he's told at the outset just what he's going to achieve, quantitatively and qualitatively. He's told what he'll have to do — step by step — in order to learn. And he's given the questions he'll answer on his final exam. He is offered all the tools he needs to learn facts and all the individual help he needs to place them in perspective and interpret them.

Where does the time-honored lecture fit into this scheme of things? It doesn't. As President John E. Tirrell says: "The medieval monks were the forebears of contemporary lecturers. They were the only people of their day who could read. So they read the few books available and *told* their students what the books said. This is still the practice in most colleges and high schools — despite the fact that most students can read — and despite the advent of television, tape recorders, films and other better means of communication. To say the least, our students do their own reading."

BY HIMSELF

None of Oakland's 4,000 students are locked up in a classroom — the least important facility on any of the school's three campuses. The old 45-minute class and three-class week have been abolished. The basis for Oakland's individualized curriculum has replaced them; it consists of each student working by himself in an audio-tutorial laboratory — open from 8:00 a.m. to 10:00 p.m. every day — with a teacher always standing by, should the student require help.

Obviously, such a program requires a complete reorganization of staff, scheduling, students and facilities. Says Tirrell: "When you're new, without traditions and customs, that's the time to break with tradition. And, while you're at it, you might as well do a thorough job. Don't stop at breaking with it — jump up and down on it, *hard.* That's what we're trying to do, not for the sake of breaking tradition but because so much tradition inhibits rather than helps learning."

The students. A student registering for one of Oakland's courses knows exactly what he's getting himself into the day he registers. At that time he receives a complete course outline, some indicators of what he should learn as a result of taking the course, and a sample final test. His first class meeting is a GAS — or "General Assembly Session." From 150 to 300 students are greeted in a large lecture hall by a master teacher who will be responsible for the academic success of each of these students.

For each course a student takes, there is a GAS session to kick things off. Students are told that they must attend the weekly GAS session for one month, after which attendance will be optional. As the first GAS session draws to a close, each student receives a sheaf of papers outlining the first unit to be studied, telling them what they will be expected to cover, how they are to cover it (step by step), and giving them a sample of a test that they should be able to pass when they have completed the unit. They're then released and are on their own.

For each major discipline — such as English, foreign languages, the physical sciences — there is one tutorial laboratory. It consists of a lounge and a vending-machine snack bar, a large room filled with study carrels, an equipment storage area and shelves holding books, tapes and filmstrips. Each floor of each laboratory also has an area used by its tutor, furnished with a seven-seat conference table and a desk.

Students enter the laboratory at any time, open their syllabus and find out what equipment they need. Using that equipment — whether textbook, tape recorder, teaching machine, film strip projector or laboratory apparatus — they "go to class" by themselves.

They're at liberty to play a tape as many times as is necessary, or to show themselves a series of film strips many times over. When the tape instructs them to take a test from their tutor — or, as in the case, say, of nursing students, to demonstrate their prowess with a stethoscope — they simply go to to the tutor's desk and do so. If they're told by the tape to meet with the tutor at the seminar table for a discussion of data processing techniques, students who are at the same stage of coursework at that moment follow through on instructions.

Students are completely free to ask a tutor for help, to get a concept explained, to ask why a specific quiz answer is wrong. Test papers are corrected in their presence and seminar evaluations are made out loud — for the benefit of the students, not for the sake of record books alone.

Some taped units of instruction merely tell a student to read a certain section in a book and then amplify on it. Others specify lab exercises or discussion. Whatever work is to be done, students do it whenever they please and at whatever pace is most suited to them. A tutor is on duty as long as the lab is open.

The faculty. While Oakland's students come and go as they please, this flexibility of schedule doesn't extend to the faculty. Their work requires them to put in about a 40-hour week although, according to Tirrell, "We actually have to force them not to work a *60-hour* week. This isn't exaggeration. We have to make them go home."

The college is staffed in a "pyramid." At the very top are a few full professors, paid on a level competitive with the nation's best four-year colleges. Below them are associate and assistant professors. These men — the school's "master teachers" — create the taped, filmed and programed courses that are used, revised and updated every year.

Below this cadre are what Tirrell calls "our bright youngsters." These people, at roughly the level of PhD candidates or holders of an MA, or even recent college graduates, are the tutors.

In addition to 25-30 hours spent in the labs, tutors attend — help to run — GAS sessions so they know what the students are being told. They devote other time to working directly with master teachers in order to see that all components of the teaching program are coordinated.

The tutors are relieved of lab assignments for three or four hours each week by master teachers — in the interest of *their* knowing just what their students' study problems are. By and large, though, master teachers spend their time evaluating the records of their students, reviewing available new material and creating and correcting master tapes that will be reproduced and placed in the laboratory's tape library. They shape all courses.

HARD-NOSED ANSWERS

So much for the skeleton of the Oakland system of instruction. It serves all 18 subject areas and is, according to the college administration, eminently successful. But "inventors" are always overly enthusiastic about their product. They seldom stay to point out where their system doesn't work. To find out what the Oakland system's weak spots are, SM's editors put President Tirrell on the spot and asked him some hard-nosed questions. Tirrell came back with some equally hard-nosed answers. The results of that exchange follow.

Q. Dr. Tirrell, the program you run sounds exciting, but where does the student come into it? Where does he get started?

A. You don't get started at Oakland unless you've been thoroughly screened. This isn't the kind of thing where a youngster sends in his records and, if he's above the median curve, we take him. Far from it. There's a battery of tests to be taken and a tough interview. The man who gives this interview is a professional counselor. We have one such man for every 300 full-time students. By the time he's through with a student, he knows him inside and out. He keeps in touch, too. In addition, we have the GAS meetings, where students get personal contact with their teachers. These go on all year, though they're optional after a month. A student who's starved for contact can come to as many of them as he wants. So he gets to see plenty of his master teacher.

Q. "1984," here we come. The master teacher stands on a platform in full view, and the student "sees" him. He might as well be a robot. Is this what you call an education?

A. Look, it's easy to carp at a concept. Copernicus ran into plenty of trouble when he said the earth spins around the sun, instead of the opposite which most people believed.

We're saying, in effect, that the college spins around the student – instead of the opposite. I call this an education. That master teacher standing in front of a GAS session is more than a babysitter. He's there to clue his students in on how they can get the most out of their education. His purpose is to motivate them, inspire them to do a better job and to like it while they do it.

Q. But this is hardly a personal contact. Does a student come into contact with the faculty?

A. The bulk of the "nuts and bolts" teaching, the coping with day-to-day problems, comes from the tutor in the laboratory. Together with the master teacher, he's part of a formidable team that has only one goal: The student's success. There's plenty of personal contact in the labs.

Q. The students see tutors when they have a question, or when there's a test to be graded. But they don't just drop over to his office to chat about the subject matter, or about their personal problems. And that *does* get done in traditional colleges.

A. That, my friend, is not correct. You should see our students. Whenever they feel like it, or whenever they need to, they stop their work and walk over to the tutor's desk — which is right where they are, not across the campus — and talk, ask questions, or do whatever they want to do. That does *not* get done in traditional colleges. The colleges only *say* that it gets done. Remember when you got some test questions wrong and you couldn't figure out why? You had to dog your professor all over the campus and finally grab him by the lapels and say, "Hey — what gives?"

Our youngsters don't have to find their teacher — he's there, waiting for them. That's his only reason for being there. And, I might add, he grades their test papers while they wait. He explains why they were wrong and tells them what they ought to do — read this book, review that tape, maybe do the whole unit over again. If that isn't personal contact — the kind you just can't even *buy* on the run-of-the-mill campus — then I don't know what is.

Q. Well, let's say that these personal contacts do go on. And suppose that a student flunks test after test, no matter how many times he repeats each unit. What does the tutor tell him then? "Go home, you can't make it?"

A. No student goes through that kind of repeated failure in total ignorance. Many of our assignments consist of taking small quizzes in a workbook, or doing lab assignments with other students and the tutor, or taking self-administered exams. The student himself knows when he's doing poorly or when he's really failing. The tutor knows too. He enters the grades for students on a running record that's kept in each individual lab. He reviews these records and has the opportunity to bring them to the master teacher's attention. And the master teacher himself does lab duty and reviews the records. He knows when it's time to bring the student in for a conference, or call a counselor into the picture. These students aren't alone.

We're not practicing anarchy, here. You have to remember that. We're trying to allow for the maximum freedom of the student — for the conditions that do away with artificial restraints handed down by tradition and academic myth — without allowing him to lose the discipline of learning. He's never on his own in an area where he's not fully capable. We're not giving up our roles as teachers.

Q. You still haven't really spoken to the main question: What's the advantage of the Oakland program in terms of the material your students work with on their own? Isn't this rote learning? And what's so good about that?

A. I thought I did answer that question. With the personal help these students receive from their tutors, their master teachers and whatever consultants are required, they *deal* with what they've learned. They use the tapes and slides and other aids to master basic information. But when their syllabus tells them to take a test or engage in a seminar, they have to *use* the facts, display a mastery of them. You can't prove mastery of a subject unless you respond to artificial academic "emergencies" with your information: A tutor tells you to deliver an impromptu speech in French, or he challenges everything the book has been telling you all along — that sort of thing. This is learning, not just memorizing.

Q. Still and all, Dr. Tirrell, there's a basic fact that doesn't ring clear in all of this. You program your courses, in effect, and you use your tutors so that a student can acquire a number of facts through sheer repetition —

A. *And* problem-solving.

Q. All right, rote *and* problem-solving give the student his facts. But the tutor responds only when the student is taking a test or asking a question — that's where the problem-solving comes in. He certainly won't go to a student and say, "Look, this course is too boring for you. Go write a paper on such-and-such a topic and meet me every other day in my office so we can discuss your problems and your progress." The nature of your program seems to eliminate the extra-ordinary. It fits students into programmed sequences. Aren't you actually dehumanizing the student?

A. No. Our set-up eliminates the "boring" course. Since the student goes as quickly as he likes, the know-it-all does not have to wait for a slower student to pick up an obvious point. If he really knows all there is to know, he goes to the tutor, asks for the final test and passes it. He is then finished with the course. In addition, extensive pre-admission screening finds out — through tests, records and interviews — those students who are exceptional in both an encouraging and discouraging sense. The counselors suggest programs, whereby students can make maximum use of themselves — whether to find the motivation that's held them back from achieving scholastically or to discover a challenge suitable to their abilities.

Q. But the student still works basically with a machine or a book, not with a person. Isn't that "dehumanizing"?

A. There's constant contact between students and tutors. I wouldn't call that "dehumanized." Look, let's get this whole thing straight. In most colleges and most high schools, there's regular contact of one sort or another between students and faculty. For example, there are lectures. The professor or classroom teacher stands up and presents information to those students who can stay awake. But there are unfortunately few really great lecturers around. We feel that there are many, many better ways of presenting this same information that are no less human.

Q. Okay, but at most colleges and high schools there is usually more intimate student contact with faculty members.

A. Right, the seminars. A group of unprepared students must meet with a faculty member two or three times a week and pretend they know what they're talking about. Some students are prepared, most aren't. We have the same seminars, but with three very important differences. First, students don't go to them until after they've prepared themselves. If they're to discuss the role of the peasants in the French Revolution, they've really studied their material before they have a conference. Second, the *student* calls the conference when he's *ready* for it, he doesn't go when the schedule says he must go. Third, the seminar will usually consist of two or three students discussing with a teacher. Most seminars are too big for real discussion — they more often become question and answer sessions. Let me add a fourth point. Scheduled seminars run for a set period of time. Ours go on just as long as necessary. If three students and a teacher get into a really interesting topic, they can keep going on it all day, if they wish.

Q. Let's talk about this faculty of yours. Your tutors get turned on and off like taps. They sit, doing whatever they want to, when the students don't need them. When the students do need them, they have to be bright-eyed, bushy-tailed, and fully informed on whatever area of their subject is to be dealt with at that moment. Doesn't this amount to something like a dehumanization of the teacher?

A. This is *not* a teacher-oriented college. It revolves around the students and their academic and — to a large degree — emotional needs. Our teachers are there to teach. That's what they want to do more than anything else. That's why we hired them. As far as they're concerned, their whole purpose in life is to be ready to help these youngsters whenever help is needed. For a teacher, that isn't a demeaning role, it's a rather happy one, I think. Doesn't that make sense?

Q. Yes, but let's face the facts, Dr. Tirrell. Your tutors, who serve by standing and waiting, are MA-holders or PhD candidates; in practice they're actually little more than graduate assistants, whether they're taking courses at that moment or not.

A. And they're all sharp. They're the cream of the crop.

Q. Fine. But graduate assistants need experience in order to get a better job later on. They want an entree to the field. What actual experience do your tutors get? They could be construed as nothing more than audio-visual aides in the labs. Designing lessons and planning what students should learn is fundamental to teaching, isn't it? These people don't get any such experience. So why should they come here? Do you make them rich?

A. No, teachers by and large don't get rich until they write textbooks and have their students buy them for a course that's taken almost word-for-word right out of the book. We pay our tutors on a competitive basis, but we don't pay them a fortune.

Q. So why should they come out to Oakland? Are they simply rejects from the graduate assistant programs of large universities?

A. They're men and women who want to teach. They're taking a breather from their personal studies, perhaps; maybe they're impatient to get into a teaching situation. Whatever their secondary motivations are, their prime one is a desire to see youngsters learn. They appreciate the chance to answer questions, to show students where they've gone wrong on quizzes, to steer them straight when they're in trouble. Isn't that what any teacher wants? And is it inconceivable that, out of all the young teachers-to-be in our universities, 60 or 70 or 80 want to come to a beautiful region and a new college where the "action is"? Where the dream-dialogues about individualized instruction get made *real?* I don't think so. And I sure as brimstone know that these people aren't retreads — you should take a look at their records. They're a Tiffany group.

Q. I would presume then that the faculty higher up on the "pyramid," the master teachers, are an even more elite group.

A. Correct.

Q. And they want to teach more than anything else?

A. Correct again.

Q. Then what possible reason could teachers have for allowing themselves to be locked away in an office most of the time while "the action" is down at the labs — where tutors are garnering the lion's share of it? Is it the money?

A. The money isn't bad, I'll tell you that. Salaries for assistant through full professor are more than competitive. But it isn't that by a long-shot. These men could get excellent salaries at any college in the nation. It *is* the chance to really teach in a truly new way — a way they agree is best for students. I know they agree because when we let the word get out that we were staffing this kind of school, we got over 3,000 applications for 135 openings. And it *isn't* a matter of being locked away from the "action." One of the fundamentals of teaching is being able to design courses, to determine what students can and should learn. That's the main concern of these people; even their GAS sessions are aimed at achieving maximum learning for their students. And the GAS sessions are far from an ivory-tower solitude. They put the teachers smack in the middle of an audience. However, audiences are really secondary to teaching. The real teaching comes into play when these experts construct courses, make slides, dictate tapes. They talk to every student in their class when that student is ready to hear that segment of the course. It's an entirely personal, one-to-one relationship. They take their students by the hand and guide them: "Now read pages 12-14 and then turn the recorder back on." "Now write two paragraphs on William Blake's philosophy of innocence." How far from being locked away can you get?

That kind of contact, and the knowledge that it's helping the students move towards greater knowledge and ability, are what net us this exceptional faculty. Again, it comes to this: Here's a chance for them to teach — not talk about their undergraduate escapades or reflect on their family life. Here's a chance for them to impart knowledge in a very pure sense.

Q. That "pure sense" is rather theoretical, it seems to me. Suppose the course isn't too pure. Suppose the course just doesn't work out midway through the year?

A. It gets changed — and fast.

Q. How? You have 10 students still on the first two or three units, maybe 50 somewhere in the middle, perhaps another 50 doing more advanced units. You can't just recall all tapes and slides. In a traditional school, a teacher *could* simply revise his notes. Isn't this a severe shortcoming?

A. We have a great advantage over tradition. If a professor or teacher botches a section of his course, it's too late to do much about it. His students have had it. Next year, perhaps, changes can be made. If our teachers botch a section, the first students to come to it would immediately tip off the tutors. They would do this because, when they had to discuss the section with the tutors, it would become obvious that they didn't know what they were talking about. The tutor would tell this to the master teacher who would review the tape, figure out where he went wrong, and cut a new section. It would be on the shelves ready for the bulk of the students who wouldn't have gotten that far anyway. One day after a poor lesson is caught, we can have corrected materials out to our students.

Q. Then this is really a hit-and-miss proposition. Material is taped and then you sit back and wait for a student to tumble. When he does you say, "Oops, excuse me," pick him up, dust him off, and cut a new hit-or-miss tape.

A. No. Tapes and other materials are evaluated by the faculty deans and department chairmen before they're ever put into use. This is one of our biggest jobs.

Q. Deans checking over teachers' lessons? You couldn't get away with that at any other college. Teachers are awfully zealous about their academic freedom. Don't you get complaints?

A. First of all, teachers know that some kind of control is necessary. Its sole purpose, however, is to see that basic ground is covered — to make certain that essential elements are in each course and well held together.

Q. What about the non-essential elements — non-essential to you, maybe, but important to the teachers?

A. You mean like a teacher's saying on a tape that the Civil War would have ended sooner if the British intervened? You mean just plain old opinion? Well, of course, we want that. We didn't hire these people to be textbooks; we want them to engage the pupils.

Q. Suppose, in a sociology course, a teacher said that drugs should be made available to addicts. Would the tape be censored?

A. Oh, look. This isn't a police state. If a teacher wants to say that, fine. But let him be *certain* that he's giving all the information that's germane to his specific sociology course. And let him then be sure that he's given his students — or led them to — all available facts. Then, if he finds it necessary to his peace of mind, let him say that, in his opinion, addicts should be given drugs. As long as he serves the students first and himself second, why should we be concerned? Incidentally, this emphasis on serving students gives us another interesting advantage. We find out pretty quickly which tutors are really helping students and which ones aren't by the way the students use them. Since students can select the tutors with which they work, it doesn't take long to identify the poor ones. The same is true with the master teachers. The ones whose courses are constantly breaking down, can't teach. Since teaching is what we hire people for, we soon know which faculty members belong and which don't.

Q. How about a teacher's serving himself — or his subject? There's obviously little room in your program for his doing research or sitting down to write articles for learned periodicals. Doesn't a teacher forsake an awful lot when he passes up this area of academic endeavor?

A. He doesn't forsake teaching, and that's his reason for being with us. You're right when you intimate that we don't push research or publication. Let me amend that to say, "We don't encourage research or publishing on *the students' time.*" Certainly, we're in favor of a man's advancement in his field, or his contribution *to* his field — once his job is done. We're finding, though, that the teaching job isn't so easily done if it's done right. So we make it possible for master teachers to have time to do research by sending them away on research leaves.

Q. It must be pretty expensive to provide a carrel for each of about 4,000 students.

A. We don't. By using computer runs based on number of students, the hours the labs are open and the average daily attendance, we decided that one carrel to every 4.5 students is sufficient.

Q. Is it really? What happens if everyone comes at once on a certain day?

A. Well, that happens — usually on the first day only, right after the initial GAS session. The students are all fired up and eager to learn and they absolutely throng into the labs.

Q. So this is your big scheduling headache.

A. No, actually not. These are intelligent youngsters, they see that the lab's too crowded and some of them drift out. They come back a few hours later and there are plenty of seats. Thereafter, when they establish their most comfortable hours — some of them work best early in the day, some late at night — or when they find out when their part-time jobs leave them free to study, the crowd thins out and the labs don't get filled up again. Incidentally, some of them work away from the carrels altogether.

Q. Are students assigned specific carrels once they decide on their hours?

A. No. That would only tie them down to a specific place at a specific time. That's what we're opposed to. We want students to feel free to come in at any time — or not to come in for weeks at a time, if they can afford not to. The labs, the equipment, the hours — these must revolve around the students; the students shouldn't have to adjust to them.

Q. Then you don't have one tape recorder, one set of slides, etc. assigned to each student?

A. No. The same formula — one piece of apparatus for each 4.5 students — prevails. And — to forecast your next question — there's never, except maybe on that first day, a time when a student can't go to a storeroom and find a recorder for himself or go to the shelves and take down a tape or slides that his syllabus tells him to use.

Q. Isn't stocking all this equipment still prohibitively expensive? How can you afford to do it?

A. The cost isn't prohibitive, but it is high. That's why we have operating costs of $1,100 per student per year. But that cost will come down to about $800 — partially as a result of our salary schedule. You see, though we pay top-ranking faculty a high salary, we don't necessarily go after MA holders to staff our tutorial positions. And, with a large number of such moderately-salaried staff members, our mean salary is rather low. Naturally, this means that operating costs are less and students' expenses are then less.

Another economy factor is actually that selfsame expensive equipment. It's not as elaborate as hardware used on a part-time basis in other schools. When we went shopping for equipment, we looked for apparatus that would serve the student – not for glamor. These really handsome machines with a hundred wheels and gauges take so long to master that they trap the student. He's more worried about working the machine right than he is about learning. The equipment we use is oriented to the student, and it's designed to do what he wants it to *when* he wants it to do it – that gives him an opportunity to progress at his own rate.

Q. When you say "progress at his own rate," do you mean that if a student takes a year to complete one term's work, you still are concerned only with the fact that he has learned?

A. That's our over-riding concern. We believe that we bear responsibility for close to 100% of our youngsters' succeeding. And, if we don't get 90% or 95%, then we're going to start evaluating our work with a microscope.

It makes me furious to travel around the country and hear college heads boast that their standards are so high, they can flunk out 35% of their freshman students. We have higher standards: We want to keep our students in school. If it takes them a month to do a term's work, or if it takes them a year, we want them in school and free to learn as best they can.

Q. If you're so interested in setting students free, why give them grades?

A. The way some youngsters react to grades, it would be nice if we didn't have to give them. But we're responsible for evaluating each student's progress in terms of his ability, the course designer's analysis of desirable terminal achievement, and the student's vocational or academic needs. We need a measurement.

We don't mete out C's as punishment or A's as reward. We do apply these notations to a student's work so that we know whether he's to continue in a certain course or major, or whether he needs help. Maybe we can get away from grades. And maybe we will. We're trying a lot of strategies and we're looking for an awful lot of answers. We've found only a few.

But what we have found, we think, is a sure way to truly individualize education. We refuse to be hamstrung by tradition – or hampered by unproven speculation. We insist that every student get all the help he needs to learn as much as he can as best he can.

(Total!!) Independent Study at Oakland

John E. Tirrell

When Oakland Community College opened in September, 1965, fifteen months from the date it was approved, it accepted on two separate campuses a record initial community college enrollment of over 4,000 students.

As president — and first employee — my immediate task was to recruit key administrative personnel and assign them the specific problems of design and planning of the campuses and the development of the functional requirements for the instructional program.

The need for innovation in instruction generally, and in higher education in particular, was widely accepted and any demonstrated achievements could be utilized beyond this one institution.

Jerrold R. Zacharias, chairman of the Panel on Education Research and Development of the President's Science Advisory Committee, stated in the committee's report: "The task of educational research and development is to learn how to provide for all students the education an exceptional teacher provides for a few."

Unfortunately, the Zacharias panel did not produce any significant plan for translating the goal of educational research and development into reality: namely, "to provide for all students the education an exceptional teacher provides for a few."

At O.C.C., we believe we have taken a significant step forward in implementing this educational innovation.

The college staff reviewed virtually all recent literature on learning theory and the application of that theory to our major objective, individual student learning. Research on class size, space and time utilization, and innovations at colleges and universities across the country were carefully studied. The success of learning techniques based on individual study was convincing and design specifications for the O.C.C. instructional methodology were derived from the information assembled.

Individual study of learning sequences developed by the instructional systems approach in a tutorial laboratory using multimedia employed at O.C.C. presents a striking contrast to the methods and techniques of conventional instruction. Conventional methods of teaching are basically teacher-oriented or "open-loop" instructional systems. The teacher plans and organizes his subject matter presentation in terms of coverage of material in specified units of time; he tells groups of students what he considers to be relevant based on his best

Reprinted from *Junior College Journal*, April 1966, by permission of the publisher.

estimate of what is important and what degree of understanding he wishes to achieve in his students. Little provision is made for directed and continued student response and correct answer confirmation as the prime criterion for the design and pacing of instruction.

The student usually plays a passive role, being neither required nor able to respond and receive correct answer confirmation in the learning process.

There is usually no finite prestatement of final or terminal performance objectives specifying exactly what the individual student must be able "to know" and "to do" to achieve acceptably.

With conventional "open-loop" instructional models, the student is evaluated by means of tests which sample the material covered during the instructional sequences. The test questions may or may not be relevant to points of significance required for the concise understanding of principle, concept, or application involved.

The instructional systems approach applied at O.C.C. is a learner-centered or a "closed-loop" model of instruction. It is a self-adjustive performance system based specifically on the pre-definition of (1) what is to be learned, (2) the required levels of terminal or final proficiency to be achieved by learners, and (3) the most appropriate sequence of instruction for learners to insure their success on each progressive step leading to the attainment of the prestated terminal performance specifications stated in behavioral terms.

Of critical importance in designing the "closed-loop" instructional model as applied in the tutorial laboratory situation is the prespecification of the "critical or optimal learning path." This learning path is limited to "need to know" instructional requirements; the use of relevant demonstrations only, exercises, etc.; the reinforcement of concepts to be learned; the sequence and order of presentation of instructional components to be included as integral parts of the instructional sequences; the prescribed role of instructor and student in each instructional setting; and, of great significance, the means for controlling pacing of learning based on the measured understanding of individual students.

INSTRUCTIONAL METHODS

In contrast to conventional methods of curriculum planning and instruction in institutions of higher learning, the Oakland Community College-designed and implemented instructional methods are primarily student- or learner-oriented. Courses of instruction have minimized traditional group teaching applications. Instead, students are provided carefully designed instructional sequences which stress supervised self-directed instruction. Learning is controlled and paced by the individual student, consistent with his abilities to perform successfully.

The model of self-directed learning at Oakland Community College is based on the work of Professor Samuel Postlethwait of Purdue University. With the audio-tutorial or tutorial-laboratory model of instruction developed by Dr. Postlethwait, the responsibility for learner achievement rests primarily with the learner himself. Instructional materials, equipment, and all other resources required for successful terminal achievement are provided each student in a specifically designed study carrel. Self-directed instructional sequences include use of multimedia such as audiotapes, visual displays, books, periodicals, laboratory experimental set-ups, programed materials and manuals. Faculty members are always available as tutors during self-directed study activities to assist students, when requested, in achieving predefined knowledge and skill objectives.

This "tutorial laboratory" environment enables the student and instructor alike to utilize their respective abilities at maximum capacity. In essence, the method places the responsibility for learning and the mechanics for study time on the student while permitting the instructor to have maximum personal contact with the student on a "need to know" basis. The instructor, then, can more efficiently direct his skills toward orientation and guidance.

Students are provided large group assemblies on a scheduled basis, mainly for motivation. A skilled "master teacher" uses this time to discuss course objectives, present new developments in the field, point out applications of the subject matter, and integrate subject matter with other areas in the predesigned educational program. Student performance is frequently evaluated by written, performance, and/or oral exams used as the basis for advancement and to furnish feedback information to the learner.

In order to insure a properly functioning system it is most critical for implementing personnel to be fully oriented to their task. At O.C.C. an in-service program covering the following areas was conducted on: (1) system design applications; (2) roles of instructors, students, and administration; (3) student performance evaluation criteria and techniques; (4) teaching strategies to meet individual student needs; and (5) operational conditions required by the field-test program.

As with any system, it can be expected that individual components will undergo a series of modifications in design. In an instructional system, the means for determining design change requirements will be based on how well specific instructional materials, sequences, etc., produce the desired terminal learning achievements for which they were designed. Normal practice requires several modifications in materials in order to insure the highest level of performance predictability. A fair test of all system components for individual courses of instruction at O.C.C. will require a minimum of two years with a third year for full-scale implementation in a new campus designed for this program.

SYSTEM MANAGEMENT METHODS AND PROCEDURES

Critical to a learner-centered systems approach is the design and implementation of management organizational principles which can truly accommodate the functions to be performed in the achievement of its objectives. At O.C.C. a significant departure from conventional systems management principles and organization was implemented.

The underlying design principle of the O.C.C. management model places major emphasis on instructional management requirements which are consistent with the learner-centered approach. Major divisions of management responsibility are placed with the offices of vice-president for curriculum and vice-president for campus administration. The former office is charged with total responsibility for the design and selection of instructional systems components (materials, people, facilities) which are required to produce the desired learner achievements. The latter office is charged with the responsibility of achieving stated student terminal performance specifications by providing independent control for the implementation of the instructional systems design completed by the office of vice-president for curriculum. Both activities are of equal significance for achieving stated systems objectives, and, as such, represent by a process of checks and balances the necessary controls to assure system integrity.

The design of an instructional system, completed by the vice-president for curriculum, must be approved by and accepted for implementation by the vice-president for campus administration. Once the instructional system is accepted for implementation total responsibility for system and student performance evaluation will rest with the vice-president for campus administration. Requested modifications in the instructional system, insertions, and deletions will be based solely on performance criteria derived from the actual process of operation. Quality assurance in the achievement of learner products becomes the central theme of this systems management model. The student is paramount in the definition of policies and procedures for total system operation. In turn, the functions performed by system support groups under a vice-president for business, including the offices of finance, systems, new facilities, and purchasing, are oriented to assist the instructional program.

DEVELOPMENT COMMITMENTS

The board of trustees at O.C.C. has plans for over $40 million for development of three campuses to be in operation in Oakland County by 1970. When fully operational these sites will serve the needs of over 15,000 full-time community college students. All campuses will be elements of a single integrated community college system under one administration. The board has further authorized interim plans for the integration of computer techniques for administrative functions and computer assisted instructional applications. Each of the campuses will be modeled after the tutorial laboratory approach presently in operation at the two existing campuses.

An extensive planning, design, and implementation program was initiated to achieve the present operational posture at O.C.C. The five major functional requirements to be completed between January, 1965, and June, 1966, are:

1. An instructional systems approach which would coordinate the management efforts of administrators and faculty members.
2. A plan for orientation and training of new faculty members in the use of the independent study approach, since no experienced staff exists.
3. The development of instructional materials which would meet the exacting specifications written by the faculty.
4. The design of an inexpensive student study carrel which would have the necessary flexibility for using all modern media.
5. The design and selection of reliable equipment to be used in the carrels.

There are two major phases of effort currently planned.

Phase I (January, 1966-June, 1968):

1. Evidence on the successes and failures of students using various approaches to learning, media, teacher and learner time, etc., and other implications for equipment and architecture will be available for dissemination to existing and new institutions.
2. Validated programs would be available for the use of other educational groups. There are significant costs of designing, writing, testing, revising, and evaluating various media and it seems unnecessary for others to duplicate this effort — even if they had the desire and financial resources.
3. A large group of faculty in the many academic disciplines and numerous technical fields would be trained in the development of effective learning materials using a multimedia approach. This could provide the basis for the immediate development of phase two materials for national community college curriculums.
4. Computer-assisted instruction is possible and awaits the training of a large group of subject matter specialists and the availability of a substantial number of programs. O.C.C. provides the first opportunity to implement computer-assisted instruction where extensive program materials were developed prior to the purchase of a computer.

Phase II (1968-1970):

By July 1, 1968, O.C.C. will be able to demonstrate objectively the effectiveness of INSTUISAMM (Independent Study with Tutors Using Instructional Systems Approach and Multi-Media) in an operational community college. In September, 1967, a third campus especially designed for this program will be opened for operation, with only three classrooms, at a cost of $13.7 million.

These accomplishments will provide the empirical criteria and necessary resources to extend the O.C.C. operation to a computer-assisted instructional environment. Recent recommendations for the development of this computer capability were postulated at the U.S. Office of Education symposium held at the University of California, Irvine, California. It was specified that the O.C.C. type of facility would be best suited to long-range community needs. The development of extensive learner-centered instructional materials for O.C.C. in phase one, in conjunction with the large O.C.C. faculty capability to produce further materials, will provide a unique operational testing capability for computer-assisted instructional applications in the community college.

Resource Centers for Teacher Education

Gayle Rahmes

After years of frustration in attempting to make sure that student teachers found every medium available for their units or lesson plans from the textbooks, curriculum guides, pamphlets, kits, tapes, filmstrips, phonograph records, transparencies, and realia — an idea dawned. Why not adapt the public librarian's "reader's interest" arrangement and make resource centers for the elementary and secondary school subjects?

The Education Division of the Wilson Library at Western Washington State College is now arranged this way. Bookstacks, files, tables, and chairs are now grouped to form resource areas for:

Social Studies
Science
Family Life, Business Ed, Industrial Arts, Home Economics, Vocations
Mathematics
General Curriculum
Art, Foreign Languages, Music
Special Education (Culturally Disadvantaged, Gifted, Mentally Handicapped, Physically Handicapped)
Language Arts (plus Reading)
Professional Teacher Education

Reprinted from *Audiovisual Instruction* 14:104, March 1969, by permission of the Association for Educational Communications & Technology.

Enough seating is supplied in each area to accommodate its use by professors and their classes for study and research. Approximately 45 groups come to the Education Librarian each quarter for instruction in the use of their areas or in the use of the entire complex. Undergraduates, graduate students, inservice teachers, supervisors of student teachers, the student teachers, extension classes, workshop and institute participants, and library and curriculum personnel from school districts and other colleges and universities come to use and view the large collection.

Included in the complex is a 10,000 book school library collection, almost 300 education periodicals (and Education Index), and the entire 370 (Dewey) and Library of Congress L's. (The library is shifting to LC.) There is also an audio-visual-production workroom for education majors which includes a duplicating machine, five typewriters with type from elite to poster size, phonographs with or without earphones, filmstrip and slide projectors and previewers, screen, staplers, three-hole punch, tape recorders and duplicator, overhead projector, magazines for clipping, and thousands of pieces of free advertising and informative pamphlets from publishers, associations, industry.

The latest guides to free and inexpensive materials and the catalogs, guides, books and pamphlets for audio-visual materials for classroom instruction and bulletin board preparation are near the workroom.

Professional teacher education materials for subjects from creativity, discipline, dropouts, to teachers' salaries, tests and testing, and workshops, are available in books, guides, pamphlets and service bulletins. ERIC (abstracted in Research in Education and on microfiche with reader), Harvard Clearinghouse for Educational Differences (Xeroxed) publications, the Curriculum Analysis Service (textbook evaluations), Automated Education Handbook, National School Law Reporter, Administrative Service, Curriculum Service, Education Summary, and NEA Research Reports are examples of services subscribed to and available in the professional center.

Encyclopedias, atlases, and dictionaries (on loan from publishers or second copies purchased by the main library) from primary to higher education levels circulate from the Education Division.

All of the materials circulate except the education periodicals. Thirty-eight duplicates of the most often used periodical titles are purchased and do circulate as single issues.

There is an excellent education reference collection centrally located in the area. A new library addition is planned for September 1970 which will double the present floor space for education.

This Division is operated by one Education Librarian, a clerk, and seven student librarians. All personnel are required to be education majors. They coordinate acquisition procedures, cataloging where necessary, arranging and shelving. They process and acquire curriculum materials for files and resource centers. They set up service catalogs, maps of the area, instructional handouts. They give reference service for the Education Division as well as location information for other parts of the library. The circulation of materials is handled by the main circulation desk.

Western's education faculty and students have indicated their appreciation of this new arrangement of their Division. Even when there is no attendant in the area most people report that they can locate the materials they need with little difficulty since all types of educational media except films are arranged similarly in each resource center. (The Campus Educational Media Center is housed in a nearby building and is open to students and faculty from 7:30 a.m. to 5 p.m. each day of the week. The Education Division is open all of the hours of the main Wilson Library.)

Thank goodness for an idea! This has been the greatest boon to good service in an education-curriculum center for teacher education that this Education Librarian has ever found! Happy re-arranging to you, too!

Mt. San Jacinto Multi-Media Instructional System

Joseph L. Bishop, Jr.

Since its founding in 1963, Mt. San Jacinto Junior College has sought methods which would improve both the techniques of teaching and the efficiency of learning. As part of this continuing search, the college has initiated a different approach to junior college instruction. It implemented a system of multi-media instruction designed to meet the college's special conditions.

The program utilizes four approaches to teaching: (1) an instructional center where students can independently study and take tests in carrels equipped with filmstrip projectors and tape recorders; (2) small group sessions; (3) individual sessions with instructor; and (4) large group sessions.

Each activity contributes in its own special way to the education of the student. The instructional center gives him the opportunity for self-training and testing with audio-visual material keyed to the courses taught at the school.

The small group sessions permit the student to come in contact with the instructor and other students. These meetings act as a bridge between the factual knowledge learned in the instructional center and the application of this knowledge.

The individual sessions offer direct communications between the student

Reprinted from *Educational Screen and Audiovisual Guide*, September 1968, by permission of the publisher.

and the instructor, and make available opportunities for personalized guidance and help.

The large group sessions are an efficient way to disseminate general information to all students enrolled in a specific course. These meetings or assemblies are ideal for first week orientation, special events, tests, demonstrations and films.

The instructional center is designed as an integral part of the college's new library. One hundred "Sabre" custom-designed study carrels have been installed and each is equipped with a late-model cartridge filmstrip projector and tape recorder. A student may go to the instruction center at his convenience, check out the appropriate materials and privately conduct a study lesson and accompanying test. He may repeat a lesson as many times as needed. And should he need assistance, he may call upon one of the credentialed instructors who is on duty.

EFFICIENCY, CLARITY, AND INTEREST

The underlying objective of the multi-media instructional system at Mt. San Jacinto Junior College is to help the student accomplish the learning task in an efficient, clear, and interesting manner. To ensure that this goal is attained, the criteria for each course are established by the instructor and are defined in terms of student behavior expected at the end of the course. These objectives are documented in writing and are made available to the students at the beginning of the term. Thus the students are more likely to perform in the manner desired because there is little room for misunderstanding the nature or purpose of the course.

Subsequently, tests and evaluations of the student tell both the teacher and the pupil to what extent both have been successful in achieving the objectives of a course. In other words, goals which are clearly and firmly established in the minds of both parties do not mislead, become irrelevant, unfair, or useless.

As soon as the goals or objectives for a course have been specifically established, the instructor then finds the appropriate media to teach that particular course. This may be a single concept film, a special magnetic tape recording prepared by the instructor in conjunction with a workbook, or other types of media. The important point is that the teaching media are the best available material that can be purchased or produced by the college for the development of that particular instructional objective. These materials are then organized and collected in the instructional center for the students' use.

Most of the instructional material (filmstrips and magnetic tape recordings) used at Mt. San Jacinto Junior College is produced by the college staff. The main reason for this approach is that commercially produced presentations normally do not match the specialized needs of the courses taught at the college level.

Filmstrips are produced by the school's photographer while the tape recordings are made by other members of the college staff. It is the responsibility of the individual instructor to prepare the filming and recording scripts and have available artwork, props, experimental apparatus and other reference material needed for the productions.

Usually about twenty copies of the filmstrips and twenty recording tapes are made for each lesson. Production costs are kept to a minimum by improvising. For example, the color masters for the filmstrips are made by using a "half-frame" 35 mm camera — shooting frames always in final sequence to eliminate the need for editing. Average cost of a filmstrip per unit is less than two dollars. The magnetic tapes are reproduced from the "master" at the college by using twenty study carrels tied together with a mixing system which was designed by an instructor.

These presentations, together with course outlines, lesson guides, tests and other printed material, are then stocked at the instructional center, and are managed and handled by the library's regular staff. Students check out lessons in the same manner as they would borrow library books.

Thus these important advantages are always realized:

- The student attends the center at his convenience as frequently as he wishes, but often enough to complete the minimum assignments.
- The materials contain the same content, quality, and objectives for every student.
- The quality of the presented media remains constant, that is, the mood and fatigue of the instructor do not change the quality of the presentation.
- The student can progress at his own rate of speed within the time limits for each unit.
- The material is repeatable. The student is able to repeat any part of the study as many times as he wishes.
- The student receives assistance when he desires it. There is a tutor (credentialed instructor) on duty at the instructional center at all times.
- The lesson presentations carry the personality and individuality of the instructor since he is responsible for creating the entire production including the use of his voice on the magnetic recording tapes.
- Each unit (activity) is done in context.
- The media which best expresses the objective of a course or lesson is employed.
- The student is active, that is, he must change the frame of the filmstrip when instructed to do so, answer written questions, etc.
- The student is able to see his progress from unit to unit.

Currently eleven survey projects are active to evaluate and analyze selected aspects of Mt. San Jacinto's Multi-Media Instructional System. The studies are being carried out as cooperative research programs with the University of California, Los Angeles, under the direction of Mr. Bruce Munroe, executive assistant to the Dean, Program on the Education of Teachers. Among the elements being investigated are the overall objectives of the program, the effectiveness of various media and methods of instruction, and the impact of the program on students.

The findings and statistics obtained from the evaluations will be used to upgrade the multi-media instructional system. The data will also be made available in future reports written by members of the Mt. San Jacinto staff.

Plans are also underway to expand the system to include other courses taught at the school such as vocational training courses.

The project was adapted from work done by Dr. Postlethwait of Purdue University; Dr. Tirrell of Oakland Community College, Detroit; Dr. Arthur Cohen of the University of California, Los Angeles; and Dr. Corrigan of Litton Industries.

Motivating the ABE Student

Ruth Goodman

Educators have recognized that individuals learn at different rates and vary in their abilities to absorb and integrate stimuli. What have educators done with this knowledge? One attempt has been through individualized instruction. Programmed materials are being used more widely. In the Wilmington Project, the learning laboratory concept is being employed in addition to small group activities which emphasize social living skills, such as health and nutrition, child growth and development, banking and budgeting, consumer education, human relations and practical government. Remedial and developmental reading, computational skills acquired in the learning laboratory situation, are brought to life, given meaning in functional application, in small group social living skills discussions. For example, computational skills are applied through the preparation of marketing lists and a comparison of prices at various neighborhood grocery stores and supermarkets. In one class, the students were prepared to go to a supermarket farther from their homes because the local grocery charged slightly higher prices on some food items — until they realized that the cost of transportation to the supermarket far exceeded the savings on food items.

Reprinted from *Adult Leadership*, February, 1969, by permission of the publisher, Adult Education Association of the USA, Washington, D.C.

In another class, students reinforce reading skills through our "Literacy through Sewing" class. By reading the pattern and instruction booklet, such words as "notch" are added to their vocabularies and words such as "bias" and "dart" are given conceptual depth and dimension. Computational skills are reinforced by the student's necessity to make pattern adjustments according to her own body measurements.

Motivation for writing is provided by having the students write a short story about the completed garment. Students of this class invited others to their "fashion show." This gave them status and recognition and made it possible to appear before a group to make a presentation. Students were particularly cost conscious; learned about the care of clothing, personal hygiene and good grooming.

The following is a story written by a student and presented at the fashion show where she modeled a dress she had altered:

> I enrolled in the sewing class because of losing weight under the doctor's care because of a bad back. Coming from 230 lbs. to 175 lbs. required a lot of alterations which I did not know how to do.
>
> I have learned how to fix my clothes that are too big as well as my son's pants. All this cost me was fifteen cents for the thread.

She signed her name and added a postscript:

> "P.S. I will be glad to come again next year!"

This student and the others in the group attend eight hours each week in ABE, four of which are in the sewing class. Several attend neighborhood classes (which may be held at a church, community center or public school building) and attend the sewing class at the Adult Center of Education. The esprit de corps and morale of this group soon spread throughout the community and calls came in expressing interest. Enrollment of fifteen students in this second class revealed that reading competency ranged from the total illiteracy to fourth grade level.

In still another class, where students expressed an interest "to learn to type," Literacy through Typing reinforced dictionary skills, spelling, punctuation, English usage and reading skills, while learning a manual skill which holds a great deal of status.

How effective is this approach? Our records reveal the following:

1. Going to the sewing class or the typing class is a face-saving device for some students who do not want to reveal their literacy inadequacies to their friends, neighbors and relatives.
2. Need for literacy training becomes more acute and is recognized by the student.
3. Fewer dropouts and higher attendance rates than other groups.

Not all students enrolling in our ABE classes are interested in sewing or typing. Some women give as their reason "to help my children with their schoolwork." However, the greatest number – both men and women – "want to get a job," "want to get a promotion in my job," or "want to change my job." In order to accomplish these goals, the student recognizes the need to acquire the high school diploma or its equivalent. In order for us to prepare the student to achieve his goal, we must resort to the inclusion of subject matter which may have no relation to being successful while on his job (such as grammar). The three areas of study undertaken are: Reading, Computational skills, and English usage. We have found that:

1. The average reading growth in 40 instructional hours is one year. This ratio diminishes as the student approaches fourth grade reading competency. One student (beginning level, 2.5; ending level, 8.0) achieved an overall average of 24 instructional hours per year's reading gain. Another student who came to us was unable to recognize all the letters of the alphabet but could write his name (never went beyond third grade in school); was able to achieve one year's reading gain in 49 instructional hours. Both of these cases are males, employed, one Caucasian who wishes to change jobs, one Negro who wishes to get a promotion in his job. All students achieving 8th grade literacy who took the GED test passed.

2. Standardized tests appear to reveal frustration levels rather than instructional and independent reading levels. It is time consuming and difficult to administer standardized tests within a system of continuous enrollment and where attendance is erratic.

3. Concentrated instruction in computational skills is most effective and rates of achievement more rapid when the student reaches seventh grade reading competency.

4. The majority of students aspiring toward high school equivalency do not need a separate course in social studies and literature. It is possible that the varied subject matter covered while in the remedial and developmental reading program provides the student with information in various fields while improving his literacy skills. Another possibility may be that the social studies and literature sections of the GED test are in fact tests of reading comprehension.

5. The learning laboratory in operation at the Adult Center of Education is open from 8:30 a.m. to 4:30 p.m. and 7:00 p.m. to 10:00 p.m. and allows the student to come at times convenient to him, and for continuous enrollment 52 weeks a year. Employed students on shift work benefit in the continuity of study.

    Students enrolled in classes held in churches, community centers, office buildings or school buildings throughout the city, twice a week at regular scheduled days and hours (determined by the group) who are unable to continue at their neighborhood location because of shift work or for any other reason, can attend the Adult Center of Education learning laboratory at hours convenient to them. We have found that the majority of students begin by attending two hours each day, but increase the number of hours per day as they recognize the progress they are making. The range of weekly attendance is from a minimum of four hours to 32 hours.

6. School grade completion does not correlate with reading achievement. Ten percent of students reading below eighth grade level were high school graduates.

Of the 251 students tested (English-as-a-Second Language students are not tested): 20% were non-readers; 35% were at the primary level (1-3); 29% were at the intermediate level (4-6); and 16% were at the advanced level (7-8).

Seventy percent of the enrollees were women of whom the majority were Negro, and unemployed; 30 percent were men (representing a 12% increase over the male enrollment since the beginning of the program in 1965). The majority of men enrolled were Caucasians. It appears that men are less reluctant to attend a center intended for adults only and prefer the learning laboratory setup to the traditional classroom situation.

At Lansing Community College: Audio-visual-Tutorial Instruction in Business

Ronald K. Edwards

Recently, a woman entered the business division of Lansing Community College with a special request. She had a job offer which she needed and wanted to accept, but it required the use of a particular business machine that she knew nothing about. Could we help her?

Under traditional circumstances an instructor would have had to spend personal time tutoring this woman at mutually convenient meeting times when the classroom was available since the school term was already three weeks old. But times are no longer traditional in the Accounting and Office Programs Department of Lansing Community College in Michigan. The woman was allowed to enroll and register that same day – not for a complete course but for

Reprinted from *Junior College Journal*, May 1969, by permission of the publisher.

one-third of the complete course in office machines, which was all she needed. She established her own schedule of training between the hours of 8 a.m. and 10 p.m. Her instruction came to her personally in a special carrel via 8mm sound films in continuous-loop cartridges. The cartridges were inserted into a rear-screen projector equipped with earphones. In less than two weeks, she had finished her one-third course, passed the final test, and accepted her new job — all without further teacher contact and no class disruptions.

Another opportunity to demonstrate the applicability of the audio-visual-tutorial program to individual needs presented itself during winter term 1968. A student who wished to enhance her typing knowledge came to one of the typing instructors with a typical problem. She had received an eight-week typing course designed to teach the keyboard in junior high school. She had learned the keyboard well and was typing approximately thirty-five words a minute. Her problem stemmed from the fact that her typing speed would indicate that she should enroll in our second term of typewriting, but she would be drastically disadvantaged by her lack of understanding of basic typing rules and forms which we include in the first term.

This is a typical situation. Students frequently arrive with a six- or eight-week junior high course or a one-semester, one-year, three-semester, or even two-year high school course. In addition, they come from high schools with varying standards and with varying levels of competency as designated by the passing grade. The range of ability and knowledge is tremendous. Our task has been to place these students initially in one of three typing courses we offer on the basis of their major needs; obviously, the only students who are properly placed are those with absolutely no typing experience.

The student we mentioned would probably not have done well in Typing II. Yet, if placed in a beginning course, she would have been bored with the initial keyboard drills; her time would have been primarily wasted, and her typing speed would have frustrated the beginning students seated nearby.

Consequently, since our typing course is divided into more than 120 individual single-concept units and has been successfully tested, we decided to add a dimension to our current experiments. The instructor outlined a course of study based on the student's individual needs as determined by a series of short objective-type tests. The requirements equalled a term's work but included units from both the traditional Typing I and Typing II courses. The units were indicated on a "prescription sheet," and the student went to the business division's audio-visual-tutorial laboratory and received the exact instruction and practice necessary for her purposes.

HOW IT BEGAN

Development of this space-age instruction began two years ago when the division received the approval of the chairman and the college president to study the possibility of automated individual instruction in the office education area.

The first task was to search for evidences of similar projects being undertaken; surprisingly, the most reasonable projects were found within our own state and even our own school. Projects included were individual instruction via magnetic tapes at Oakland Community College, California; televised instruction at Michigan State University; and the newly completed natural sciences courses on slides with accompanying tapes for individual study at Lansing.

None of these projects met our specific requirements, however. The taped individual learning system, even with slides, did not offer opportunity for demonstrations which we considered necessary. Televised instruction has this facility, but such a method would be financially prohibitive on an individual instruction basis.

We wanted and needed a system that had the many advantages of the classroom teaching situation and yet none of its restrictions. We hoped to teach each student the skills and abilities necessary for him, at his own pace, and without including redundant practice and information. We wanted to give the student the opportunity to repeat certain segments of courses as needed or skip unnecessary parts without penalty. We wanted to assure faster students that they would not be held back by any policy of everyone practicing a specified number of hours regardless of ability. At the same time, we wanted those who would learn concepts or skills more slowly to be assured that they would not be penalized by arbitrary time limitations established for administrative purposes.

For our purposes, then, we needed a medium which would permit demonstrations on an individual basis. Slides would be ineffective because no movement could be shown. Closed-circuit television was eliminated because of its expense and limitation for individual instruction. Single-concept films were considered, but the aspect of requiring students to synchronize an accompanying tape for sound was unrealistic. We needed the single-concept 8mm film in cartridges but with sound as well. And we found it. A newly designed rear-screen 8mm projector which would accept a cartridged, continuous-loop film with a magnetic strip for sound was marketed during our search. With this medium to provide the demonstration ability, we were in business.

Professional photographers were hired to produce the first filmed demonstrations as we had neither the knowledge nor the equipment to do it ourselves. We have since acquired both. We designed an individual study carrel which included a unit housing the cartridge-loading 8mm sound projector, a slide projector, and a cartridge tape recorder. The carrel, itself, was made spacious enough to hold an office machine, i.e., calculator or typewriter, or to spread out an accounting project.

THE EXPERIMENTAL PLAN

The first experiment was a beginning course in office machines held during the winter quarter, January through March 1967. The basic operations of three types of machines, the ten-key adding-listing machine, the rotary calculator, and the key-driven calculator are included in this course. Through two control groups and one experimental group, we found that students learned more in less time with the new method of instruction.

The second project was a beginning typewriting course and was completed for the fall term 1967. Again, the experimental group exceeded the control group, measured in both speed and accuracy of typing skill and knowledge of typewriting fundamentals.

Programs in Typewriting II, Typewriting III, and Office Machines II have been tested since with equally successful results. Shorthand, business mathematics, accounting, economics, and other office education courses are being planned for future inclusion in A.V.T. methodology. The objective is to provide an office education curriculum that can be completely individualized for every student participating. No two students will be required to follow the same path nor progress at the same speed, yet all will be striving for the same goal and will reach it with better skills, more competencies, and fewer "gaps" in their knowledge than the present traditional curriculum and methods can ever produce. This will be possible because the entire office education curriculum will be divided into hundreds of programmed tutorial units on audio-visual media lasting from five to seven minutes each rather than through a relatively few blocks of related information units of thirty or forty hours' duration.

DIRECT INSTRUCTION

The new plan of individualized instruction is direct; consequently, little time is wasted. The amount of material which can be given to the student can be increased so that greater coverage of the subject matter will be possible. Any "gaps" or weaknesses in prior education can quickly be eliminated by assigning or repeating specific individual units; likewise, any strong areas in an individual's skills or knowledge from prior education can be eliminated from his program, allowing him to progress faster and without needless repetition.

The traditional classroom, even with all its refinements, is rendered obsolete by this new system. It is expected that large laboratories or library-like areas will be created in which students will study various levels of typewriting, shorthand, accounting, and other subjects simultaneously.

Courses begin on the command of each student rather than on an arbitrarily established date required for all persons involved. The course ends for individual students when a specified level of competency is reached and not at the completion of a set number of hours or days. Students are beginning and graduating from the curriculum every working day of the year. We have already experienced success with this system of continuous enrollment at Lansing in our key-punch operator training program.

The role of the teacher is expanded from the present one of lecturer, demonstrator, and paper checker to one of counselor, coach, and tutor. The teacher's time is spent with those students who need additional help and encouragement. Teacher-student contact is on an individual basis. Questions which remained unasked in the past because of a fear of peer ridicule in the class situation are fully discussed under this new tutoring system; consequently, every student gains a more complete understanding of each subject-matter area.

HOW IT WILL WORK

A student wishing to take a secretarial course or curriculum at Lansing will, after being accepted in the normal way, go to the Department of Accounting and Office Programs for an interview and test. An educational specialist in the secretarial science area will interview her to help determine the specific program she will need in order to prepare her for her chosen occupation. At this interview, the student will also be introduced to the unique type of laboratory learning she will be undertaking. Together, they will arrive at decisions concerning which "traditional" course sequences she should follow.

After this preliminary interview, the student will take one or more placement tests to determine how much of each sequence she actually needs for top performance. For example, a girl with one and a half or two years of typing from high school may be adequately prepared as far as speed and accuracy are concerned but may not be sufficiently familiar with specific business forms for the type of work she plans to enter. In such a case, she would be given instruction only on those business forms necessary for occupational competence as determined by the placement tests.

Another illustration might be made in the area of office machines. Perhaps the student has had a machines course in high school and received excellent training. The college, however, has a much greater variety of office machines than the area high schools. The course sequence, then, can eliminate those machines on which the student is already competent. At the end of the sequence, the student will be just as familiar with all machines, in less time, as another student who might need instruction on all of them.

The area of business mathematics can conceivably present a case for further illustration with a little different view. A student with a good high school mathematical background might very easily pass a placement test which would indicate that a course in college business mathematics would not be necessary. This could be done without the student knowing the time-saving procedures of aliquot parts or the sixty-day, 6 per cent method of calculating interest. If this situation is confronted, as it so often is at the community college level, the student concerned could obtain instruction in each of these areas without sitting through a full course in mathematics.

Under our present classroom systems, a student finishing an economics class with a grade of "C" is thought to have an average knowledge of the entire course. Very often, however, that student has a better-than-average knowledge of parts of the course and almost no understanding of certain other segments. Presently, there is no recourse for the student unless he sits through the entire class again to obtain "patches" of information he missed during the first time through. Under the A.V.T. method, however, once the weak areas are determined, he can obtain the exact instruction he needs to fill the "gaps" with a minimum of time, effort, and cost.

This last illustration is important in its implication that, with the audio-visual-tutorial method of teaching, more students, through sufficient repetition of instruction in their weak areas and elimination of instruction where the knowledge is complete, can conceivably finish as what we now call "A" or "B" students.

After the placement tests have been evaluated, the student will be given a "prescription sheet" for each course sequence chosen. These sheets will have the code numbers of all the units of instruction within a particular sequence. The specific units required of the student will be indicated by a checkmark in a space preceding the code number.

The student will take the checksheet — authorization to use the laboratory facilities as well as the designed course outline — to the audio-visual-tutorial laboratory. The lab technician will give the student either a cartridge containing sound film or a set of slides with an accompanying tape, the first instructional unit checked on the sheet. Subsequent units are given the student as he is ready, but only one unit at a time; units may be given the student a second time, but the student allowed to skip any units which are checked on the sheet.

The student will take the cartridge or slides to an individual learning carrel, place it in the projector or tape recorder provided, and receive a short, clear lesson. The instruction, presented on a center screen and through earphones, is concerned with a single concept. When the instructional phase of the unit is absorbed, the student returns it to the lab technician. Related work indicated on an assignment sheet is then completed in another area of the lab. This method frees the carrel equipment for use by other students while practice work is completed.

The ratio of time in a carrel to related practice or work outside the carrel is approximately one to four. The instructional units are five to ten minutes in length, with an average of about seven minutes. Students will then spend thirty to forty minutes in the lab area completing a specific related assignment. If difficulty is encountered, there are two alternatives available: One is to review the short instructional unit in the carrel; the other is to get assistance from one of the instructors in the lab. These instructors are qualified college teachers who are available for individual help and who will also examine work with students immediately upon completion.

Progress checktests are included intermittently throughout a course. The tests are self-administered; an answer sheet is provided so that the student can check his own paper. When completed and checked, the test is left with the technician who forwards it to the departmental office for review by the student's adviser and for subsequent filing in the student's personal academic file.

If a student neglects going to the lab on a regular basis, an attempt will be made to determine the cause. He may be invited to a counseling session with an adviser. The adviser also will be available on appointment at any time the student desires or needs additional help with a program.

Upon completion of all segments of a particular course outline, the student will take a test for the complete course. This test will be administered by the department and checked by the student's adviser. If the test indicates that there are still areas of weakness in the student's knowledge or ability within the scope of the course, the adviser may recommend repetition of a specific segment. In the event that everything is satisfactory, the student will receive the same credit as any other student who completes the test with a similar score. In the final analysis, the only difference between the two students is the time required to arrive at the desired level of ability.

The project might be best described as an attempt to put programmed instructional units on automated audio-visual media for individual use, with qualified tutorial assistance whenever necessary. The units are being made available fourteen hours a day, five days a week and Saturday mornings. Each course begins when the student is ready, is taught when the student commands, and ends when the student is competent.

Multicampus Instructional Resources Services

Robert C. Jones

The expansion of junior colleges across the nation has now assumed an

Reprinted from *Junior College Journal,* March 1966, by permission of the publisher.

dded dimension in the form of multicampus institutions. Single campus disricts are re-forming; new districts which are being established either plan to have more than one campus or begin that way. The Junior College District of St. Louis-St. Louis County is certainly not the first multicampus institution, but it has set a pattern for new districts which are being formed.

The administration and organization of a multicampus district also takes on added dimensions, especially in the area of central, instructional resources services for the campus libraries. By the same token, multimedia services have replaced the single-concept, "library and books" services.

The Junior College District became law in 1962 and fact in early 1963 when two campuses opened in rented quarters; a third campus, in temporary quarters, opened early in 1964; and now, three years later, 7,000 students are enrolled at the three institutions, permanent sites have been acquired, and the three campuses have master plans permitting immediate construction.

Starting a new institution without the restrictions of outmoded faculty and facilities is perhaps easier than trying to straighten out the mess of some established institution; this is particularly true of the libraries. When the colleges opened the libraries opened — paneled shelving, tables, and chairs had been installed; 200 periodical titles were on hand, with back issues on microfilm and reader-printers for their use. Some 2,500 new books were on the shelves, cataloged and processed, ready for circulation on machine charging equipment. The 200-volume revolving McNaughton Collection of latest fiction and nonfiction had been acquired for each library, as had the periodical indexes and standard reference works; and, there were no conventional card catalogs. Multiple copies of printed book indexes were provided; easy to use and distribute, they also represented saving in cost and space.

The district organization includes a central office separate from the campuses; the campus organization includes a director, deans, counselors, librarians, and faculty. The central office, with the district president, a vice-president for business, coordinators for physical facilities, development, systems, student personnel, and instructional resources, is organized to provide both leadership and services for the campuses.

In turn, the Instructional Resources Center at the central office is organized to order, receive, process, produce, and distribute all instructional materials: books, periodicals, records, tapes, slides, transparencies, films and filmstrips, programed materials, AV and tutorial equipment. The equipment includes tape recorders, record players, slide and filmstrip projectors, slide viewers, 8 and 16 mm movie projectors, the Dialog Learning Labs, and audio-tutorial equipment. The Central Instructional Resources also provides an AV technician to service equipment and facilities, and a photo technician to make and copy slides, transparencies, and tapes. All materials, books included, are delivered daily to each campus, ready for students' and faculty use. The librarians are thus free to devote most of their time to serving students and faculty.

Having no books or periodicals, selection of a basic core of general and reference books was relatively easy; we needed some of everything. More specific titles were selected to support the anticipated curriculums, and incoming faculty members were ordering books and materials before they reported for duty. To avoid having to hire numerous catalogers requiring desks, typewriters, and super vision, all books are ordered through a book-processing center, where books including foreign and out-of-print volumes, are procured from all publishers, and delivered fully cataloged and processed, with plastic covers, cards and pockets ready for circulation.

Another time-honored waste of time in libraries is the binding and shelving of periodicals. This has been eliminated by not binding any periodicals; instead we have selected titles from the 300 periodicals we now take, and have back issues on microfilm. Reader-printers are provided so that the student may either read the article or push a button and get a hard copy to keep.

As librarians know all too well, one of the biggest headaches in a library is the care and feeding of the card catalog. The cabinets, themselves, are costly and cumbersome, seldom if ever up to date, and difficult for students and faculty to use. Consequently, we didn't buy any cabinets and we do not have card files. This, again, is an advantage of not having precedents or established routines

After considerable research and experimentation, we arranged for the same company which catalogs and processes our books to produce our book catalogs by camera and computer. The company is sent one Library of Congress card for each book in the district collection. The cards are laid out in sheet form, each sheet having a page number and space designation for each card. Thus, a code number "70R" would mean page 70, space R, which would be a photograph of the entire Library of Congress card. From these sheets, which are retained in the form of a book, keypunching is done and the information then transferred to 1401 computer tape for print-out by author-title, and by subjects. The print-out is photo-reduced for clarity, and the pages hard-bound into book indexes.

Each entry in the indexes contains the author, title, subjects, editor, edition, and date, and the classification number for locating the book on the shelves; students can go directly to the open shelves and obtain the book.

But each entry also includes the code number mentioned above for reference to the full Library of Congress entry if needed. Campus locations are also given if the book is not in all three libraries.

CHANGING CIRCULATION SYSTEMS

The indexes are kept up-to-date by cumulative supplements issued at intervals, depending upon acquisition; each year a total cumulation is produced. Each campus has fifteen sets of three volumes each (author-title index, subject index, and the Library of Congress card catalog volume), for distribution throughout the libraries and in faculty offices. The indexes are as easy to use as a telephone directory.

Cost comparisons are difficult to make because one bulky card file cannot be compared to multiple sets of the book indexes. The fifty sets of three volumes each which the district has cost less than the card file cabinet for one campus would have cost. Once the computer tape is made, any number of the indexes can be produced at little extra cost and, for reruns, the cost is mainly that of punching the new acquisitions.

Further developments of this process are already evident. When the Junior College District and the processing company both acquire a full complement of computer equipment we can tape book orders here, connect our computer to theirs by data phone to place the order, have their computer call ours back with billing information, and print-out the new catalogs.

Another built-in advantage is that we have all of our titles on tape so when, and if, we wish to convert to some form of computer circulation, we can simply call for a runoff of the author entries on prepunched cards, and change circulation systems in a few days. At present, we are returning an approved Library of Congress card to the company as the books are received; they keep the keypunching current and can thus produce a cumulated supplement on short notice.

The McNaughton Collection is a revolving selection of 200 titles of the latest fiction and nonfiction, for which we pay a nominal rental fee. Each month twenty new books are received and twenty slow movers returned. Best sellers are available at the time they are hot, and we have not tied up funds for purchasing and cataloging of books which may shortly be of little value. Books which do have lasting value can be purchased at 70 per cent off after six months, and being ready for circulation when received, require no further processing.

PROGRAMED INSTRUCTION AND EQUIPMENT

In view of making use of multimedia instruction, we are currently developing outside reading and some programed lessons on micro-cards, and will equip carrels in the libraries with small readers. Students now check out small slide viewers or a deck of slides from the libraries for programs in art, humanities, or science. Carrels are also equipped with Craig Readers and with E.D.L. pacers, with a full range of programs and tests available in the library. Audio-tutorial labs have also been programed with a recorded lecture on tape synchronized with an automatic slide projector or correlated with slides, transparencies or pictures, or filmstrips; programs, so far, include biology and chemistry labs, art, remedial reading, English composition. "How to Use the Library" is in the works.

Libraries on two campuses contain an advanced version of the language lab. The Dialog Learning Labs can be used in the conventional sense with the instructor playing tapes or records or talking and listening to the students. But, each station in the lab or in the library contains a headset and a dial, so the student simply consults a listing of programs and dials the desired lesson, which may be Spanish, French, German, Russian, humanities, music, art, shorthand at various speeds, composition, sentence structure, etc. The remote tape deck cabinet stores 120 simultaneous programs, any of which can be changed in seconds. One program last semester included a workbook in sentence structure which was checked out from the librarian, and a taped lecture which the student dialed. When the lesson was completed the student was given a test, after which he dialed another number and got the answers with explanations. This program has been very effective in bringing students up to an acceptable level of performance. When suitable videotape recorders are available, the carrels will be wired for video and TV programs. The next step will be to run all audio and video programs through the computer, and have hundreds of listening and viewing stations throughout the libraries.

Numerous experiments are being conducted by faculty on released time to develop Dialog Programs, audio-tutorial programs, videotape and TV programs. Grading student papers on tape recorders has proven very effective. The instructional resources staff is assisting these efforts by continuous research and demonstration of latest AV equipment and its uses, and by producing color slides and transparencies, and making taped programs. The faculty on each campus, however, is directly involved in initiating and carrying out programs. From a situation of wondering how faculty would take to all of the innovations, we have come to a point where they are cooperating us to death.

The central office staff consists of a coordinator of instructional resources, an assistant for AV, and an assistant for technical processes, the AV and photo technicians, and three library assistants. Each campus has a librarian, an assistant librarian with the library certificate, library assistants, and student-help to shelve books and deliver AV equipment.

These staffs will be increased when we move into permanent buildings but we do not envision the customary order and catalog and serials librarians; the prime function of the campus librarian is to work with students and faculty, and a major effort is now being made to involve the faculty in ordering books and materials in their fields.

The prime function of the central staff is to provide services so the librarians will have time to work with faculty and students.

INSTRUCTIONAL RESOURCES BUILDINGS

The instructional resources buildings planned for each campus offer little that is new except that each will house a vast complex of audio, video, and programed labs; numerous individual listening and viewing stations; plus darkrooms, preview rooms, recording rooms, faculty and AV workshop.

The other floors will house more conventional library materials, will be fully carpeted, contain 90 per cent carrels and carrel tables, some of which will be also wired for listening and viewing.

To go into more detail, the Forest Park Community College building, which is being constructed, will ultimately house 500 individual listening and viewing stations at the basement level, and seat over 1,000 individually on the other floors. It will hold 80,000 volumes. The building takes shape as a split-level, with a platform in the center for circulation, reference, and browsing, and upper and lower mezzanines for intermingled seating and shelving. The circulation desk, which we have designed, will accommodate periodical indexes and the printed book indexes on its outer sides, with circulation equipment and reserve books inside. The person or persons on duty in this area will, thus, have close at hand everything students are likely to need help with. Circulation files and returned books will be kept in the workroom, leaving the circulation area free of desks and clutter. Everything will be on open shelves, and there will be no fines or turnstiles; the in and out doors will be electric to control traffic flow and help students coming in and out with armloads of books.

CENTRAL OFFICE – CAMPUS RELATIONSHIPS

In addition to the mechanical assemblage in the library, each classroom will have receiving and initiating capabilities for audio and video tapes, and, perhaps, permanent projection equipment. The halls in each classroom wing will be studded with small alcoves, some as lounges, others wired for audio and video programs. Students need not cross the campus to read or listen to assignments.

Basic to the operation of a multicampus college are the relationships, established by chart or practice, between the administration at the central office and on the campus. The upper-level mode of operation between the district president and the campus directors applies to the relationship between the central instructional resources staff and the instructional resources staff in the campus libraries. There are two extremes, both unsatisfactory: complete authority at central, or on campus.

In order to preserve the initiative and creativity of all staff and faculty, complete autonomy at either end of the organization is inconsistent with district philosophy. But so is total freedom to run off in all directions. It would appear that a central administrative staff and services are necessary for efficient and coordinated district-wide operation, and it would appear that campus freedom to operate independently within district policy and procedures is also necessary. And it would appear that no one solution need apply to all or any other institutions. Just as junior colleges across the nation differ in philosophy and purpose, they must also select that type of organization which best suits their purpose.

Electronic Learning Center

R. Stafford North

Colleges must change if they are to meet the challenges of exploding knowledge, increasing enrollments, and shortages of competent teachers. They must be willing to change, to explore new techniques of instruction — and colleges and universities all over the country are doing just that. They are experimenting with instruction by television with multimedia laboratories that utilize all types of audio-visual equipment, some simultaneously; with programed instruction; and with many other methods of extending the influence of the teacher.

One of the most interesting new experiments is occurring at Oklahoma Christian College near Tulsa, Okla. The college is small and young, only 16 years old. It is a four-year liberal arts college, offering degrees in five major fields and preprofessional training in several others. Its first degrees were conferred in 1963. This year 788 students are enrolled and in each of the past five years there has been an enrollment increase of 20 percent. Half of the students are from out of the state. Its present campus consists of four classroom buildings, a small auditorium-library building, and two dormitories. Three years ago, plans were begun for the new $1 million, three-story Learning Center, located in the center of the campus quadrangle. The center comprises a library, faculty offices, and learning carrels in its 57,000 sq. ft.

The Learning Center is unique in that its heart is an electronically equipped, private carrel assigned, full time, to each student enrolled as his own private study area. The second and third floors of the building accommodate more than 1000 carrels, with room for expansion as the campus grows. The first floor is a library with space for 50,000 books, plus periodicals and reference works. There is seating for 100 students, a special microfilm reading room, and an area for library services. Thirty students can be seated in a special viewing room equipped with dial and loudspeaker so students can gather in groups to hear tape-recorded lectures or participate in "telelectures" featuring off-campus authorities.

A PRIVATE WORK CENTER

In addition to the 1000 carrels on the second and third floors, there are 12 faculty offices, three conference rooms, an office for the center's director, a control room for recording equipment, and two recording centers. Each student carrel has sound-absorbent walls, bookshelf, desk, typewriter stand, chair, and locked cabinet. Through an electronic computer system, each carrel is connected to a variety of audio-taped materials. The student merely dials the program number listed in a bulletin, puts on his headset, and gets to work. The carrels are meant as a personal work center for the student, where he can read, write papers, listen to taped lectures or music, or view slides, filmstrips, or movies.

"The Learning Center is designed to make the most effective use of all sources of knowledge — the teachers, books, and audio-visual materials," says Dr. R. Stafford North, dean of instruction and principal planner of the center.

The dial-access electronic learning system permits teachers to prerecord those portions of their courses that lend themselves to audio-workbook presentation. This enables students to supplement their required class attendance by studying independently at their convenience.

TWO TYPES OF SYSTEMS

The DATAGRAM learning system includes two studio-tape systems — individual or group listening tapes. For both types of programs, the student merely puts on his headset, dials a three-digit number, and is connected to one of 136 taped programs. "Group listening" tapes provide lectures at a prescheduled time to a large number of students, who may listen in their carrels rather than in a large, crowded lecture hall. Sometimes students follow the lectures using a workbook prepared by the teacher and keyed to the audio-tape lecture.

The DATAGRAM system is now being utilized for courses in public speaking, English, world literature, American government, political science, art appreciation, music appreciation, general biology, introduction to the theater, introduction to business, Old Testament survey, and intermediate algebra. Other course materials are being developed. The type of course material determines the best method of presentation. In no case, however, is a course entirely on tape. The student continues to have direct contact with the teacher; however, those portions of a course that are suitable for a programed presentation are transcribed to tape and workbook. The discussion is handled by the teacher directly with the students.

The "individual listening" tapes are reference tapes or lectures assigned in addition to regular lectures. At the end of the program, the tape automatically rewinds and is ready for another student.

"The dial-access system offers many advantages," explains Dr. North. "The tapes can be used over and over and are easy to update. The recording equipment and related materials are relatively inexpensive and tape recordings are less difficult to prepare than other types of instructional materials. A wealth of material is available for the various prerecorded courses.

"Music appreciation courses will include the world's outstanding symphony orchestras; history courses will include significant speeches, while literature courses can offer dramatizations of Shakespeare."

COMPUTER RELAYS REQUESTS

The Oklahoma Christian learning system is the result of extensive research and planning for quality education by Dr. North combined with the technological know-how of North Electric Company of Galion, Ohio, a telephone-equipment supplier. The center of the DATAGRAM system is a computer in the control room. It connects the student to the material he wants to hear. Nine machines can each play four lectures simultaneously, while five additional machines are connected with recording and duplicating tapes. By using a play-back machine with the five recorders it is possible to make three copies of three different tapes or as many as five copies of one tape at a time. The recording console also contains an AM-FM radio tuner and turntable, making it possible to record radio programs or records. The console can also be used for telephone hookup with off-campus lectures anywhere in the world.

A similar system in use at Ohio State University has about half of the student positions centrally located in the listening center, while others are remotely located in other campus buildings. A third application of the DATA-GRAM system is at Oral Roberts University in Tulsa, Okla. In addition to the audio capabilities, it will provide dial-access video programs.

Learning Resources Approach to College and University Library Development

Fred F. Harcleroad

Recently, in the foreword to an important book written for the Council on Library Resources, Verner W. Clapp defined "library work" as "the operations connected with assembling information in recorded form and of organizing and making it available for use."[1] In the introduction to this same book, J.C.R. Licklider, the author, wrote, "The 'libraries of the future' may not be very much like the present-day libraries, and the term library, rooted in book, is not truly appropriate to the kind of system on which the study focused."[2] In a sense,

Reprinted from *Library Trends,* October 1967, by permission of the publisher.

these two somewhat contrasting statements epitomize the difficulty of modern library theorists and their concerns for "learning resources."

Today's problem is one of abundance — abundance of printed materials and of information stored in non-print form. One hundred years ago, the Harvard Library contained approximately 120,000 volumes. In this year alone, Harvard Library expects to accession more than 120,000 books. Because of the increasing flow of printed materials, even Harvard Library's accession rate is too slow for a great university library which hopes to meet its research function; maintain constant, comprehensive growth in its book and periodical collections; and continue its reputation for high standards. With the development of the computer and the resultant systems for rapid information storage and retrieval, forward-looking librarians have focused their attention on the problems of cataloging, storing, searching for, and reproducing this mammoth amount of information. It is perfectly logical that the major focus of the scholars of the library world, working in large research institutes or universities, should be on ways to cope with the massive flow of new information and its proper storage and use in meeting the research function of the university.

At the same time, the technological improvements in photography, magnetic recording, and pictorial transmission have reached a confluence with the increased research on the "learning process." Several libraries have added materials which are preserved by these methods. However, in many established libraries they remain outside the pale and are operated by units independent of the library. These new materials and techniques for storing and presenting knowledge to students and scholars have brought about an emphasis on independent study and learning far greater than was possible before. In addition, they have made it possible for students and professors on many campuses to produce their own materials to meet local needs. Such demanding work is considerably beyond the concept of a library which assembles material prepared previously by others.

Several factors make a difference in the development of learning resource programs on various campuses and their relationships to library development: (1) the size, (2) age, and (3) major purposes of the institution. Small institutions with relatively limited financial backing and building space tend to include very few of the newer learning resources among their book and microform collections. On the other hand, comprehensive institutions with large libraries tend to have separate television and radio units, audio-visual service units, programmed instruction centers in many departments, and duplicating centers all over the campus. Older institutions with long-established libraries do the same, adding new units for technological developments such as television, audio-visual services, programmed instruction, computer and data processing operations. Some new institutions incorporate all these operations within the library and develop a Division of Educational Services or of Learning Resources. The type of institution also appears to make a difference, although this factor is associated with the size and age of the institution. Institutions which emphasize instruction over public service or research tend to combine their services in some fashion. The great research universities of the United States have massive libraries – and massive problems. They tend to leave television, video-tape, audio-visual and photographic services to other units of the university. Specialized research services provided by these other technological areas usually remain outside the university library. Also, extension divisions of large research universities often offer the additional film, television and photographic services to the public and then add such services for their campuses. Although these generalizations have many specific exceptions, they are worthy of careful analysis and further study.

A few illustrations will provide some indication of the variations between institutions and of the importance of size, age and objectives. Illustrations selected are: (1) two community or junior colleges – the new Brevard Junior College in Cocoa, Florida, and Stephens College in Columbia, Missouri; (2) two small liberal arts colleges – the Oklahoma Christian College and the Oral Roberts University, both in Oklahoma; (3) a new expanding state college – the California State College at Hayward; (4) a university in transition – the Southern Illinois University; and (5) two older established universities – the University of Minnesota and the University of California.

These descriptions are not complete and are quite brief, but will provide enough information to indicate some of the directions in which learning resources programs have been developed on various types of college and university campuses.

Brevard Junior College, Cocoa, Florida. Brevard Junior College has developed a Division of Educational Services with a Director who is immediately responsible to the President. Seven different departments or units are part of this Division, including (1) the Office of Institutional Research, (2) the Office of Data Processing and Technical Research, (3) the Library, (4) the Television and Radio Center, (5) the Audio-Visual Resources Center, (6) the Study Skills Clinic, and (7) the Language Laboratory. The Language Laboratory, Audio-Visual Resources Center, and the Television and Radio Center were first brought together in 1964. In 1965, the Library was added as a fourth unit. Then, in 1966, the other three units were made part of the Division.

In describing the functions of the various units one important difference distinguishes the Library from the Language Laboratory, the Audio-Visual Resources Center, and the Television and Radio Center. The Library "selects and acquires recorded knowledge, catalogs it and makes it readily available for retrieval – or retrieves it and circulates it." The other three units do this for commercially-prepared material, but they also originate and store information materials which they develop themselves on the campus.

The Audio-Visual Resources Center and the Library have been located in a new "Learning Center." A new communication center is proposed, which will include new facilities for the Television and Radio Center and the Study Skills Clinic. They already have developed a group of specialized booths for self-study which are called "inquiry modules." These modules allow the student to use films, video-tapes and live, closed-circuit telecasts on a dial-access basis, and give them access to stereo-tapes, language and other general taped materials containing tests or classroom lectures. In the modules the learner can watch color movies, study microfilm, use controlled reading scanners or read printed materials which have been checked out of the Library section of the Division of Educational Services.

Descriptions of the Brevard Junior College program emphasize the fact that it is attempting to innovate in education, as well as to integrate the use of media; it is interested in pioneering new approaches to learning processes, coordinating all the interrelated professional resources, and using all the appropriate new technology for the welfare of students and faculty. In this relatively young junior college the Library has become only one of seven units in a Division of Educational Services, but it is an exceedingly important unit. Nevertheless, the new technological aids to learning and the production of local learning materials were developed outside the Library and gradually have been amalgamated into a total Division which includes the Library as one of its component parts.

Stephens College, Columbia, Missouri. In the last decade, Stephens College has studied extensively the use of all types of learning resources and has planned and built the James M. Wood Learning Center to incorporate the results. Two useful reports[3,4] and one magazine article[5] present good descriptions of the development at Stephens.

The Learning Center includes at its core a library for books and other educational media. The total design attempts to provide flexibility in use of space for many purposes, a great variety of learning resources for several educational purposes, and close proximity among the spaces, resources and persons working together for teaching and learning; it also tries to make resources easily available which may improve the educational process.

This Center includes five buildings: an old one which was remodeled, and four new ones. The heart of the Learning Center is the dissemination system which originates in the television, radio and film department — a building which also houses the audio-visual center and a 300-seat classroom. Nearby is the humanities and communications department building with classrooms and faculty office space. On the same mall nearby, is the "resources library" which houses the general library, five divisional libraries, some faculty offices and seminar rooms, and a large collection of audio-visual materials such as motion pictures, slides, filmstrips, records, and tapes. The other two buildings, housing the art department and the religion, philosophy and language departments, are connected to the television, radio and film building by coaxial cable.

In this Center the faculty have planned many projects. They have used amplified telephone lectures for instruction in a variety of fields. Tape-activated, rear-screen slide projection is planned and used by the humanities division. There are listening tables (audio-lab facilities) in several divisions including theater arts, speech, business education, social studies, and the humanities. The language laboratory and programmed instruction materials are used for testing and teaching in communication, mathematics, foreign languages, and the humanities, with an emphasis on the aural-oral, reading, and writing approaches to languages.

However, the most important point about this new Learning Center may be that the entire operation is organized under a Director of Educational Development, emphasizing its close relationship to the instructional program of the college. Leyden and Balanoff[4] repeatedly emphasize the need to reexamine course objectives, analyze methods currently being used to achieve these objectives, identify educational media being employed in the teaching, and, finally, identify those methods, materials and media which the faculty consider critical in meeting their course objectives. The instructional emphasis at Stephens is obviously strong and the organization of their Learning Center has evolved as a result.

Oklahoma Christian College, Oklahoma City, Oklahoma. Oklahoma Christian College, a fifteen-year-old liberal arts college, developed a learning center in 1962, although it was started originally as part of a plan for a new library. The result of the planning is a three-story building with the first floor allotted to a library of 50,000 volumes, with seating for 110 students, a microfilm room, a reference area, periodical room, and technical processing area. The other two floors house more than 1,000 study carrels, the offices of the Director of the Learning Center, faculty offices, conference rooms, two recording studios, and a control room for electronic equipment.

Each student pays a thirty-dollar fee per semester to rent a carrel and guarantee his private, specially-designed study. The student has direct dial-access to three different types of recorded materials: (1) taped lectures, often used with workbooks, prepared by faculty to serve as instructional material for certain portions of a course; (2) dial-access "taped exercises" which are largely drill material needed in such subjects as language, math or science; and (3) dial-access "aural material" — such as music, poetry, drama, speeches — which must be heard for optimum learning. In addition, the student may check out small projectors and view films or single-concept film cartridges. He can look at filmstrips and slides in the carrel or check out a portable recorder for language laboratory listening, recording and/or playback.

Oklahoma Christian College is an example of a liberal arts college which encourages development of teaching materials by its own professors and students. The carrels or "study spaces" are used heavily during most of the day. As late as 4 p.m. one-third of the students will still be using them. A traditional library is located nearby and has a few additional seating spaces for people who wish to use them. However, the fundamental organization is that of a learning center of which the library is but one part.

Oral Roberts University, Tulsa, Oklahoma. Oral Roberts University has developed a new Learning Resources Center six stories high with very extensive electronic aids. The library is a critical part of the Learning Resources Center and includes "nests" of audio-video carrels. The entire Center is based on a dial-access, audio-video system, with television studios, tape and film rooms, a science laboratory with a closed-circuit television loop, and specialized programming possibilities for film change with slides, filmstrips, video-tape clips or audio materials without the video. Furthermore, the building provides for use of both audio and video response systems for individual or group evaluation of success in learning from programmed materials. In addition to the carrels in the library, there are audio-video carrels in the learning laboratory and audio carrels in the language laboratory. On the whole, this center is used as a supplement to normal instruction. However, there has been some experimentation with its use as a complete self-teaching system. Classrooms with a specially prepared teacher's desk are able to receive any programmed materials that can also be channeled to the audio-video carrels.

Comparing Oral Roberts University with Oklahoma Christian College, one sees that Oral Roberts University provides for extensive transmission of video material to study carrels, while Oklahoma Christian College has audio materials available and is using these materials for certain phases of instruction which are almost "total." Oral Roberts University, however, is still using its Learning Resources Center mainly for supplementary instruction. Once again the emphasis must be on materials which have been developed within the institution and are made available for study through a dial-access system. The library – the book library – is still available as a part of the Learning Resources Center.

California State College at Hayward, Hayward, California. The California State College at Hayward started in 1959 and now has 5,000 students, enrolled in twenty-nine undergraduate and ten graduate degree programs. Two divisions make up the total learning resources program: first, there is the Division of the Libraries and second, the Division of Learning Resources (which is actually a misnomer, since it does not provide for those learning resources in the library). The Division of Learning Resources includes (1) the Audio-Visual Utilization Service; (2) the Audio-Visual Technical Service; (3) the Materials Preparation Services, including film and filmstrip production; (4) the Instructional Television and Radio Services; (5) the Instructional Publication Services, including duplicating and stenographic services; (6) the Audio Laboratories which provide for the audio retrieval of foreign language, music, and speech materials; and (7) a Center for Independent Study. The Center for Independent Study enables students to study programmed materials with a variety of different mechanical and electronic machines. It provides for (1) students who want prerequisite background for courses (such as trigonometry, needed for calculus); (2) parts of courses (such as genetics or chemistry in a film series); (3) credit by proficiency examination after studying full course materials; and (4) remedial or developmental work (such as a course in slide rule, which is not given for credit and must be taken on the Autotutor with programmed materials).

Organizationally, the Division of Libraries and the Division of Learning Resources are parallel, and the Directors of both report to the academic dean of the College. Information regarding the background for this program and plans for its future development in terms of buildings and operation are found in the book *Learning Resources for Colleges and Universities*, a project completed at the California State College at Hayward for the United States Office of Education. This was published in September, 1964, and suggests future roles which digital computers can play in the learning resources center. At present, there is no provision for their direct use as part of computer-assisted instruction at the College.

Southern Illinois University, Carbondale, Illinois. Southern Illinois is a developing university with a long history. While its library is not large in comparison with the biggest university libraries in the United States, it has grown enormously in the last decade and recently accessioned its millionth volume. In 1964, a study was made of the interrelationships of the various learning resources on the University campus. As a result a number of these resources — for example, the audio-visual services, materials preparation services, and the self-instruction center — have been incorporated into the library organization as operating units. There are audio-tutorial services in the self-instruction center where a great deal of programmed tape material is provided for students. Combination audio-tape and two-by-two slide series are available for group instruction. Also, students can study film materials in the self-instruction center after checking them out from the center or the audio-visual services. Students taking large courses in art history use the center's self-contained slide projectors, while those in biology use a variety of materials including 8mm single-concept films, slides, tapes, laboratory materials and models.

A new large general classroom building has been completed recently and makes use of multi-media instructional support provided by the audio-visual section of the library. It has extensive potential for large-group instruction. Student response systems are planned for this building so that professors can have instant feed-back on the learning which is taking place within their classes.

This university's experience exemplifies incorporation in the library of a part of the learning resources on the campus while certain other resources still remain independent and have only limited relationship to the library. Examples are the closed- and open-circuit television facilities, the film production center, and the data processing or computer center. Nevertheless, it represents a way in which learning resources developments can take place in the library of a large university with a rapidly expanding book collection.

The University of California, Berkeley, California. Recently the library at the Berkeley campus of the University of California was rated second in the "overall library resources index" list which was prepared by the American Council on Education. In June, 1966, the Berkeley campus library had about 3,200,000 books and was receiving 45,000 periodicals. Nevertheless, in December, 1966, the academic senate library committee stated, "Substantial improvements will be necessary if the Berkeley library is to meet the challenge presented by new areas of study, new teaching methods and an increasing emphasis on the search for knowledge by students, faculty and the many other users."[6] The *Daily Californian* Weekly Magazine devoted four pages to discussing the problems of the "rich but frustrating" library at Berkeley.

The library obviously has so many problems in maintaining its stature and accommodating the enormous load of book and magazine acquisitions that developments in other technological forms of information storage have been delegated elsewhere.

For example, Berkeley, through its television office, provides a library of video-tape and film for faculty and student use. These materials are available on an interbuilding random-access, closed-circuit television communication system. The television office has 350 reels of recorded video-tape and film inventoried to departments and on deposit in its library. Various materials are prepared by television and film coverage, both in and outside the studio. The office develops thirty-minute lectures and demonstrations for such departments as industrial processes, optometry, and engineering graphics. Shorter modules (programs) of fifteen minutes or less are often made for the life sciences, such as physiology and biology. Documentaries of thirty minutes or longer are prepared for such fields as sociology, criminology, forestry, speech and law. The video-tape and film library is part of the master distribution center of the television office. This master distribution center serves twenty-eight different instructional rooms in five different buildings, with permanent equipment available in each. The television center is but one illustration of the many different "learning resources" which are available on the campus, but organized completely separately from the book library.

The University of Minnesota, Minneapolis, Minnesota. The University of Minnesota is another example of a strong, developing university with a large library and strong research program. Over the years the University has developed a unit called "university services" which includes the Audio-Visual Education Services and the Printing Services which normally might be considered part of the learning resources division of a college or university. The Audio-Visual Education Services include a production department which provides motion picture films, teaching filmstrips, microfilms, and copies of opaque and recorded materials. One phase of their production service, the Artist Service, designs and constructs charts, graphs, exhibits, displays; models animation material for motion picture production; and prepares almost any other kind of graphic art required by the university faculty.

The Audio-Visual Education Services are expanding the language laboratories and closed-circuit television; doing programmed material research; working to provide learning resources in the campus dormitories and study centers; and developing facilities for self-directed learning and independent study. Plans are under way for construction of a central learning resource center where a student can obtain both audio and visual reinforcement by dialing proper code numbers on a dial-access system, including closed-circuit television, film and tape playback, recording devices for both visual and auditory materials and for language lessons. Audio-Visual Education Services hope to have home dialing systems for audio-response materials, including language lessons or capsule reviews of lectures given that day. Once again, new technological means of storing or producing information have developed outside the aegis of the book library.

It seems obvious that great research libraries and the professional leaders from these libraries must continue to spend most of their energy and attention on the book and periodical collections, and on the enormous outpouring of new materials which are to be stored for posterity. Recent books on such subjects as "libraries of the future," "libraries and automation," or "information retrieval and storage" indicate the enormous complexity of the problems which face this portion of the learning resources area. Swanson's recent paper on "Design Requirements for a Future Library,"[7] contains no mention whatsoever of materials described in this article as parts of learning resources, other than books, magazines, and microfilm. In fact, the 258 pages in *Libraries and Automation*[7] include practically no reference to any learning resources except books and magazines. Licklider in *Libraries of the Future*, does describe the schemata of the body of knowledge as including "strings of alphanumeric characters, and the associated diagrams, graphs, pictures, and so forth, that make up the documents that are preserved in recognized repositories."[8] He also discusses briefly "the problems and developments in the use of computers as aids in teaching and in learning, and as a basis for group cooperation in the planning and design of buildings."[9] However, most books in the library field which describe themselves as dealing with the libraries of the future or the state of the library are concerned basically with punched cards, electronic searching, notched cards, feature cards, microphotography, national library systems, indexing, information frameworks, file storage access, automated storage and access, output printing, interface problems, principles of design, and choice of equipment.

One of the few contemporary articles which goes beyond these problems is Osborne's paper on "The Influence of Automation on the Design of the University Library." He states that, "University libraries of the year 2000 to 2100 will look very much like the newer libraries of today. They will be more complex in their organization because the bookstock will be greatly splintered, because they will be interconnected nationally with other repositories, and because they will even more than today rely on a multitude of forms, including A-V and TV devices, over and above the microforms and other non-book materials now available."[10] In further discussion, he indicates that "the university library of the future . . . can be anticipated as a still more sophisticated complex of the traditional bookstock, plus A-V, plus IR [information retrieval]. And this means in particular: (1) an intensification of the trend towards individual accommodations such as wired carrels; (2) all conceivable wiring and equipment for technical processes, as well as reader services."[11]

Chart 1 — Learning Resources Organization Plan A

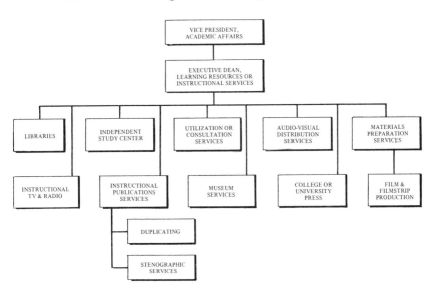

But even Osborne, although he noted the importance of A-V in varied forms and the need for wired carrels, did not consider the problem of producing local, personalized, and individualized teaching materials on the college and university campus. Ideally, a library will be associated with the total learning resource capability of the university or college and this organization (as suggested in Chart 1 or Chart 2) should be quite comprehensive. Although the large libraries may have to be separate because of their large book collections and enormous problems of storage and retrieval, ideally there should be some relationship between the other learning resources on the campus and the basic part of the learning resource of any campus, the book and magazine collections. At the present time, however, the most promising organizational developments for using learning resources are taking place outside the library in large research universities, and in a new division of educational services or learning resources which include the library in smaller, instructionally-oriented colleges and community colleges.

Chart 2 – Learning Resources Organization Plan B

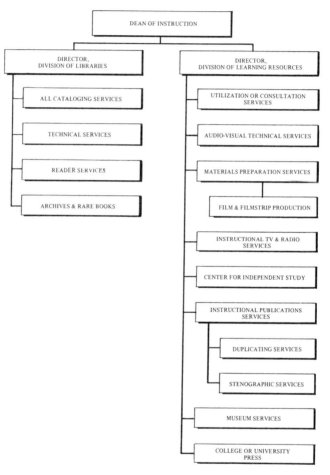

REFERENCES

1. Licklider, J.C.R. *Libraries of the Future.* Cambridge, Mass., M.I.T. Press, 1965, p.v.
2. *Ibid.*, pp.1-2.

3. Mayhew, Lewis B., ed. *New Frontiers in Learning.* (Report of a conference.) Columbia, Missouri, Stephens College, 1959.
4. Leyden, Ralph C., and Balanoff, Neal. *The Planning of Educational Media for a New Learning Center.* (A preliminary report by Stephens College, Columbia, Missouri, to the U.S. Department of Health, Education and Welfare, Office of Education, Nov. 1963.) (Processed.)
5. Balanoff, Neal. "James M. Wood Learning Center, A Saturation Experiment at Stephens College," *Audio-visual Instruction*, 8:226-229, April 1963.
6. *Daily Californian* Weekly Magazine. January 10, 1967.
7. Swanson, Don R. "Design Requirements for a Future Library." *In* Barbara E. Markuson, ed., *Libraries and Automation.* Washington, D.C., Library of Congress, 1964.
8. Licklider, *op. cit.,* p. 24.
9. *Ibid.,* p. 170.
10. Osborne, Andrew E. "The Influence of Automation on the Design of the University Library." *In* Allen Kent, ed., *Library Planning for Automation.* Washington, D.C., Spartan Books, 1965, p. 72.
11. *Ibid.,* p. 73.

CMSC's Self-Instruction Center

It's a long way from the little red school house to Missouri's up-to-date electronic learning center, opened this year at Central Missouri State College. Campus experts in audio-visual education and in instructional engineering have pooled their talents to create a Self-Instruction Center that's unique in Missouri in the use of audio and visual techniques for learning. Open to all students and faculty, the Center offers unlimited opportunity for the creative exchange of knowledge and ideas.

Whether he's looking for help in art, home economics, languages, industrial arts, child psychology, you name it, a student can tutor himself through use of audio tape, video tape, film, and slides. He can hear last week's lecture again, supplement his professor's instruction with lectures by well-known authorities, see a play on film, test himself, or check his lecture notes.

He can choose from a library of 275 titles on audio tape and 250 on video tape, some recorded by CMSC instructors and some taped commercially. New tapes are added to the library almost every day. The center is equipped with 100 listening stations, where the student has a choice of audio-tape decks or video-

Reprinted by permission from *School and Community*, April 1970, pages 16-17 and 26-27.

tape monitors. The audio-tape decks are equipped for stopping and replaying. Students say it's the only opportunity they have to control the lecturer. Many students practice and check their shorthand using the stop and start device. Earphones supplied with the tape decks have microphones attached, especially useful when the student wants to practice his foreign language pronunciation.

The bulk of the laboratory is the bank of 34 tapes in high-demand by instructors for special instruction which can be heard in any of the carrels. Other tapes, in less demand, are placed on reserve, and tapes are changed daily to meet the needs of the students. Tapes are activated in each carrel by a dial system and are heard through headphones; this system is called dial access.

Ten study carrels are equipped with individual tape decks in addition to a dial-access console. These tape decks are manually controlled by the student. Reserve audio tapes are used in these carrels.

Video monitors as well as a dial-access console are provided in five carrels. The video tape is placed on a video-tape recorder in the control room and transmitted electronically to the study carrels. The sound for the video monitor is received by the student via headphones.

The most popular subject in the dial access system has been music appreciation, followed by English literature. Students take their books with them and listen to the professional character recite his part while they follow in the book. The printed page comes to life and becomes more meaningful to the student. Speech, study skills, public speaking, science for general education, and professional orientation are also very popular.

Specific assignments account for the volume of use of many tapes. A professor may send a whole class to the Self-Instruction Center to supplement class instruction with a lesson on tape. Or he may recommend to an individual student that he use the Center for research or to bring up a grade.

While many tapes available in the Center are made on campus, others are speeches and lectures recorded by nationally known persons in government, industry, and education. Followers of Eugene McCarthy might enjoy his talk on "Industrial Arts and Economic Growth," a 30 minute tape recorded in 1964. Education majors might enjoy Robert M. Hutchins' "On Education." Also available are "The Responsibilities of Television," by Newton N. Minow; "Tangents of Technology," by Aldous Huxley; and "Labor Looks at Itself," by delegates from United Auto Workers.

"The Role of Government in the Economy," by Gunnar Myrdal, and "The Prospects for Democracy Around the World," by Adlai Stevenson, might interest a social science major. A series of Spanish lessons and French lessons are designed to help the foreign language student broaden his knowledge of spoken language.

Students may take home a copy of any recording in the catalog; they must furnish their own tape, but there is no charge. The Center is equipped with a sound recording studio where faculty members make instructional tapes.

The Central Missouri State College Library had been appointed by the U.S. Department of State as a regional depository for tapes released for distribution by the U.S. State Department. Included among the tapes are speeches and announcements by major government figures on contemporary issues. Copies of the tapes are made at the College and made available to any school within the region, and a current list is available to social science classes at the College.

Also incorporated in the Self-Instruction Center are five group instruction rooms for five to twenty persons. They are equipped to take advantage of all the video and audio equipment in the center. Each room has a wall mounted console, permitting students to dial for audio-tape recordings. Large TV monitors are part of the electronic equipment within each room. Sound for the above mentioned equipment is amplified through a loudspeaker. Each room is equipped with 8mm single concept and 16mm film, film strip, and slide projectors; record players and portable tape recorders.

The single concept projector is a recent development in presenting three to five minute films concentrated on one subject. The small light-weight projector uses cartridges in which the film is a continuous loop.

The latest addition to the College's electronic learning facilities is a two-way Tele-writer system connected with the Jackson County Residence Center in Independence. Classes in both schools can be taught simultaneously by a teacher in one class. The other class hears the lecture through an amplification system, sees notes written by the lecturer on an overhead projector, and joins in the discussion through the use of microphones.

The Tele-writer system was introduced through the auspices of the Kansas City Regional Council on Higher Education. It can be used in exchange with any other school that has the facilities.

Mobile video-tape recorders are available from the Self-Instruction Center for use in classrooms. Especially valuable for immediate playback, use of the mobile units gives both students and instructor a visual and verbal critique of classroom work. One style of mobile unit fits on a wheeled cart, another is small enough to fit in a back-pack.

Charles L. Honeywell, assistant professor of education, is director of the Self-Instruction Center. Mr. Honeywell holds Bachelor and Master of Science degrees in education, and during a leave of absence last year studied instructional media at Southern Illinois University. He was an ideal choice to head the new Center, which opened in September.

The manager of instructional engineering, and designer of many of the electronic systems on the campus, is Jerry Hildebrand, who not only incorporates his own improvements into much of the audio-visual equipment, but also doubles the amount of equipment the College can afford to own by building components himself.

Staff members in the Self-Instruction Center are available to help faculty members with audio-visual aids to be used elsewhere on campus. One teacher of technical arts, for example, has completed an introduction to his course using slides and audio tape. Teachers are finding that the use of media in preparing lectures helps them not only to sharpen their lectures, assuring that nothing is left out, or unnecessarily repeated, and that explanations are clear and concise, but also to present accompanying pictures, doubling the impact of their presentation and broadening the students' understanding.

Another teacher has used audio tape for instruction in how to write a theme, and prepared written material to be used as the student listens. Professors say they see improvement in the grades of students using the laboratory, and students develop enthusiasm for subject matter that includes relevant and current documents.

Students' interest in using the laboratory grows from hesitancy to enthusiasm, reports Honeywell. He sees a natural reluctance to tackle unknown equipment blossom into enthusiasm and initiative once the student masters the machines and sees the potential for himself.

Teachers report that recording themselves on either audio or video tape is an enlightening process, and hearing or seeing themselves as the student sees them often makes them improve their presentation. Competition with the recorded experts for the students' interest and respect sharpens their classwork.

A student who finds classwork dull and too theoretical is almost sure to see more relevancy to his studies as he listens to an expert in management, the practitioner in public relations, or the politician discuss the practical aspects of their jobs.

The Self-Instruction Center is one area in a learning center that includes many other up-to-the-minute devices. In addition to microfilm, Ward Edwards Library offers microfiche, and microprints. One classroom, seating 60 students, is equipped with a Raytheon learning system, a tape console and answer recording device, which can be programmed to automatically give the lecture, then the test, and record the answers activated by push-buttons at each student's desk. The Instructional Resources Center, on another part of the campus, is the repository for the video tapes and the workshops for making them. Here also are all the tape recorders, projectors, and other individual classroom instructional aids available to teachers. A closed circuit television system has been in use on the campus for several years, and is used for instruction, observing, and testing in many fields.

In an era when students are seeking answers outside the textbook and the traditional classroom program, Central Missouri State College is taking giant steps in the direction of supplying relevant alternatives.

Self-Instruction Lab Teaches Communication Skills

Lucius A. Butler

It has been the policy of many teacher training institutions to include a segment of audio-visual instruction in one of the teaching methods courses or as a separate audio-visual course. Most often a segment of the course is concerned with the learning of audio-visual equipment operation and basic production techniques.

Because it would be virtually impossible for all education students at the University of Hawaii to receive small-group or individual machine-operation instruction, it was decided in 1966 to devise an individualized program in equipment operation as part of a course in audio-visual techniques.

Six student stations were provided for self-instruction. Each station was equipped with a manual of instructions, tape recorder, filmstrip projector, 16mm motion picture projector, and associated instructional materials. An additional station with an overhead projector and an opaque projector is set up during part of each semester.

There was no attempt in the beginning to expose the student to any of the advanced techniques of preparation of materials for these projectors. They were told of the many uses which each projector has and were encouraged to learn the simple techniques involved.

Programs were constantly revised and rewritten to make each step clearer to the student and to include various new modifications in the equipment. Sets of flip-card programs are now being developed as an alternate format. Also, new flexible stations have been designed to allow more space for students.

With full-time supervision, the self-instruction laboratory is capable of serving 500 students each semester in machine operation. At present, the laboratory is operating at approximately half of its potential, with plans in the next few semesters to increase the operational level as full-time supervision becomes possible.

A new development in individualized self-instruction of educational communications skills was begun the spring semester of 1969. Basic graphic skills, including lettering, mounting, laminating, and transparencies have been included in 27 self-instructional learning display stations. A second series of 27 learning displays dealing with presentation boards, audiotape recording, and basic photographic techniques are also being introduced during 1970.

Reprinted from *Audiovisual Instruction* 15,2:55-57, February 1970, by permission of the Association for Educational Communications & Technology.

The learning displays are constructed of two sheets of 22″ x 28″ gray chip board made into three panels by cutting one sheet in half to form the two side panels. Book binding tape is used to form a continuous hinge.

The nine lettering learning displays are free hand, stencil guide, rub-on transfer, stick-on pre-cut, trace and cut, quick-cut, charts, graphs, and posters.

Some of these are not used by beginning students unless they have completed all the other units and want to use a particular skill in their semester project.

The nine mounting and laminating learning displays are rubber cement mounting, spray-adhesive mounting, dry-heat mounting, laminating by machine, spray-protective laminating, dry-heat laminating, pin mounting, hidden mounting, and picture display techniques. The second, fourth, and fifth are used only by advanced students.

The nine transparency production learning displays are handmade, thermofax, diazo-ammonia, adding color, mounting, masking, rubber-cement color-lift, laminating color-lift, and overlay.

Only the thermo transparency, mounting, masking and color adding are required by beginning students. The others are accomplished by students as they take the basic graphics course.

The operational aspect of these learning displays is unique in two respects. First, the display is self-contained and is set up or taken down in less than one minute. Second, the materials needed by the student are contained in discarded shirt boxes of the same size which are kept in two larger boxes. This permits storage and distribution to each display area with no time loss. Equipment assigned to a learning display station is kept on a projection cart for the week of its use in the basic course in audio-visual techniques.

Initial response from students indicated that these learning displays will replace the small-group demonstrations of graphic skills, some of which will now be given in the large group sessions by slide-tape and 16mm motion picture presentations.

The second series of self-instructional learning displays deals with presentation boards, audiotape recording and photographic techniques. The nine units in each area are as follows:

Presentation Boards: chalks and chalkboards, permanent chalk, pounce patterns, templates, projected picture enlarging, grid picture enlarging, magnetic board, flannel and felt board, and hook and loop board.

Audio Recording: audiotronic reel-to-reel, Sony reel-to-reel, Wollensak reel-to-reel, Raytheon large cartridge, Panasonic small cartridge, record to tape dubbing, speaker to tape dubbing, tape to tape dubbing, and multisource dubbing-mixing.

Photography: basic still camera, choosing films, Ektographic instamatic copy, planning still picture sequences, close copy camera, making titles, basic motion picture, planning motion picture sequences, and shooting motion pictures.

Some of these include tape-slide units which may be used in the large group and/or the individual self-instructional learning strategy.

The extended utilization of self-instructional learning displays, together with the improved self-instructional machine-operation stations, will permit the teaching staff to spend a greater portion of time helping students plan and evaluate their semester media utilization projects.

SECTION FIVE / APPLICATION OF LEARNING RESOURCE CENTERS IN SPECIAL AREAS

Implementing the Media Program in Schools for the Deaf
Richard L. Darling

Media Production Facilities in Schools for the Deaf
William D. Jackson

Remedial Labs Try to Cure Classroom Troublemakers

Where Do We Go From Here?
Stephen D. Berry and Charles I. Miller

How to Design a Working IMC
David S. Porter

A Review of Services Offered Through the IMC Network

Leroy Aserlind

The unavailability of adequate instructional materials for use by the teacher in the special classroom was cited by the President's Panel on Mental Retardation as being a "major barrier" to education of the handicapped. Subsequent legislation, PL 88-164, was passed in 1963 which provided funds for an innovative approach to the problem.

Heretofore instructional materials centers had been from a more or less traditional mold — libraries of instructional materials available for loan to teachers. The special class teacher often had to rely primarily on her own collection of materials, with this collection supplemented by that of a city, county, or district library. For the most part the materials that were more generally available to this teacher were those materials which had been developed for the child with no perceptual, learning, or behavioral handicaps. These materials often contained intrinsic elements incompatible with the learning characteristics of the handicapped child (Aserlind, 1968).

Under Title III, Section 302, of PL 88-164 two Centers were funded — one at the University of Wisconsin and one at the University of Southern California. One of their express purposes was to enlarge the concept of a Special Education Instructional Materials Center (SEIMC). The SEIMC's were initially seen as being in a position to offer a number of services beyond that of housing a basic collection of materials. By 1964 both Centers were in their first stages of operation. From these early operational experiences several general goals of Special Education Instructional Materials Centers were proposed, most of which were service oriented. These were:

> First, a center must have an operational radius. If only local clients are served, many teachers in small towns and rural areas will be deprived of services . . .

> Second, a center should be in a position to remark to clients on the effectiveness and characteristics of materials . . .

> Third, such centers must offer workshops, conferences, and ultimately, as accumulated information increases, credit courses . . .

> Fourth, such a center should have a consultative staff. This would include a field man who could guarantee a constant and vital rapport within the center's operational radius, including consultation with field clients . . .

Reprinted from *Exceptional Children*, December 1968, by permission of the publisher.

Fifth, such a center should issue, at regular intervals, a publication or newsletter containing at least two things: an acquisition list and an evaluation section . . .

Sixth, the center should have, ideally, a search and retrieval system so that among increasing masses of materials, certain items can be identified and located . . .

Seventh, and the final basic characteristic of such an ideal center, the center's staff should have the motivation and ability to engage in design and arrange for the production of educational materials [McCarthy, 1966, pp. 27-28].

On such a basis the two initial Centers predicated much of their developmental activity over the first years. By 1965 it became evident that these Centers were able to provide needed services to special education personnel within a relatively circumscribed area. Because of their apparent success and the approval of an ad hoc advisory committee on instructional materials centers, the U.S. Office of Education drew up a plan for expanding the program (Olshin, 1967). The expansion program called for establishing a number of regional Centers in the United States; these Centers then were formed into the Instructional Materials Center Network for Handicapped Children and Youth, funded through the demonstration phase primarily by the United States Office of Education.

Each basically operates as an independent Center, offering direct services to special educators and to the satellite centers being established in its region. Each of the independent Centers, however, coordinates its activities with those of the other Centers and the Network in general. Vital to this coordination is a continuing communication maintained through reports and meetings.

As previously stated, the principal goals of these Centers are largely service oriented at the present time. A number of the services were orginally envisaged as having an empirically demonstrated need. Others have been developed through continual field operation and evaluation; still some services were designed to meet new needs which have been created by the existence of the Centers themselves. The present article deals only with the general services offered within the Network Centers and will not discuss the more unique, specific aspects of individual Center servicing, which are discussed in the articles by Rotberg and Ensminger elsewhere in this issue.

LENDING

Almost without exception, the service of lending is seen as the most important function of a Center in its early stages, since it is of the most immediate benefit to special class teachers and answers one of the persisting needs in special class. All of the Centers, with the exception of the Reference Center at the American Printing House for the Blind, maintain an acquisition, cataloging, and shelving operation for the purpose of providing a lending service. The general policy of the Centers is to lend books and manipulative material for a short term period. IMC's do not supply materials for total school year classroom use, but give the teacher the opportunity to use materials in practice and to make judgments in terms of future purchase. Exception to the short term use of single copy material is found in the fact that several of the Centers supply classroom materials for the blind (Illinois, Michigan, and American Printing House). The loan periods for materials in the Centers generally range from two weeks to a month with both renewal and recall privileges available.

A variation of the lending services, necessitated by the size of the regions, is mail order lending, which Centers now provide. Some, such as the Kentucky Center, allow a longer lending period for mail order loans. Similar special arrangements are made by Centers servicing an extraordinarily wide geographic area — for example, the Oregon Center of over 840,000 square miles.

The lending service is important because it entails a direct and vital contact between the Center and the teacher in the field and, conversely, between the teacher and the Center.

SEARCH AND RETRIEVAL

Search and retrieval will undoubtedly gain in importance. Two factors leading to this are the increasing number of materials, methods, and pertinent research studies and an increasing attention to the concept of diagnostic, precision, or prescriptive teaching. From this will emerge materials and references with a high degree of specificity to individually diagnosed learning problems and with an attendant academic prescription.

At the present time the principal purposes of search and retrieval are to supply teachers, administrators, or classroom researchers with lists of shelved or cataloged materials relevant to a particular need or problem. This type of service is still in its relative infancy. Three Centers — California, Texas, and Michigan — have independently developed computer programs and compatible cataloging systems which are specially designed to perform a search and retrieval operation. These systems have a number of possibilities. Some requests received by the computerized centers require searches and retrievals by author, title, grade level, subject matter, activity level, etc., and numerous combinations thereof. Traditionally, teachers browse through the shelves or look through the card catalogs. Computers now print "browser's catalogs," making available to the Center user discrete listings directly applicable to his immediate interests.

Other Centers such as Wisconsin maintain a search and retrieval system based on IBM machines such as the keypunch, sorter, and printer. At present a number of the Centers are relying on manual searches, but it seems likely from existing trends that all Centers will eventually have a direct tie to a computer center with a cataloged program which will be developed within the Network. CEC-ERIC is presently compiling a library of computer retrievable abstracts provided by the regional centers. In the near future, print-outs of these abstracts will be available to special education practitioners.

RESEARCH DESIGN

This is an available but little used service offered by a number of Centers to special education teachers and administrators. One of the purposes of this type of service is based on the fact that the special education classroom and teacher are potential sources of a great amount of practical, *in situ* information. The "teacher as a researcher" is one of the concepts accepted by the Network. To encourage the teacher to enter into some type of research activity or commitment, Centers will offer consulting services to the classroom practitioner on basic elements of experimental design, measurement, statistics, and evaluation of results. As more satellite centers are developed through the regions it may be anticipated that the regional Centers will be devoting more energies to the development of the special classroom as a prime research site.

MATERIAL DEVELOPMENT AND DESIGN

The original purpose of this category of service was to help and encourage the special class teacher to design and develop materials for her own special situation. Also, it was felt that the Centers would be in excellent position to enter into experimental creation of special education instructional materials which, if successful, would become public domain. Again, attention to other immediate problems and to copyright problems has precluded a great deal of activity in this service area. Perhaps some of the existing materials developed by Centers may well be considered as unique projects, although falling under the aegis of particular services.

As originally premised, the Centers were to offer this service to help make up for the lack of special materials developed by commercial producers. Present indications are that within a comparatively short time more commercial producers will begin to market materials developed expressly for use in special classrooms.

EVALUATION

All Centers in the Network accept evaluation of instructional materials as one of its services to special educators. Several of the earlier established centers — Wisconsin, California, Colorado, and Michigan — have done preliminary work on establishing an effective evaluation model. A Network committee is currently functioning toward this end. Independent efforts of several Centers have suggested approaches to the critical but difficult evaluative process. To date most efforts, such as those at Oregon, involve the use of teacher evaluation groups which use and discuss materials to arrive at a consensus regarding the effectiveness of the materials. California also is concerned with developing methods of utilizing teachers' judgments and ratings and validating these procedures against the more typical pattern of professional evaluation by supervisory or curriculum specialists staff.

It is evident from initial approaches that the use of practicing teachers in field evaluation of materials will be increasing in all regions of the United States.

MOBILE VANS

Both empirical and research evidence suggests that use of lending facilities of an IMC decreases in direct proportion to the distance away from the Center. Means of nullifying this distance effect which have proven to be effective are increased field consultant activity and the use of mobile vans.

The Colorado Center pioneered in the mobile van concept. The vans bring materials directly to schools and teachers in outlying, and in many instances, remote locations. The teacher is offered the opportunity to see, discuss, and select materials that may be of immediate interest or need. Other Centers are adapting the mobile van idea to private or state automobiles or other means of first hand dissemination. Wisconsin, while not using the mobile materials van as a direct service, is supporting the use of these vehicles in subregions served by satellite centers.

CONSULTATION

Consultation services offered through the Centers can take many forms ranging from consultation and participation in full year training programs under ESEA Title I (such as the California Center), to on the spot document specialists to consult with users who come to a Center (such as Kentucky). Presently most of the consultation services offered through all the Centers in the Network consist of direct consultation with state and local administrative personnel on programing and consultation with teachers on the selection of methods and materials for use in the special class. Increasingly, the consultation expertise efforts of the Centers have been instrumental in developing state plans for the establishment of satellite centers (New York, New England) and for consultative help in the preparation of satellite center grants (Texas, Kansas, Oregon, Wisconsin, etc.).

Eventually a point will be reached at which a number of the direct services in a region can be taken care of by proximally located satellite centers. The areas of programatic, research, educational, and developmental consultation will fall increasingly upon the specially prepared personnel at the regional Centers.

MATERIALS DEMONSTRATION AND DISPLAYS

A significant portion of the direct services offered by all Centers in the Network relates to material demonstration and display. Each Center perceives this as an important service and develops its programs accordingly. Through direct display a larger number of teachers are acquainted with the purposes of a Center as well as with a particular Center's acquisitions. Demonstrations are most often conducted either by Center field and specialist personnel or by master special education teachers enlisted for that purpose. Records kept at Wisconsin indicated a rise in usage of lending services from a subregion following a materials demonstration or display program in that area.

Oregon, Kentucky, New York, New England, and California Centers have prepared, or are in the process of preparing, videotapes or other audio-visual presentations of materials demonstrations and displays. This is expected to further enhance the distribution of these services which is limited by the number of materials available for display and the amount of professional time for preparation and demonstration. Particularly effective videotapes will be reproduced and made available to all Network Centers for distribution throughout their regions.

CONFERENCES, INSTITUTES, AND INSERVICE PROGRAMS

All Centers are involved in an active program of offering conferences, special institutes, and inservice programs. Many inservice programs are related to preparation and use of materials, as well as to learning theory, reinforcement, research findings, etc. Most of the programs are developed in cooperation with school administrators, supervisors, and universities. An increasing number of administrators are allowing and suggesting that a portion of the school allotted inservice training time be spent at one of the Centers working with its staff on some previously determined topic or area of study.

Institutes and conferences, along with lending, display, and demonstration activities, are another means of offering services to current and potential users of the IMC's. Examples of recently offered programs are: Education Rhythmics and Motor Development for Exceptional Children (Oregon), Materials for Teaching Children With Learning Disabilities (Kentucky), Materials Used in Self Directive Study (New York), Teaching Mathematics to the Exceptional Child (Wisconsin), and Institute for Special Education Administrative Personnel (California). These topics represent only a portion of the offerings made through the Centers as, for instance, Florida, Kansas, and Texas each conducted approximately 25 of these special programs.

In addition, all Centers have supplied speakers for a significant number of programs sponsored by other professional, public, and private agencies on local, regional, and national levels.

CURRICULUM AND CREDIT COURSES

A number of the Centers associated with colleges or universities are in the process of developing on-campus and extension courses relating more directly to instructional materials for the handicapped children than do many existing courses today. The Centers realize that service should be offered to students in preparation for careers in special education. It is anticipated that within two years the majority of the university affiliated Centers will be offering credit courses based extensively on knowledge gained through research and through Network accumulated findings on selection, utilization, and evaluation of these special materials.

PUBLICATIONS

All Centers have developed or are in the process of developing some type of publication for the teacher readership within their particular region. Two examples are *The Winnower* (Wisconsin) and *The Torch* (Oregon). These publications contain articles on issues in the field of special education, informative and educative articles, and discussions of materials. *The Winnower* maintains an acquisition list for the purpose of bringing the readers up to date on the latest holdings in the Center.

An essentially similar function but somewhat different format is seen in the *UKRSEIMC Quarterly* (Kentucky), *IMSCE Communicator* (California), and *IMCing in New York* (New York). In two of the older Centers (Wisconsin and

California), circulation runs approximately 3,500 and 8,500, respectively. The advent of a national publication will preclude and eventually replace extensive publication services on the part of the Centers; however, all of these Centers will continue to offer a newsletter service containing primarily regional information.

ABSTRACTING

As mentioned earlier under search and retrieval, one of the functions of CEC-ERIC will be to maintain a constantly updated file of pertinent abstracts. These files will be accessible to the practitioner in special education. The Centers will supply abstracts and evaluations to the central file using a Network thesaurus as the basis for selection of key descriptor terms.

OBTAINING SERVICES

In order to make use of the IMC Network, it is important that special educators contact the Center servicing their region (see Table 1). If that Center is not yet operational or does not have the desired material or service, the request will be referred to another Center known to be able to answer the request.

It is important that requests be as specific as possible; for example, asking for "materials for teaching arithmetic to the retarded" will probably be met with a request for further details. Asking for "samples of workbooks for teaching arithmetic to the intermediate level educable retarded" will more likely bring the desired material or service.

As this article has described, the IMC Network provides numerous services to special educators. The Centers lend out materials; supply listings of materials by area, level, and subject, etc.; send out field consultants and mobile vans to local areas; set up courses; provide consultative assistance for instructional materials use, evaluation, research, programing, and development; send out newsletters informing of available services and acquisitions; and set up inservice training programs and workshops.

REFERENCES

Aserlind, L. "Research and Instructional Materials for the Mentally Retarded." *In International Association for the Scientific Study of Mental Deficiency, Proceedings of the International Association for the Scientific Study of Mental Deficiency.* Amsterdam: Excerpta Medica Foundation, 1968 (in press).

McCarthy, J. "Educational Materials for the Mentally Retarded: A Quandary." *Education and Training of the Mentally Retarded,* 1966, 1, 24-31.

Olshin, G. "IMC Network Report." *Exceptional Children,* 1967, 34, 137-141.

Table 1

Instructional Materials Center Network for Handicapped Children and Youth

Center and Director	*Region served*	*Services*
AMERICAN PRINTING HOUSE Mr. Carl W. Lappin, Director Instructional Materials Reference Center American Printing House for the Blind 1839 Frankfort Avenue Louisville, Kentucky 40206 502/895-2405	National	Visually Handicapped
CALIFORNIA Dr. Charles A. Watts, Director Instructional Materials Center for Special Education University of Southern California 17 Chester Place Los Angeles, California 90007 213/749-3121	Arizona California Nevada	All areas of exceptionality
COLORADO Dr. William R. Reid, Director Rocky Mountain Special Education Instructional Materials Center Chairman, IMCNHCY, 1967-1969 Colorado State College Greeley, Colorado 80631 303/351-2681	Colorado Montana New Mexico Wyoming	Physically Handicapped Mentally Retarded Emotionally Disturbed Hard of Hearing
ERIC Dr. June Jordan, Director ERIC Clearinghouse on Exceptional Children The Council for Exceptional Children, NEA 1201 16th Street, N.W. Washington, D.C. 20036 202/223-9400, ext. 601	National	All areas of exceptionality
FLORIDA Dr. Marvin Gold, Director Southeastern Materials Center University of South Florida Apartment 44 Tampa, Florida 33620 813/988-4131, ext. 815	Alabama Florida Georgia Mississippi South Carolina Puerto Rico Virgin Islands	Mentally Retarded Emotionally Disturbed Speech Impaired

Center and Director	*Region served*	*Services*

ILLINOIS
Mrs. Lenore E. Powell, Director — Illinois — All areas of
Instructional Materials Center — exceptionality
726 South College Street
Springfield, Illinois 62706
   217/525-2436

Miss Gloria Calovini, Director — Visually
Instructional Materials Center — Handicapped
410 South Michigan Avenue
Chicago, Illinois 60605
   312/427-3387 (Chicago)
   217/525-4552 (Springfield)

KANSAS
Dr. Eugene Ensminger, Director — Iowa — Emotionally
Special Education Instructional Materials Center — Kansas — Disturbed
University of Kansas — Missouri — Learning Disabilities
1115 Louisiana — Nebraska — Orthopedically
Lawrence, Kansas 66044 — North Dakota — Handicapped
   913/864-4158 — South Dakota — Mentally Retarded

KENTUCKY
Dr. A. Edward Blackhurst, Director — Kentucky — All areas of
University of Kentucky Regional — North Carolina — exceptionality
  Special Education Instructional Materials Center — Tennessee
641 South Limestone Street — West Virginia
Lexington, Kentucky 40506
   606/258-9000, ext. 2764

MASSACHUSETTS
Dr. Harold Ruvin, Director — Connecticut — Mentally Retarded
New England Materials – Instruction Center — Maine — Physically
Boston University — Massachusetts — Handicapped
704 Commonwealth Avenue — New Hampshire — Emotionally
Boston, Massachusetts 02215 — Rhode Island — Disturbed
   617/353-3266 — Vermont — Speech and Hearing
                                            Learning Disabilities

MICHIGAN
Mrs. Lou Alonso, Director — Indiana — All areas of
USOE/MSU Instructional Materials Center — Michigan — exceptionality
  for Handicapped Children and Youth — Ohio
343-B Erickson Hall
Michigan State University
East Lansing, Michigan 48823
   517/353-7810

Center and Director	*Region served*	*Services*
NEW YORK		

Mr. Raphael Simches, Director, New York
  SEIMC
Mr. Maurice D. Olsen, Coordinator
Special Education Instructional Materials Center
New York State Department of Education
800 North Pearl Street
Albany, New York 12204
  518/474-3995 (Simches)
  518/474-7690 (Olsen)
	Central New York
	State
		All areas of
		exceptionality

Mrs. Elizabeth L. Ayre, Regional Coordinator
Special Education Instructional Materials Center
State University College at Buffalo
1300 Elmwood Avenue
Buffalo, New York 14222
  716/862-5506,5507
	Western New York
	Region
		Mentally Retarded
		Physically
		  Handicapped
		Emotionally
		  Disturbed
		Speech and Hearing

Dr. Gloria F. Wolinsky, Director
Regional Special Education
  Instructional Materials Center
Hunter College
Box 563x
695 Park Avenue
New York, New York 10021
  212/360-2304
	Eastern New York
	Region
		All areas of
		exceptionality

OREGON		

Dr. Wayne Lance, Director
Northwest Regional Special Education
  Instructional Materials Center
University of Oregon
1612 Columbia Street
Eugene, Oregon 97403
  503/342-1411, ext. 2021
	Alaska
	Hawaii
	Idaho
	Oregon
	Washington
		All areas of
		exceptionality

TEXAS		
Dr. Claude Marks, Director Special Education Instructional Materials Center University of Texas 304 West 15th Street Austin, Texas 78701 512/471-3145, 5722	Arkansas Louisiana Oklahoma Texas	All areas of exceptionality

Center and Director	*Region served*	*Services*

USOE
Dr. George Olshin, Chief
Research Laboratories and Demonstration Branch
Division of Research
Bureau of Education for the Handicapped
US Office of Education
ROB – 7th and D Streets, S.W., Room 2010
Washington, D.C. 20202
  202/962-6370

Mr. Mel Appell, Research Coordinator
Research Laboratories and Demonstration Branch
Division of Research
Bureau of Education for the Handicapped
US Office of Education
ROB – 7th and D Streets, S.W.
Washington, D.C. 20202
  202/962-7693

WASHINGTON, D.C.

Dr. Raymond Cottrell, Director	Delaware	Mentally Retarded
Mid-Atlantic Region Special Education	District of Columbia	Crippled and Health
Instructional Materials Center	Maryland .	Impaired
George Washington University	New Jersey	Emotionally
820 20th Street, N.W.	Pennsylvania	Disturbed
Washington, D.C. 20006	Virginia	Speech Impaired
202/676-7200		

WISCONSIN

Dr. LeRoy Aserlind, Director	Minnesota	Physically
Special Education Instructional Materials Center	Wisconsin	Handicapped
Chairman Elect, IMCNHCY		Mentally Retarded
University of Wisconsin		Emotionally
415 West Gilman Street		Disturbed
Madison, Wisconsin 53706		Speech Impaired
608/262-4910		

COORDINATOR
Dr. Don Erickson, Coordinator
Instructional Materials Center Network
  for Handicapped Children and Youth
1507 M Street, N.W., Room 207
Washington, D.C. 20005
  202/223-9400, ext. 601

A Technology-Resource Center for Vocational-Technical Education

Milton E. Larson

TRC — Technology-Resource Center for Vocational-Technical Education — is a concept for strengthening in-service teacher education. The nature of in-service updating activities in technology, built into a series of short-time experiences with hardware applications and related sciences, does not fit into most existing facilities for higher education. Therefore, a unique physical facility is desirable.

The search for a good educational facility is an outgrowth of the housing need for that kind of program and activity. Supported by a grant under 4 (c) of the Vocational Education Act of 1963, a research effort was given to this need. The problem was to develop the educational specifications, the preliminary architectural plans, and an outline of the construction specifications for a center to serve the needs of educators in the vocational-technical field.

The task force tackling the problem included representatives of each division of the vocational-technical field as well as specialists in the fields of architecture, building construction, and educational media. The principal investigator and architectural consultant visited educational and industrial facilities throughout the nation. Then two group sessions were held (totaling seven days) and, along with considerable individual effort, the development of very complete educational specifications resulted. Applications of architectural competencies to the educational specifications through a series of space-relationship studies resulted in a design highly creative and functionally efficient for the unique purpose of the project.

The center was designed to provide a maximum of service and to represent the most advanced in educational innovations. Its aims are to motivate, enrich the background and broaden the scope of scientific and technical knowledge, and to increase ability to apply the skill and knowledge gained in practical situations. Active participation in laboratory-shop situations and observations of demonstrations, both important learning experiences, are built into the center.

The curriculum for such an institute could be developed through the combined efforts of a technology-resource center programmer and representatives of industry and education. The approach to education will be on an adult basis, employing media such as rear-screen projection, closed-circuit projection television, and instructional materials, providing a step-by-step development of the operational sequence based on analysis of the job.

Reprinted from *School Shop*, Ann Arbor, Michigan, April 1966, by permission of the publisher.

The instructor or instructors will be specialists in the field assisted by technicians wherever necessary. Students will have the benefit of first-hand contact with an industrial approach, using industry-type equipment in a superior teaching-learning environment.

For example, assume that an institute is offered for machine-shop teachers on the fundamentals of numerical-control machining. Specialists in numerical control are brought in as guest instructors. Numerical-control equipment is brought into the module. The concept is presented. Each teacher not only sees demonstrations of the various phases of numerical control, but through actual participation he has an opportunity to actually perform the sequence of programming, tooling of the equipment, and operation on a production (short-run) basis.

Or, imagine that the electronics instructors in the area have been invited to participate in a three-day workshop. The best instructors will be individuals specializing in the field of transistor-circuit design. Laboratory activities will be coupled with presentations and class discussions. Both class and laboratory activities will be focused on such topics as small-signal transistor amplifiers, transistor power amplifiers, high-frequency transistor amplifiers, transistor oscillators, and transistor-frequency converters and detectors.

Student participation activities within the module will involve determination of component values, connection of the circuit, measurement of the circuit operation conditions, changes in components, and observation of effects. The center will incorporate the features of a planned operations "update" for vocational-technical educators in a concerted, continuous manner. It will have much more flexibility and adaptability than common college and university laboratories. The facilities will be designed to expedite moving new "hardware" in and out, to meet the needs for short-term updating activities and to accommodate a variety of learning activities not suited to the traditional college pattern. While some offerings will undoubtedly carry credit, many of the short-time activities will not be so encumbered. The center rather than offering a single summer institute will offer a complement of coordinated institutes, workshops, clinics, and seminars. These will be based on the needs in the field and the new developments in industry.

However, this center is planned to supplement and not supplant the present offerings of industry and institutions of higher education. A small base staff will serve on a full-time basis and be supported by a much larger supplemental call staff composed of specialists from agriculture, business, and industry. Curriculums will need to reflect both horizontal articulation (expressing the concept of broad implications across instructional fields) and vertical coordination (which indicates a level of program descriptive of "depth").

ONE CENTER – TWO DIVISIONS

The center consists of two main divisions: (1) the technology complex and (2) the resources complex.

The technology complex. – This area is designed to expedite effective instruction in a series of institutes or workshops of from one to eight weeks in length, clinics from one to five days, and seminars of from two- to four-hour duration. Therefore, the building must provide for convenient loading and unloading, handling, moving, and other activities. Essential power supplies and other utilities must be accessible and convenient. Little fixed equipment will be retained in the modules. Convenient to each module is a staging area for preparing the equipment for demonstration or participation activities.

The resource complex. – This complex provides a concentrated approach to increasing the quality and quantity of instructional materials. Essential to the center is a professional library, spaces for curriculum-research activities, writing rooms for curriculum development, equipment and space for minimum reproduction and dissemination, and facilities for evaluating curriculums. Model development to expedite availability of mock-ups, models, and prototypes will constitute another service. It is hoped that mass production and marketing of the models would become the function of an industrial firm. Another feature of the proposed plan is for a unit of the resource center to be given over to innovations, discovery, and development.

AREA SERVED

The technology-resource center should be located centrally and conveniently to the area served. A minimum site of ten acres is desirable to provide for the structures, demonstration area, parking, and expansion.

With modern transportation the center can easily serve an area encompassing several states. For longer institutes a commuting distance of 300 miles is not excessive. However, the density of population within the area as well as the concentration of industry, business, and agriculture will be factors in the proximity of adjacent technology-resource centers. A single large metropolitan area could utilize such a center effectively. Certainly, a single large industrial state will have a potential need for such a center. Two, three, or more smaller states could be served by such a center.

In today's highly complex and increasingly technical industrial, business, and agricultural fields, vocational-technical educators hold the key to a significant manpower problem – providing technical personnel equipped to meet the challenge of today and tomorrow. Speaking before the National Education

Association Convention in July 1965, President Johnson announced his support of " . . . a program of fellowships for elementary and secondary-school teachers so that they can replenish their knowledge and improve their abilities." TRC will do just that. In addition, it will provide more and better instructional materials and aids. Immediate action is essential if the eight out of ten students who do not graduate from college are to find opportunity and if our employers are to find needed workers competent for our space-age society.

Gary Goes into Action

Edwin Carmony and Leila Ann Doyle

The school's media program (library-audio-visual) has the potential to provide educational experiences that are relevant to the needs of today's youth through individualized or group instruction. The new media standards may, at first glance, seem visionary. But if we look back over the road we have traveled to arrive where we now are, we may well decide that these goals can be reached. Both the quality and extent of the media services accepted today were a few years ago considered beyond attainment.

Just where are we now? In Gary, Indiana the integration of library-audio-visual services has been the informal policy for a long time and the official policy for the past five years. The degree of integration of library and audio-visual services and the extent of the services offered vary, due to space limitations in older buildings and to the unhappy fact that staff allocation has not kept pace with the growth of the program and the demand for services.

Major steps were taken in an effort to improve the educational experiences for children through the implementation of the philosophy, program and services outlined in the 1960 *Standards for School Library Programs* released by the American Association of School Librarians, and the quantitative standards published by the Department of Audio-Visual Instruction in 1966. Nine new centers were organized in elementary schools so that now all schools are served by centralized media centers staffed by qualified professional personnel.

With the acceptance of the philosophy represented in the 1960 standards publication and the official Gary schools' policy on integration of services, the growth of the media program has followed at a pace, which, if maintained, would soon take us beyond the 1960 standards and well on the way to the 1969 standards.

Reprinted from *Educational Screen and Audiovisual Guide,* June 1969, by permission of the publisher.

The centralized media services provided by the Gary Public Schools include:

- a professional library which serves the professional staff of the school system.
- a 4500 print 16mm film library with daily delivery to each school.
- facilities for maintenance of equipment by three highly trained electronic technicians.
- materials duplication and production services.
- the technical service area which serves as an acquisition, cataloging and processing center for all printed and audio-visual materials.

Also a part of the media services for teachers and students are:

An instructional radio station, TV distribution systems, twenty-two language laboratories, reading laboratories, speech laboratories, recording studios, and room darkening facilities and projection screens in all classrooms.

The budgets provided by the city for library books have been doubled since 1964. In addition, $410,455.30 was received from Title II of the Elementary and Secondary Education Act. Each school center has been given a second budget, which is controlled by the media personnel, for the systematic acquisition of audio-visual materials.

Secretarial help has been provided for secondary centers and adult aides for the Title I school centers. Although far from adequate, the need for and value of para-professional staff is being demonstrated. Supplementary assistance was given by the students in the technician training program of the Technical-Vocational School. This program was organized when the school opened in September, 1968. The success of the program during the first six months of its existence has been far beyond our expectations. It is proving to be an almost ideal setup for the training of para-professional media personnel.

So as we review the development of the media program that has taken place, particularly since the publication of the 1960 standards, we are encouraged to plan for further progress.

In Gary the major problem is not philosophy, nor equipment, nor materials. Our need is for qualified staff in adequate numbers and for the space for that staff to function, thereby expanding the media program and services so necessary for a quality educational program.

The needed space is most easily acquired when new buildings are being planned. Central staff personnel must accept the leadership role and major responsibility at this point. The allocation of staff is the prerogative of the principal within each building. The principal who knows the value of the services which can be provided by the dedicated media staff will request and assign adequate staff to this area as rapidly as possible.

All of the Gary schools will not meet all of the standards in the foreseeable future. However, we can continue to work toward them. Many standards require only short-range goals; others take long-range planning.

How do we proceed? First we study the standards. We accept the challenge of setting up timetables for progressive steps toward reaching the standards. We identify the position of each school and school system with respect to our goals. A point by point comparison of present position with goal should result in realistic requests for budget, personnel and space for a step by step movement toward the goals. The schools which now have adequate facilities and for whom building programs are now planned should approach the standards within a three-year period. The major expenditure will be for personnel-professional and para-professional.

When we believe in something we do something about it. When we believe in an educational program that provides both teachers and students with the instructional materials and equipment needed for effective teaching and learning, we will take the necessary steps to initiate the implementation of the program. In the final analysis the survival of civilization is dependent on the education given our youth: on their ideals and ideas, on their knowledge and skill, on their ability to *think*. The children in our schools pass this way but once. Tomorrow will be too late; they'll be out of our reach. Today they are ours. Today is our only hope.

Regional IMC Built on Cooperative Foundation

Melvin Mead

Education today is beset by many problems and subjected to many criticisms. Some of the problems are self-created, as are many of the criticisms justified; examples of both exist in numerous instances because of one fundamental lack — *cooperation.*

Cooperation among school districts can benefit nearly every area of the educational program — joint development of special curricular programs, mutually agreeable personnel policies, and pooling of purchasing power suggest but a few. The Lane County Cooperative Instructional Materials Center is a story of cooperation in one special area — the provision of audio-visual and other instructional materials, and the supporting services which these require.

The Lane County Cooperative IMC story is one of *cooperation* from its inception, involving the eighteen public school districts of the county and the

Reprinted from *Educational Screen and Audiovisual Guide*, November 1967, by permission of the publisher.

Lane County Board of Education for the Rural School District (successor to the office of County School Superintendent; and since restructured as the Lane County Intermediate Education District). The kind of cooperation involved in conceiving and establishing an instructional materials center such as the Lane County project is not suddenly created in a vacuum, however. It was generated from a background of mutual effort and help that is perhaps the most outstanding feature of public education in Lane County. The district superintendents of the county have for a number of years met monthly at informal luncheon sessions; from these have come many actions, including the establishment of the Lane County Cooperative IMC. Other county-wide educational organizations, some formally constituted, some not, aid such cooperative ventures, as does the state department of education.

The need for adequate, full-scale instructional materials services had been recognized and voiced by individual educators over a long period of time; the fact that a state-wide film rental library, limited almost entirely to 16mm film, was not the ultimate answer was widely recognized. Individual districts, notably Eugene Public Schools and Springfield Public Schools, made attempts to rectify the problem. Eugene, with 40 percent of the 45,000 students in the county, was able to establish a rather sizeable (1,000 prints) film library and some other vestiges of an IMC program.

FOUNDATIONS AND FUNDS

Action began in earnest, however, in the pattern that had accomplished results in earlier experiences. A committee was appointed in 1960 from the superintendent's organization. Its goal — to study and plan for the establishment of an instructional materials center. The committee, consisting of top administrative personnel, and assisted by various consultant authorities, spend a year in studying the role and function of the IMC, and the second year in actual planning.

To create sufficient impact to insure at least significant service rather than merely adequate service, an initial operating budget estimate of approximately $100,000 was deemed necessary. Since initial capital requirements were high, only $25,000 of this first budget was earmarked in the planning stages for acquisition of materials.

To compensate for this relatively small acquisition budget, two factors were included in planning. First, potential N.D.E.A. Title III matching funds were sought and banked upon where possible. Strong support within the limits of the act for regional center development has been a continuing Oregon State Department of Education policy since initiation of the Title III program, and N.D.E.A.

has continued to be a significant factor, although the local community has assumed a steadily increasing fiscal responsibility as the years have passed.

The second factor included in initial planning was the use of rent-to-own acquisition from the major film producers. Through this avenue, an initial library "significantly large to make a substantial impact on education" was possible.

Actual development of the Center began June 1, 1962, with all effort concentrated on the development of a "significantly large" 16mm film library. Service to the schools began about September 20 of that year. Although the Eugene and Springfield districts continued to provide from their district libraries the basic services to their schools, the Lane County Cooperative IMC immediately served as an important backup source. Even before the acquisition of films for the Lane County collection was begun, planning was undertaken to coordinate the evaluating and buying for the three film libraries in a meaningful way.

CONSOLIDATION AND MERGER

On August 1, 1963, another long step down the road of joint effort was taken when the IMC functions of the program of the Eugene Public Schools were merged with the Lane County Cooperative Instructional Materials Center. The two centers were rehoused in remodeled space in the ground floor of an apartment building adjacent to the administrative offices of the separate operations brought together under one director.

Immediate benefits were discernible to both agencies in terms of more effective deployment of staff, easier coordination of effort, and financial savings in capital investment. As an example, the audio-visual consultant of the Eugene Public Schools, freed of the time-consuming responsibilities of operating a central circulating collection of materials, has been able to concentrate a great deal more effort on the development of instructional materials programs in individual buildings.

Today, after five years of rather phenomenal growth and expansion, the Lane County Cooperative Instructional Materials Center provides the 50,000 students, 2,500 teachers, and 16 local districts of the county with an audio-visual collection of nearly 11,000 titles. The 16mm film collection, the base of the initial development, continues to constitute a large and fundamental segment, numbering presently approximately 4,500 titles. The collection has expanded to include almost all other media, however, with the notable exception of videotape. Some media appear in only nominal quantities, where it has been felt that they were basic to the collections of individual school buildings. In such cases, every encouragement has been given buildings to develop these media. Examples are filmstrips, records, and study prints.

Special emphasis has been placed on development of comprehensive collections of media which are felt to have particular potential and significance. The current medium of emphasis is the Super-8 single concept film. Undoubtedly, as a pattern of standardization begins to appear, the videotape will also assume a role of importance in the Center.

To make the large collection of audio-visual materials significant to classrooms and children, an effective scheduling system and fast, frequent delivery have been essential. A standing rule governing the handling of requests since the first years of operation has been that no request would be in-house longer than 48 hours before it had been processed and the requester notified of the action. In most cases, such "turn-around" is accomplished in 24 hours or less. The system and equipment used for booking has changed once during the five years; the probable next step, being tentatively planned to occur within the next two years, will be an IBM 360 computerized booking system, incorporating telecommunication units in the larger schools. (The 360 is presently used for the storage, assembly, and production of the Center's catalogs of various types.)

Availability further depends on an extensive truck delivery system, involving four vehicles. The two largest districts each provide a truck which delivers to each school daily. Thus about 60% of the students and teachers in the county have daily access to the Center. The remaining classes are served at least twice a week, with a number receiving a third delivery. In a county as geographically large as Lane (100 miles by 60 miles), this delivery involves truck runs of as high as 240 miles per day.

Efforts to maintain effective booking and delivery methods, though demanding substantial commitment on the part of administration and real dedication from staff members, have played a great part in a very rapid and widespread acceptance of the Center's services by teachers. *The rate of increase in circulation has never fallen below 20% in five years of existence.* The *overall growth* in the five year period amounts to *more than 300%.* The 1966-67 school year saw scheduled uses reach the 64,000 level, with each scheduling resulting in from three to four showings, on the average.

KEY SERVICES

Supporting services have a broad range, including an active program of in-service functions, a full-scale local production program, equipment repair and maintenance services, cooperative bidding and purchasing of equipment and supplies, and consultant assistance to teachers and administrators covering nearly any type of media problem conceivable.

In-service activities have been varied, both in content and in their intended patronage. A significant aspect has been a deliberate close cooperation with the

School of Education of the University of Oregon; Center staff members have joined in teaching numerous courses and have readily provided tours and briefings to many other University class groups.

Local production services augment and expand on those found in typical school buildings, and are used extensively. Five staff members, aided by student part-time help, provide tape duplication, artwork, transparency reproduction, photographic services, and bulk (volume) lamination. In every case, the school is charged only for the actual cost of raw materials.

Equipment of the production department includes an offset press, Ampex 3200 series tape duplicators, tape recording and editing equipment, a diazo printer, a laminating machine, a dry mount press, a Heiland Repronar, completely equipped darkroom, and camera equipment which includes a Roleiflex 3.5 F, Nikon F Photomic T, Bell & Howell 16mm camera, and Bell & Howell Super-8 camera. All in all, the production department is the scene of a great deal of activity.

It is noteworthy that the operating budget and the support it has received from local districts and the I.E.D. board has grown apace. From an initial $100,000, the 1967-68 budget has become $341,118. From an initial acquisitions budget of $25,000, the 1967-68 figure for materials is $168,112.

THE ESSENTIAL INGREDIENT

The key to the entire scope of activity in the Lane County Cooperative Instructional Materials Center, however, and the truly signal aspect of its operation, is the breadth and amount of cooperative effort involved in its many functions.

Cooperation brings its advisory committee together regularly to review and establish policy for its operation. Cooperation (presently involving more than 150 teachers who are paid for their efforts) selects its materials. Cooperation marks its support of the development of those parts of the media program which operate at the district and building levels. As an illustration, in 1960 two districts — Eugene and Springfield — had staff members assigned responsibility for development of the instructional materials programs. At present, at least seven of the 16 districts have such assigned responsibility.

Cooperation supports its budgetary requirements. Under Oregon law, such a Center can be financed by two methods: Local districts can contract for such services, paying predetermined amounts from district funds for services received; or a Center can be financed by an ad valorem tax levy if local districts support and request its services by resolution. Such support requires resolutions from two-thirds of the districts involved, which must enroll at least 51 percent of the student population. The Lane County Cooperative Instructional Materials Center has happily been supported since its inception by resolutions from every one of the districts in the county, at all times.

The Center has even encouraged and facilitated cooperation in the curriculum-development activities of the entire county, working directly with such groups as the local A.S.C.D. group, subject matter groups, and the school librarians' association. A significantly greater enthusiasm has existed for concerted effort in curriculum development when it is known that the essential specialized materials can in all probability either be purchased or created through the regionally-organized program of the Center.

All in all, much of the success story, if success story it is, of the Center hinges on the word "Cooperative," from its title. Cooperation can occur wherever educators are willing to look for ways to work together, rather than for reasons why they can't or won't.

The Educational Resources Information Center

Stanley M. Grabowski

Lack of communication is one of the biggest problems in modern society, according to many leading sociologists and psychologists. There is no wonder that this lack of communication exists in the educational community considering the new curriculums, new media, and new teaching methods being designed and developed in laboratories and classrooms throughout the country. These developments and research are going on at a rate unprecedented in the history of education.

All this recent and expanding activity has produced a large number of valuable documents; a conservative estimate is that as many as 75,000 quality documents are produced each year in education. Many of these do not reach the people who need them. Conferences, conventions, meetings, seminars and professional journals reach only a small percentage of educators, and at best report only a tiny fraction of the literature.

In the light of the knowledge explosion, Samuel Johnson's observation that "knowledge is of two kinds: we know a subject ourselves, or we know where we can find information upon it," is especially relevant today. Obviously, there is no simple, or easy, or even a single answer to this tremendous problem. How-

Reprinted from *Adult Leadership*, January 1969, by permission of the publisher, Adult Education Association of the USA, Washington, D.C.

ever, a nationwide agency to provide a comprehensive system to make information available to educators is the best possible partial answer at this time.

ERIC (Educational Resources Information Center) is the first such nationwide comprehensive information system designed to serve American education. ERIC was established in 1965 in response to the ever-growing need for a system which would collect, process, and disseminate information on "fugitive" literature relevant to education. Through a network of 19 specialized centers of clearinghouses, each of which is responsible for a particular educational area, the information is monitored, acquired, evaluated, abstracted, indexed and listed in ERIC reference products. These reference publications provide access to reports of innovative programs and the most significant efforts in educational research, both current and historical.

In addition, each clearinghouse generates newsletters, bulletins, bibliographies, research reviews, and interpretative studies on educational subjects to satisfy the needs of the educational area it serves.

The ERIC Clearinghouse on Adult Education (ERIC/AE) is concerned with literature of practical use to adult education agencies in business and industry, churches, the military and other governmental and community organizations, as well as in schools and universities. It covers the following areas.

1. The intellectual, psychological, social and physical *characteristics* of adults which significantly affect their learning processes;
2. The combination of career and *personal interests and motives* which influence educational needs of adults.
3. The *methods* of instruction, independent study, program planning, and evaluation which are effective in the education and training of adults;
4. The *system of institutional arrangements* for providing adult education and training, as well as the economic, social and philosophical factors which govern the operation and growth of this system.

In the past 18 months ERIC/AE has processed nearly 3,000 documents. Many of these abstracts have appeared in various ERIC/AE publications such as the Current Information Sources and Information Analysis Series, the Annual Register of Research and Investigations (published by the Adult Education Association of the U.S.A.) as well as in articles in professional journals.

In addition, many of the abstracts of documents handled by ERIC/AE, together with those from the other Clearinghouses, are published each month in *Research in Education*, a monthly bulletin containing 200-word abstracts of most of the documents entering the system. *Research in Education* is the principal product of the ERIC network at this time. It also includes research in progress; and author, subject and other indexes are cumulated semi-annually. It is available from the Government Printing Office, Superintendent of Documents, Washington, D.C. 20402, for $21.00 per year ($26.25 outside the U.S.).

Many documents announced in *Research in Education* may be purchased from the ERIC Document Reproduction Service (EDRS) in microfiche or hardcopy reproductions. A microfiche is a four by six sheet of film containing up to 70 pages of text in a reduction ratio of 18 to 1. It has an eye-legible citation at the top for convenient filing, provides compact storage, is inexpensive (25 cents each) and is easy to use with any standard microfiche reader. Hardcopy reproductions are six by eight inch print-outs costing four cents per page.

This EDRS service makes it possible to obtain an important part of the educational literature produced in the United States at very small cost. For example, the entire ERIC collection consisting of nearly 16,000 documents may be purchased in microfiche for about $2,000. Nearly 500 documents on adult education alone are available in microfiche for less than $150. A library in educational literature can be maintained with microfiche, using *Research in Education* as an index, eliminating the usual cost of cataloging, indexing and other processing.

Although the ERIC system has been operating for a short period of time, here are indications that it is being used. For example:

- Sale of *Research in Education* has jumped from 208 subscriptions in January, 1967, to 4,550 in June, 1968;
- The number of reports in RIE rose from 67 to 795 during the same period of time;
- Sale of microfiche totalled 330,000 for all of 1965; during the first six months of 1968 almost 1.5 million microfiche were sold;
- Sales of hardcopy reproductions amounted to 2,050 during 1966, and increased to 5,700 during the first six months of 1968.

By June, 1968, *Research in Education* had become the best seller among all abstract-index R & D bulletins published by federal agencies. It outsells the comparable volumes published by NASA, AEC, or the Federal Clearinghouse for Scientific and Technical Information. In addition, over 1,000 copies are distributed free to state libraries, state and some local education agencies, professional organizations, federal agencies, and some colleges and universities offering a doctorate in education.

It is noteworthy that more than one-fourth of the subscribers to *Research in Education* and the subscribers to standing orders for all documents cited in RIE are accounted for by local school units and state agencies.

In recognition of the progress made by the ERIC system, the Office of Education's Superior Service Award was given to Central ERIC last June, "for the outstanding achievements and contributions that it has made to the Office (of Education) and to the educational community as a whole."

Further information about the work done at ERIC/AE as well as a list of publications available from ERIC/AE may be obtained from:

Roger DeCrow, Director
ERIC Clearinghouse on Adult Education
107 Roney Lane
Syracuse, New York 13210

There are a number of special ERIC products which may be helpful to adult educators. These may be obtained from the U.S. Government Printing Office, Washington, D.C. 20402.

OFFICE OF EDUCATION RESEARCH REPORTS, 1956-1965 RESUMES.
Abstracts of approximately 1214 research reports received by the Bureau of Research before the start of publication of *RESEARCH IN EDUCATION*. Order number, OE-12029; price, $1.75.

OFFICE OF EDUCATION RESEARCH REPORTS, 1956-1965 INDEXES.
Indexes reports by author, institution, subject, and report numbers. Order number, OE-12028; price, $2.00.

ERIC CATALOG OF SELECTED DOCUMENTS ON THE DISADVAN-TAGED, NUMBER AND AUTHOR INDEX.
1746 documents dealing with the special educational needs of the disadvantaged. Order number, OE-37001; price, $0.65.

ERIC CATALOG OF SELECTED DOCUMENTS ON THE DISADVAN-TAGED, SUBJECT INDEX.
Order number, OE-37002; price, $3.00.

PACESETTERS IN INNOVATION, FISCAL YEAR 1966.
Resumes of projects to advance creativity in Title III educational resource centers approved during fiscal year 1966 indexed by subject, local educational agency, and project number. 1075 documents covered. Order number, OE-20103; price, $2.50.

RESEARCH IN EDUCATION, ANNUAL INDEX – 1967 (PROJECTS).
A cumulative index which provides access to research projects announced in the monthly issues of *RESEARCH IN EDUCATION*, from November 1966 through December 1967. The volume contains indexes by subject, investigator and institution. Price, $1.50.

RESEARCH IN EDUCATION, ANNUAL INDEX – 1967 (REPORTS).
The reports contained in fourteen issues of *RESEARCH IN EDUCATION* from November 1966 through December 1967 are indexed in this volume. It constitutes a useful tool for those individuals who have access to copies of the monthly issues of *RESEARCH IN EDUCATION*. Price, $3.25.

MANPOWER RESEARCH, INVENTORY FOR FISCAL YEARS 1966 AND 1967.
Order number, OE-12036; price, $2.75. 393 reports from projects funded by OEO and the Departments of Labor, HUD, and HEW.

HOW TO USE ERIC.
A self-instructional manual on how to use ERIC written from the viewpoint of a nontechnical person. Order number, OE-12037; price, $.20, 12 pages.

William D. Grindeland and Richard Bliss

The main thrust in science education today is toward more student involvement and higher teacher competency in science instruction. Such efforts are accompanied by many new requirements, including logistics, which we have tried to manage through an instructional materials center (IMC) serving our entire district.

The Unified School District No. 1 of Racine County, Wisconsin, has a student enrollment of approximately 30,000 and is increasing by more than 1,000 students each year. A district of this size has a major problem in providing adequate instructional materials services, especially since the advent of the newer media of communication and the rapidly increasing volume of ideas and activities that students must experience if the best learning is to occur.

A few years ago we began a very small program to provide multimedia kits for a few areas. These original kits, designed primarily for the science and social studies areas, were merely cardboard boxes labeled with the unit and other appropriate information and filled with assorted books and charts on the topic to be studied. The initial reception was favorable, and the district moved into the program on a large scale.

Today, our early attempts appear very simple and mediocre. Individual science kits now enable us to meet the reading-level needs of all students. The kits also expose students to many different viewpoints on a particular topic. This is especially important in trying to develop objective views. Instead of cardboard boxes, we now use collapsible wooden boxes with covers, reinforced bottoms, and hand grips. These have proved most suitable for shipping in trucks and storing in classrooms.

A typical multimedia kit for a science unit will contain two to five color filmstrips, tape recordings, transparencies, charts, artifacts, equipment, 20 to 35 hardbound books, paperbacks, and other softbound materials. Perhaps the only major audio-visual aids not put into science kits are 16mm films; 30 identical kits would require 30 prints of 16mm films, which would prove too costly. Currently the center has over 1,800 16mm prints and 8,000 multimedia kits, increasing at the rate of about 500 kits per year.

Many of the filmstrips in the kits have been produced by our audio-visual production department. Our media specialist meets with the consultant of the science department and teachers. Together they plan a filmstrip to go with a particular unit — for example, a Racine water-treatment plant filmstrip was

Reprinted from *Science Teacher*, October 1969, by permission of the publisher.

produced for the sixth grade kit entitled Community Health. The center has also developed science equipment kits, three-dimensional models, and a collection of 16mm films.

To be effective, the science center kit program must be publicized throughout the district. A handbook is furnished for each teacher for every grade level covering all subject areas.

In the science center we employ a science teacher on a half-time basis to deal with the numerous requests for many types of apparatus and equipment. His major responsibility is to keep the testing equipment, science supplies, and materials in the various science kits functioning and replenished. A few years ago, our IMC tried placing science equipment and science supplies in individual school buildings, and to a certain extent schools still do have cabinets containing some supplies. In the average elementary school, however, it is almost impossible to have on hand the equipment and apparatus necessary to coordinate with the multimedia kits available. It is easier and far more economical for the IMC science center to supply the whole package of materials and their related equipment. This serves as a budgetary help in that materials can be supplied without detailed requisitions and red tape.

The science center also houses several units which are not found in the typical materials center. A recent addition is the Hamilton Animal Care Center, thermostatically controlled and vented to provide an enclosed environment for animals. The center sends out white mice, gerbils, rats, and other similar animals. Here our animal care case projects itself into the life of the classroom. We maintain interesting animals that can be checked out into the classroom. The animals can be observed by the students until interest wanes or a new unit begins. Then the animal either goes back to the science center or is transferred to some other school. Living materials to set up science interest centers within the classroom are available throughout the year.

The center has been able to supply biological materials such as: protozoans, mealworms, bacteria, algae, fungi, and a variety of reagents to the various elementary and secondary schools in the system. A refrigerator-freezer for storing some of the cultures and materials is of considerable value because it provides a central place for teachers to obtain these materials without having to wait for purchases or to raise their own cultures, which in most cases is almost impossible.

Materials can be delivered on the exact day that they are needed, thus allowing for increased flexibility in planning on the classroom level. This also alleviates the storage problem, particularly at the elementary level where storage facilities are not adequate for maintaining strong chemical reagents. Supplies can be delivered to the teacher when needed, thus reducing the need for storage of hazardous materials in the school.

A second, very useful function of the science center is that of teacher training. The science center has an autotutorial arrangement, whereby individual teachers can come in and program themselves through various units in the elementary science curriculum. Presently we have developed tutorial units in chemistry and electricity, both of which are presented via cartridge tapes and slides. We hope to add another dimension to the tutorial system by the use of videotape playbacks picked up from actual classroom units.

In a team-teaching schedule, it is possible to release a teacher to come to the science center and go through a complete unit with the help of the autotutorial and the multimedia kit. The team representative for science can then offer not only more practical leadership for this unit but more conceptual goals and realistic objectives.

Even in these early stages of development, the tutorial system realistically extends the arm of the consultant and helping teacher. One trained specialist operating in the science center can be of considerable aid to three or four unit leaders simultaneously. His presence is needed only for the rough spots. Thus the center is more efficient in terms of time than are visits to the individual schools.

While adequate materials, programs, and staff are important in an IMC science center, the spirit of cooperation that presently exists among persons involved in the center is by far the most pertinent factor. If we continue to enjoy this complete cooperation and involvement of our staff, the center will continue to be an important factor in the developing science program.

A Regional Complex of Supplementary Educational Services

Ira J. Singer

At long last, regionalism has achieved respectability in education. It is now obvious to the most provincial school district that, unless it has achieved considerable size and wealth, it cannot offer certain unique and innovational programs. It was precisely this fact that motivated the New York State Education Department, in 1948, to organize boards of cooperative educational services (BOCES) throughout the state. Initially, the plan was to bring shared teacher services in such subjects as elementary art, music, and physical education to small rural districts unable to hire full-time personnel in these fields. Soon, however, the prospects of sharing other services in vocational and general education appeared desirable and financially advantageous. The financial incentive was provided by the State Education Department in returning increased state aid to those districts "buying" services from BOCES.

In Erie County's First Supervisory District, eighteen school districts in suburban Buffalo participate in a cooperative program offering services in (1) vocational education, (2) services for physically and mentally handicapped children, (3) curriculum development and teacher training, (4) electronic data processing, (5) shared teaching personnel, and (6) pupil personnel.

The school superintendents supporting these programs started by sharing special teachers, vocational facilities, and a film library. It became evident that, through cooperative effort, sufficient numbers of handicapped children could be identified, properly grouped, and placed throughout the enlarged district. Competent directors and staff were hired to plan the challenging and expensive programs ($500 to $2,000 per pupil) for youngsters suffering from brain damage, sight and hearing impairment and loss, emotional disturbances, and other handicaps. The program was placed under the BOCES organization, which now sponsors forty-seven such classes held within district school buildings serving 600 handicapped students.

Another natural area for cooperative activity proved to be vocational education. Operating two area technical and trade schools, a carefully screened BOCES vocational faculty instructs 1,000 students for two to three hours per day. Constantly expanding, the BOCES vocational program offers trade courses in auto body repair, auto mechanics, commercial art, cosmetology, electronic maintenance, heating and air conditioning, machine shop practice, and practical nursing. Technical courses are offered in microbiology, mechanical design and construction (including numerical tape control), and technical electronics.

The participating high schools transport their youngsters to and from the area schools for these special subjects only. All other instruction, academic and extracurricular, is given at the local level. An important adjunct of the vocational program is the adult program in occupational education, serving employed persons in need of retraining or upgrading. These courses are offered in the evening and include auto collision repair, auto mechanics (basic and advanced), electronics (basic and advanced), computer circuitry, and fundamentals of refrigeration. Many area industrial firms send workers in need of training to the BOCES program. In support of the entire vocational program, federal assistance has been gained through the Manpower Development and Training Act, the Vocational Rehabilitation Act of 1963, and the Economic Opportunity Act (through its work-study provisions).

A computer center was marked for coordinated effort when the early unit-record equipment utilized by individual districts proved severely limited in function and capacity. A 1440 computer was installed in the Harkness Center.*

---

*Harkness Center is the headquarters building of BOCES, housing the administrative offices as well as those services described in this paper.

The computer generates school schedules, report cards, payrolls, appropriations accounts, census records, test scores, transportation records, and attendance reports for district schools.

A staff of twelve full-time individuals, including two programers, is on hand to operate the center on a 16-hour-day basis. Schools may "buy" any one or any combination of computer tasks from the BOCES now performing various operations for 60,000 students attending schools in three counties.

Perhaps the most fascinating potential for cooperative activity lay in curriculum development and teacher training. Innovational projects in content, method, and media applied to samples of a student population of 67,000 and a teacher population of 3,500 proved an intriguing prospect to the schools of the First Supervisory District.* Therefore, in 1962, BOCES employed the writer to design, organize, and promote this new instructional service.

It was agreed that despite the abundance of challenging new curriculum concepts and teaching techniques, the impact on actual classroom practice had been disappointing. Also accepted was the premise that a major reason for the existing gulf between educational research and classroom practice was the lack of communication between researchers and innovators on the one hand and local teachers and administrators on the other.

Therefore, the BOCES Curriculum Development and Teacher Training Program was organized with the following objectives in mind: (1) to reduce the gap that presently exists between educational research and classroom practice; (2) to provide the practicing teacher with support services essential to the transformation of innovations in content, method, and media into instructional realities.

The Curriculum-Communications Center for Innovations in Education has been designed to encourage the dissemination of significant curriculum developments within the framework of effective teaching techniques and communications technology. The hypothesis for this approach is that teachers participating in integrated curriculum-communications programs are more likely to transfer new ideas and materials to daily practice than are teachers introduced to "audio-visual," "methodological," and "curriculum" concepts as separate and distinct entities. In other words, teachers are taught innovational ideas in innovational ways by innovational people using innovational things.

The center features large-group, small-group, and independent study facilities. A "teaching wall" in the large-group area is equipped with a remote control console activating various combinations of five audio-visual sources, a rear-screen overhead projector with ceiling-mounted mirrors, a combination of seven sliding surfaces (chalkboards, flannelboards, front screens, custom overhead screen),

---

*The First Supervisory District includes the school systems of Akron Central, Alden, Amherst, Cheektowaga, Clarence, Cleveland Hill, Depew, Frontier, Grand Island, Hamburg, Lancaster, Maryvale, Sweet Home, West Seneca, and Williamsville.

black fluorescent lights, and full control of room and wall lights. A grant from the Division of Educational Communications of the New York State Education Department defrayed all expenses for this unique facility.

Telelecture equipment is also installed in the large-group area, enabling teachers in training programs to hear and interview consultants "live" from any point in the nation or overseas via telephonic hookup. For example, conversations between fifty teachers at an economics workshop in the center and Drs. John Coleman and George Bach at the Carnegie Institute of Technology in Pittsburgh contributed significantly to the success of the program.

In the independent study area teachers use carrels equipped with a variety of auto-instructional devices, programed texts, audio-visual instruments, and curriculum materials spanning all grades and subject areas. Approximately 100 programed texts as well as a variety of "teaching machines" are available on loan to district teachers.

The center has been the setting for recent workshops in dramatics, biochemistry, politics and government (in association with the Taft Institute of Government), economics (in association with the New York State Council on Economic Education), the High School Geography Project, Mathematics, the BSCS (Biology), and industrial arts. The workshops are organized at *any* time during the year in response to instructional needs identified by on-the-job teachers, administrators, and curriculum specialists. Outstanding consultants are hired temporarily from throughout the nation because of their close involvement with the project to be studied at the BOCES seminar. These consultants are urged to use the multimedia facilities of the center as a direct consequence of our BOCES experience that utilization of innovational materials by a prestige figure (usually a "content expert" in the eyes of workshop teachers) has an immediate effect upon post-workshop classroom practice; teachers attempt to emulate the methods employed by the consultant.

During the first two years of the program, approximately 500 district teachers have participated in BOCES-sponsored in-service workshops ranging from ten to fifty hours in length and approved for in-service salary credit. This approach is seen by many local administrators as superior to the university in-service or extension program. The BOCES program has four distinct advantages over the university approach: (1) Workshops are organized in prompt response to expressed needs at any time during the year. (2) Consultants with recent experience and knowledge of the workshop topic are employed on a fee basis. (3) Teacher incentive is supplied by the awarding of in-service salary credit. (4) Unique facilities and services are available for the workshop and follow-up periods.

In brief, the ingredients of need, timeliness, supervision, incentive, and follow-up assistance form the core of the BOCES program. Although the Fund for the Advancement of Education has assisted in establishing this program, the

BOCES districts have assumed full costs and have expanded the program considerably.

Acting on the hypothesis that teachers will use visuals more frequently and effectively if such visuals are professionally prepared products of their (the teachers') own ideas, and assuming also that teachers have neither the time, talent, patience, and/or funds to create and utilize visuals to any significant degree, the BOCES hired a full-time artist (expanded to three for the 1965-66 school year) and installed a darkroom and studio for the purpose of producing "custom-made" visuals. Teachers submit a written idea in narrative terms for the art staff to recreate in visual terms. Transparencies, slides, posters, photographs, and three-dimensional displays have been included in some 3,000 visuals distributed during the first year of operation. This regional Materials Production Center has been producing the evidence necessary to "sell" the building instructional materials center concept. As individual buildings assume the burden of short-term production tasks, the BOCES Center can undertake such complex tasks as 8mm and 16mm film production, videotape production, tape duplication, and publications services.

The BOCES film library houses 2,400 16mm prints and 8mm cartridges, delivery vehicles, automatic film inspection equipment, and five full-time employees. The Harkness Center library contains such quality prints as "The Humanities Series," "Project 20," "NBC White Paper," "CBS Reports," "Walt Disney," etc. The library was made possible by a 1959 agreement between participating districts to contribute $25,000 per year for a ten-year period toward the purchase of new films. This formula has been followed through the 1965-66 school year. There will be further development during the coming years due to the addition of new school districts to film library membership and expanded NDEA financial support. Utilization of the library is reflected in some 20,000 film orders filled during the past year.

Finally, teachers are supplied with the names of community agencies willing to send speakers and consultants for large- or small-group classes at all levels. Such groups as the Bar Association, medical societies, orchestral societies, newspapers, mental health organizations, governmental agencies, and industries have been extremely cooperative in supplying speakers.

The Curriculum Development and Teacher Training Program has been instrumental in development of the following cross-section of innovational activities adopted by local school personnel:

1. The teaching of a course in computer mathematics to twenty high school students via the auto-tutor in one area high school.
2. The design of independent study carrels copied and utilized by five elementary schools.
3. A "teaching wall" design adopted in modified form for several new building projects.

4. The construction of a teaching machine designed by a first-grade teacher of reading for her students.

5. The filming of a series of 8mm film loops for the elementary science program of a member district.

6. A supplementary grant of funds to several language teachers traveling to France and Russia on NDEA grants for the purpose of reproducing and distributing films and tapes made during the trips. These were made available to the entire BOCES district.

7. A monthly principals' seminar with such guests as Lloyd Trump, Gardner Swenson, Eugene Howard, Lloyd Michael, and others sharing new ideas in half-day sessions.

8. Organization of an in-service program for two member districts embarking on district-wide nongraded primary programs.

9. Conducting a combined telelecture-electro-writing (dataphone-controlled stylus) for two-way long-range audio-visual communication with the State Education Department in Albany.

10. Providing programed materials for students at various grade levels where teachers "want to try something new."

11. Using 8mm film loops in art and social studies for mentally retarded and brain-damaged children.

12. Designing multimedia packages in 16mm slide, filmstrip, and tape formats to be tested on the center "teaching wall" and distributed to district classes.

13. Planning with Computer Center staff members the introduction of the GASP program for class scheduling.

14. Writing a proposal for a four-channel 2500 mg. closed-circuit ETV system for two member school districts.

15. Suggesting team teaching patterns and consulting on new building designs.

The foregoing are some of the functions open to a regional, innovationally oriented curriculum development center dedicated to the proposition that essential educational decisions should be based on utilization and evidence rather than fear and rumor.

Problems in communication and coordination do occur in the State Department-BOCES-local district three-way exchange. However, improved data-processing procedures are helping to ease these problems for all cooperative services. Furthermore, the standardization of certain administrative procedures becomes necessary and desirable. These have in no way inhibited the spirit or application of innovators, either in instruction or service. Operating as a service and instructional center for the past three years, the BOCES is in an excellent position to meet three necessary criteria for consideration under Title III of the Elementary and Secondary Education Art of 1965, namely: (1) to expand existing services to new student populations; (2) to introduce new services to diverse populations; (3) to operate model instructional programs for adoption by community school districts.

As costs for supplementary educational services become progressively higher, the need for cooperation between large and small school districts alike becomes increasingly apparent. The economics, quality, diversity, and overall collective strength of regional programs provide the natural setting for innovation in service and instruction too often out of reach for the individual district.

The City-Wide Instructional Materials Center

Fred Urban

Today, life in the classroom is far more complex than ever before. The curriculum has expanded and it is under great pressure to change. The recent explorations to the moon, as an example, will have a tremendous impact on the current teaching of the universe, astronomy, and space exploration. The classroom teacher cannot do the job alone.

In Norwalk, the Central Instructional Materials Center is a true extension of the modern classroom. The CIMC has a one-word motto, Service, and is dedicated to helping the teacher individualize instruction. Located in the approximate center of the school district, the CIMC makes available weekly more than 100 hours of videotapes, over 900 films, more than 2000 teaching tape kits, hundreds of recordings, over 2000 filmstrips and some 8000 transparencies to its 800 teachers serving 17,000 students.

The Professional Library and materials processing laboratory is an integral part of the center. Over 4000 volumes of educational materials are available for staff research. Last year 7000 volumes were circulated to administrators and teachers throughout the school system. In addition, 6000 books were processed and distributed to the elementary schools. The library staff visits the schools on a regular basis and conducts monthly workshops for the library clerks and school volunteers.

In order to fully understand the organization and operation of the CIMC, the three areas of software service, hardware service, and human service will be reviewed.

Reprinted from *Audiovisual Instruction*, May 1969, 14:25-26, by permission of the Association for Educational Communications and Technology.

SOFTWARE SERVICE

The closed-circuit TV studio is located in the lower section of the CIMC. This well-equipped studio produces both locally prepared and commercial video-tapes for system-wide consumption. Local teachers are trained to develop television scripts and appear in their programs. Many of the films used are supplied free of charge, some are rentals from New York's Channel 13, and the balance are prepared locally. Instant programing has been possible; for example, a weekly program highlighting the actions of the local board of education is presented the morning after the meeting. On the days following the tragic assassinations of Martin Luther King and Robert Kennedy video programs were available for the entire student population.

Superintendent of Schools Harry A. Becker has used this medium most effectively for inservice programs and addresses to the student body.

One teacher in charge coordinates the efforts of this studio.

The preparation of overhead transparencies is perhaps the busiest operation. A full-time visual materials specialist is employed to service administrators and teachers with black-and-white or color overlay transparencies for use on the overhead projector. All transparency masters are centrally stored at the CIMC and a call or written request for a newly created visual can be processed in 72 hours.

If the teacher requests a copy of a commercial transparency, a copy can be made with permission via its transparency copier, the only one in a Fairfield County School System.

The magnetic recording tape department is also a busy place. The tape specialist is continually updating the collection of 2000 master teaching tape kits. The packaged material contains not only the tape, but also the script and student worksheet. Although each school contains a basic collection, duplicate tapes must be made from the master copy to replace missing or defective discs. In preparing a complete kit, the master tape is attached to the tape duplicator, copies of the worksheets and script are reproduced, and the kit is assembled. The tape kits are then used in the classroom and returned to the individual school library to become a permanent part of the catalog collection.

The making of photographs, slides, filmstrips, and 16mm motion pictures for a variety of curriculum needs is in the hands of a staff photographer, printer, and cameraman. At the present time a 16mm motion picture depicting a water filtration system is under way.

The clearing agent or booking clerk is responsible for arranging an equitable distribution of the available software. The film collection, filmstrips, records, displays, models, and available transparencies are ordered by phone or written request by the school faculties. In order to standardize the requests the form illustrated is used.

INSTRUCTIONAL MATERIALS CENTER MATERIALS REQUEST

School	Teacher	Grade	FOR IMC USE ONLY
			to be delivered
Catalog No.	Title		
			to be returned

NOTE: This form used as requisition for one instructional aid, or several filmstrips marked "FS"

Date Wanted

Fill out after using material:
CONDITION OF MATERIAL

_____ Needs Repair _____ Parts Missing

_____ Material in wrong container

**MATERIALS MUST BE
RETURNED ON THIS
DATE UNLESS RENEWED**

Not available Reorder _____
Given first avail. date _____
Title or catalog No. _____
Not correct check cat._____
This is a duplicate request ___
Requested too late for_____

DO NOT REMOVE CARBONS

Many teachers plan their units in advance and reserve material months ahead. When an item is ordered and not available the teacher receives it at the next available date. Films having a seasonal or specific interest during a particular week are shown over the closed-circuit TV channel.

HARDWARE SERVICE

The CIMC prepares a list of available hardware and the specifications. These lists are sent to the schools in the budget packets assisting the department heads and principals in the purchase of equipment. The lists are then returned to the purchasing office and ordered.

All portable pieces of hardware are serviced at the center. A trained technician overhauls and replaces parts before the machines are returned to the school. Periodically the schools are visited for general machine maintenance.

The TV technician is on call to visit the schools and repair the television sets or the closed-circuit TV network. Roton Middle School, for example, has the equipment to originate and telecast programs. The staff technician is available to service the system. In addition to the hardware at the schools, the CIMC has a complete collection of graphic arts, tape, TV, and repair equipment to maintain for use at the center. A teacher previewing room is also equipped with the many varieties of hardware.

HUMAN SERVICE

Essential to the effective use of media are *understanding* and *availability*. If a teacher has an understanding of multimedia and the hardware is available, effective use can be expected.

Through the efforts of the director of the CIMC, inservice workshops have been held on a city-wide basis, grade level basis, content area, or by individual faculty request.

Emphasis has been given to the reasons for using media and the expected outcomes. Teachers are becoming more selective in their use of instructional materials. The movement is toward individual assignments to individual students. Children are assigned cassette type tape recorders, filmstrips, or recordings.

The TV studio has just completed a workshop for administrators. The use of the camera, videotape recorder, lighting, and production was presented. The administrators learned about the components of a studio, maintenance techniques, and production. Each participant had the opportunity to actually operate the equipment. A comprehensive guide book was prepared by the TV studio director.

The publication *Media-Happenings* serves as an avenue of understanding among staff members. Published at the CIMC, it reports new approaches and projects in our schools. Every member of the staff receives this publication. A recent publication reported on the use of wireless headsets at the Jefferson Elementary School.

The availability of materials is most critical in the everyday operation of the teacher and the classroom. The CIMC has developed primary and secondary catalogs for every staff member. These catalogs are arranged by subject area and include all media that have a direct application. For example, the intermediate catalog contains a listing of 5 filmstrips, 16 transparencies, and 2 motion pictures under the heading "Mathematics," subtitle "Graphs."

Each day the school delivery truck makes the rounds to all 28 schools delivering requested instructional materials and picking up the returns. This process assures the teacher of 24-hour contact with the center without their leaving the building.

The TV studio issues a weekly guide of the programs available on the closed-circuit network. The programs are shown at different times enabling the teacher to choose the most appropriate day or time for his class. Each teacher has a copy of the area educational TV station Channel 13's guide book through the efforts of the CIMC. This tool provides the teacher with pre-telecast information, the telecast itself, and follow-up material.

Director Harding sums up the operation in this way: "Every school media center is really a branch of the CIMC with each one growing as a resource center.

All are starting to help the teacher provide more materials for individualized instruction for their pupils and in an endless variety of methods."

Reading Center Fills Needs

Anne Way

From seldom used girls' shower room to well lighted reference study and reading center — this is the transformation which took place last summer in the G.D. Jones Elementary School basement in Wausau.

A reference study center was needed in this area since the Wausau Public Library is two and one-half miles away, and there is no transportation after 6:00 p.m. Some of the children have no quiet place for study at home because of large families and television. A boy who is a junior at the Wausau Senior High School remarked, "I surely appreciate the quiet atmosphere of the study center and its nearness to my home."

The new library provides a reference study and reading area from 4:00-9:00 p.m. and all day Saturday from 9:00 a.m.-4:00 p.m. It doubles as the Jones School elementary library during school hours. The project was financed through Title I of the Elementary and Secondary Education Act of 1965, under the supervision of Harry W. Jones, director of special programs for the Wausau District Public Schools.

The library is open to adults and to public and nonpublic elementary and secondary students from grades 5 through 12. A librarian and a custodian staff the center.

There is no worry about due dates or fines since the books, magazines and newspapers are used in the library. They may not be drawn out. Students sign a guest book on entering in order to check on the attendance. A book or magazine is signed for on a book card as used and checked in when the student has finished using it to find out what titles are used most frequently.

This procedure has been successful, judging by the last inventory — there were no books missing. A student may use the reference books, study his own textbooks, read the magazines and fiction for enjoyment, or he may type. It is also possible for forensic contestants to have their selections recorded. A junior

Reprinted from *Wisconsin Journal of Education,* April 1967, by permission of Wisconsin Education Association.

high school student states, "I surely like the study center! I have so many little brothers and sisters at home that I can't study."

The decor of the library with its pale yellow walls, blond tables and chairs, avocado drapes, and an easy chair makes this an attractive and restful place to read or work. Posters advertising books and urging the pupil to read are on display and changed each month. New books are ordered as funds are approved. To encourage attendance, a book will be given away at the end of this school year to the student attending the center the greatest number of times.

The success of the center may be evaluated from a statement by a university student, at her home in Wausau for the weekend, who came to study on Saturday: "This is the most peaceful place to work; I have never studied as long at one time before." Hopefully the center's users will continue to feel this way.

A Material-Media Laboratory To Train Special Education Teachers

Helen Juliar

Initial germinal federal funding for an in-house instructional materials center as a satellite of one of the major special education materials center and a considerable departmental commitment allowed the Special Education Department at the University of Minnesota to adapt and redefine traditional IMC functions. The aim has been to improve and innovate in instruction and curriculum in teacher education.

Federal support for improved education for handicapped children climaxes a history in the field of special education of search for ways to help children for whom usual educational approaches are inadequate. Teacher education in this field has both the obligation and the opportunity to innovate with implications beyond the specialized area.

Resources have been coordinated to form an Instructional Improvement Laboratory that proposes to exploit materials and media as tools for change in teacher education. From the passive concept of a materials depository has grown active involvement in providing service to students and staff, supporting and initiating research, searching for relevant material, developing curriculum and curriculum tools, sharpening educational diagnosis and prescription skills, broadening the base of practical preservice experience and disseminating findings and sharing talent with neighboring institutions.

Reprinted from *Audiovisual Instruction* 14,9: 38-40, November 1969, by permission of the Association for Educational Communications & Technology.

This paper will attempt to outline the functions and directions of the developing University of Minnesota laboratory supporting teacher education.

There is a need for better teacher education. A recently published two-year USOE study on teacher education (Taylor, 1968) called the field obsolete in both method and content, and charged that many students reject teaching because courses do not have serious intellectual content and because the system has a set pattern to which they must conform. This report calls for a program that speaks to the concerns of the involved students. The primary purpose of a teacher education program is to interest and involve the creative potential of young people in the search for partial solutions, bringing highly motivated, high-ability people into creative interaction with problems.

The teacher of the future will never "graduate" but will need to continue learning and innovating as long as he teaches. Change is the mission of the special educator, and plans for obsolescence must be built into all programs to help the child cope adequately. Lack of meaningful structure in teacher education programs, obscuring long-range problems and goals, lack of extensive immediate involvement and interaction in situation, theory, and research may all select-in those candidates who are intellectually comfortable with certainty, selecting-out those who are willing to live with the scheme of uncertified possibilities (Wm. James, 1955) that special education mandates.

More trained teachers are needed. Less than one-half of the nation's five million handicapped youth are getting the education they need (*American Education,* July-August, 1967, pp. 30-31) and a critical factor is the shortage of well-trained personnel.

The regular educational system needs to become more accommodating to individual differences in learning styles and needs, since the accommodative capacity of the regular system is often definitive of special education in an area. Educational crippling may occur at the point of identification.

Societal changes demand a relevant education. Increasing amounts of information and a growing technology offer challenge and opportunity for change. Increased rates of change demand that information-acquiring strategies and problem-finding skills become an integral part of teacher education. Instruction used to mean putting information on the sense receptors of passive students. Technology can extend the reach of *the student* to interpret his world instead of providing longer arms for supervisors and teachers to handle the students.

Institutions of higher learning need to assume leadership in development of creative educational materials. Teachers need not be at the mercy of competitive commercial development which results in perception of the field of education as a domain for investment (Stiles, 1967).

A report on teacher education (Smith, 1969) identified teachers of teachers as one of the main causes of the failure of teacher education, and called for a new social mechanism for training, run by colleges and universities, school systems and the local community, based on actual classroom situations. Increased size and bureaucratization of educational systems increases communication problems. In special education, professional isolation is an especially acute problem.

The laboratory attempts to provide the best material available through the most effective media, in individual, small-group and classroom settings for departmental students and staff. A computerized information storage and retrieval system is being implemented, part of a growing nationwide network aiming toward a link with the Education Resources Information Center (ERIC) Clearinghouse and the major instructional materials centers in the field. The aim is to provide students access to the materials that form the historical and emerging written structure of their field (Bruner, 1960). Goals should be self-pacing, with student-posed problems and the opportunity to share the thinking of leaders in the field.

The lecture provides opportunity to hear a person who is particularly knowledgeable discuss his subject, but communication of actual material may be more effectively and efficiently accomplished in other ways. A review of forty years of research (Dubin and Taveggia, 1969) failed to find any one method of college teaching that did a better job of conveying subject matter than another. These authors urged researchers to explore the links between teaching and learning, to analyze the consequences of differences among teaching methods. Closer school district-college collaborations in training provide a variety of urban ghetto, suburban, and rural teaching settings calling for different instructional modes and organizational structures. Credential specifications are being explored in Minnesota that permit explorative approaches to defining competencies as bases for certification.

The laboratory provides opportunity for students to become thoroughly familiar with special equipment and the software related to the field of special education, not replacing basic audio-visual course offerings, but reinforcing and supplementing. It is hypothesized that the educational levels of pupils would be raised if teachers were thoroughly familiar with the best in materials and media in their field of specialization. This "package" can be part of all methods courses taught in the department.

Research is stimulated by the laboratory in areas of course evaluation, styles of teacher preparation, innovative educational practices, teaching procedures and applications of technology to teaching. Evaluation is ongoing in an attempt to determine the impact of the laboratory on the curriculum and instruction of the department. Empirical study of instructional materials evaluation in special education is a necessity. Search efforts are being initiated to utilize teaching procedures and products that have been developed at other institutions, to avoid trite educational offerings and duplicated effort.

Curriculum materials still lacking in some areas should be developed, tested, and made available for dissemination by the laboratory. For example, analysis was made of the instruction in one of the courses in the department, leading to development of transparencies and other materials for better teaching. This provided "encapsulation of instructional procedures in specific media which are mechanically reproducible [giving] a degree of control over the variables involved in presentation, exposition and instruction . . ." (Lumsdaine, 1968).

The laboratory does not attempt to offer separate courses, but through service efforts in the department provides components for special education teacher training. A continuum of practical experiences in preservice and inservice training is the goal, breaking the walls between in and out of school. A departmental advisory group and a university-wide policy group help provide realistic institutional direction.

A statewide advisory group under the leadership of the state department of education is developing guidelines for regional diagnostic-prescriptive centers. The future direction of materials centers is influenced by the need to help teachers behaviorally define learning objectives and curricular organization, to collect behavioral data about the learning characteristics of the student and to provide evaluation for controlled intervention and adaptation of programs. Educational tests lead to diagnosis-specific prescriptions of materials and resources for learning.

Experience with this diagnostic prescriptive approach to teaching is to be provided in the Instructional Improvement Laboratory. This approach is currently being used at the Educational Modulation Center in Olathe, Kansas, and at the Educational Service Center at Mason, Michigan. The planning includes a statewide network of information-sharing in the field of special education involving state teacher training institutions, sharing computerized information storage and retrieval, developing active laboratories in direct action programs to improve instruction in teacher education, and supporting local service agencies to provide individually responsive settings for preservice and inservice training.

The Instructional Improvement Laboratory combines experiences with material and media, diagnosis and prescription, service and research, development and dissemination in efforts to change teacher education.

"Teacher educators should, in a number of specific ways, instruct teachers in the same way that those teachers will eventually instruct their pupils . . ." (Robert F. Peck and Oliver H. Brown "Research and Development Center for Teacher Education," *Journal of Research and Development in Education*, Vol. 1, No. 4, Summer, 1968, 106-127).

REFERENCES

Bruner, Jerome S. *The Process of Education*, New York: Random House, 1960.

Dubin, Robert, and Taveggia, Thomas C. *The Teaching-Learning Paradox*. University of Oregon, Eugene: The Center for Study of Educational Administration, 1969.

"Education of the Handicapped," *American Education,* July-August, 1967, 30-31.

James, William. *Pragmatism*. New York: World Publishing Co., 1955. 191 pp.

Lumsdaine, Arthur A. "Instructional Research: Some Aspects of its Status." *Journal of Experimental Education,* 37:95-101; Fall 1968.

Smith, B. Othanel. *Teachers for the Real World.* Published by the American Association of Colleges for Teacher Education, based on research by the task force of the National Defense Education Act's National Institute for Advanced Study in Teaching Disadvantaged Youth. (*The Chronicle of Higher Education.* 3:6; February 24, 1969.)

Stiles, Lindley J. "Policy and Perspective." *Journal of Educational Research,* 60:front cover; January 1967.

Taylor, Harold. *The World and the American Teacher.* Washington: American Association of Colleges for Teacher Education and the U.S. Office of Education, 1968.

An Overview of the IMC Network

James J. McCarthy

The Instructional Materials Center Network for Handicapped Children and Youth (IMCNHCY) is a federation of regional Instructional Materials Centers (IMC's) whose primary client is the special educator and whose region of service is the continental United States, Hawaii, Alaska, Puerto Rico, and the Virgin Islands. Although there is a lag between the Network's accomplishments and aspirations, this gap is closing at a rapid rate as new service and research roles are being assimilated. The Network can be a boon to special educators who know how to use it and what it can do for them.

To many special educators hearing about it for the first time, the Network may seem to be a complicated monolith which is sprung suddenly full blown from the impersonal council of the omnipresent federal government and which really has litle personal value for them. Nothing could be further from the truth.

The purpose of this article is to dispel this concept by providing an overview of the Network's development. It should be stated at the outset that the Network is designed to become a permanent organization locally controlled and locally funded. It is to serve and be guided by special educational personnel to

Reprinted from *Exceptional Children,* December 1968, by permission of the publisher.

help them better serve handicapped children. Network services are, or will be, available to every special educator in the United States.

HISTORICAL PERSPECTIVE

The Network consists of 14 Instructional Materials Centers (IMC's) and CEC-ERIC. Each regional Center is developing regional satellite centers, which may be stationary or mobile and have simple or elaborate service structures, depending on local needs, resources, and commitments. In some cases, Centers are hundreds of miles away from clients in their region and a satellite center is the only means of providing personalized service.

The IMCNHCY has a federal advisory board which is developing an information storage and retrieval system and a system of communication and coordination whereby all parts may be articulated. It is analagous to a corporation in which the stockholder is the special educator.

The beginnings of the Network were quite unelaborate, although they did contain the seeds of the growing and evolving structure seen today. That a Network such as this could develop was, I feel, foreseen in the beginning. What was not foreseen was the spectacular and unprecedented growth of a new type of major and permanent element in special education which appears to be a uniquely American contribution.

In 1964, two prototype IMC's were funded by the U.S. Office of Education under PL 88-164, Title III. President Kennedy's Task Force on Rehabilitation and Education had originally conceived the idea of Instructional Materials Centers in Special Education from its inspections of overseas nations. Traditionally, continental special educators have made more of their own instructional materials than have their American counterparts and many European special educators are actually certified to teach because, in part, of their skills in materials production. The midtwentieth century attitude in the United States seemed to be that commercial America had the resources to design and produce instructional materials in special education and that this task, properly executed, required expertise and resources (e.g., advanced psychology and learning courses, statistics and experimental design, and production facilities) not available to teachers. Moreover the teacher was considered a practitioner, not producer; his or her time was to be actively spent in the teaching role. The teacher was seen as analogous to the physician who uses surgical instruments and drugs, but doesn't usually design, create, or test these things.

Although the President's Task Force did not specify the nature of IMC's, the prevailing American attitudes in special education strongly suggested directions. The original IMC's would collect extant instructional materials in or related to special education; catalog, loan, store, and retrieve such materials;

consult with teachers and student teachers; publish acquisition lists and informational pamphlets; hold inservice meetings; help others who wished to initiate their own Centers; and even attempt to produce an item or two. They promised attempts at materials evaluation and design.

Within 2 years, these prototype Centers had demonstrated that they could prepare themselves to provide needed services in special education. However, they had not convincingly demonstrated the ability to design, evaluate, or produce instructional materials. In addition, though various experiments had been tried (e.g., mail order materials borrowing), the prototype Centers' services were restricted to a relatively small geographical region. Certainly, for the Centers to be of value, services needed to be extended to wider areas. Thus, in 1966, 8 additional regional Centers were funded, bringing to 10 the number in existence at that time.

Although every regional Center will eventually be locally funded, the initial years were largely funded by federal dollars. The government's mounting investment resulted in considerable planning at the federal level which, in retrospect, can be viewed as the next developmental stage of the Network. In 1966, a meeting of Center directors was held in Madison, Wisconsin. At that time, an organization was formed (later called the IMCNHCY), and a chairman was elected. Simultaneously, an IMC Advisory Committee was formed with the U.S. Office of Education.

At this time:

1. Definitive service regions for each Center were agreed upon in order to avoid overlap and to identify parts of the country yet unserved.
2. Each Center declared those areas of handicap for which it would process instructional materials (e.g., mental retardation, visual impairment, etc.) according to the competencies of its staff. This knowledge made it possible to refer client requests to appropriate Centers should the Center originally queried not stock the desired materials.

Through the establishment of more regional Centers, the number of special educators reached with services increased; however, this still represented a small percentage of the total. It was apparent that hundreds more of these Centers would be needed to cover the country adequately, and this was patently impossible. The solution came from the IMC Advisory Committee, which advised:

1. The regional Centers should assist in establishing satellite centers within their respective regions, adequate in size and scope to collectively service all clients in their regions. These centers would eventually be locally funded, locally controlled, responsive to local needs, and related to respective regional Centers. This last point is critical for it allowed great economies. It meant that expensive consultation, assistance with inservice training, search and retrieval of information on materials, and

other services were freely available to each satellite center which could, therefore, retain a fairly small staff and a locally responsive collection of materials with the assurance of help from the regional Center when special needs arose.

2. Evidence of regional preplanning must be required of proposals for regional Centers from areas of the country not yet covered, so that parts of large states (or several small states) would agree upon how their entire region was to be served.

Thus, by 1968, 14 IMC's collectively service the entire country. About eighty satellite centers have been established and 300 to 400 professional staff persons are devoting all or a portion of their time to operating this system. A major problem has now become one of alerting special education personnel to the availability of these services.

THE FUTURE OF THE NETWORK

The Network is an evolving structure and can be responsive to emerging needs. Its directors and advisory board meet periodically to assess progress and plan the future. The present stress is upon:

1. The rapid development of satellite centers. When these are established, special educators can receive all their services in or through these local centers. These centers, in turn, can act as sensors to detect current needs and transmit them through the Network to the Bureau of Education for the Handicapped, U.S. Office of Education. For purposes of training, materials evaluation, and activities yet unforeseen, the completed Network will provide a remarkable communication instrument with the individual special educator at one end, the federal government at the other, and all other levels of the profession plugged in somewhere between those two terminals.

2. Increased coordination among regional Centers. To sense the urgent need for precise intercenter coordination, one need only contemplate the value of (a) joint production of inservice training sessions, (b) uniform publications, (c) cooperative exchange of staff and materials among Centers, and (d) the need to speak as one with commercial producers, foreign nations, and others who are interested in the Network. Obviously, attempts at research and evaluation, materials design and evaluation, and data storage and retrieval are also enhanced through close intercenter coordination. Accordingly, this coordination is of great current importance. Steps to achieve it include the appointment of a Network coordinator and uniform procedures in reporting, data retrieval, and abstracting.

3. Stress on local funding. It is clear that as the Network grows, the federal government will find it increasingly difficult to support. No

Instructional Materials Center Network for Handicapped Children and Youth

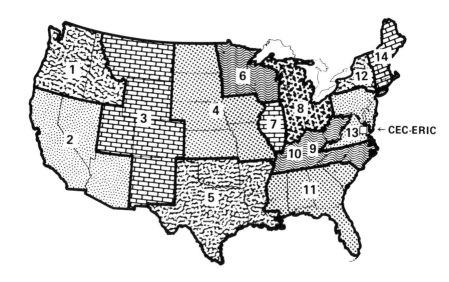

Key to IMC's, with Regions Served

1. University of Oregon, Eugene: Alaska, Hawaii, Idaho, Oregon, Washington

2. University of Southern California, Los Angeles: Arizona, California, Nevada

3. Colorado State College, Greeley: Colorado, Montana, New Mexico, Utah, Wyoming

4. University of Kansas, Lawrence: Iowa, Kansas, Missouri, Nebraska, North Dakota, South Dakota

5. University of Texas, Austin: Arkansas, Louisiana, Oklahoma, Texas

6. University of Wisconsin, Madison: Minnesota, Wisconsin

7. Illinois State Department of Public Instruction, Springfield (The two Illinois Centers are located at Springfield and Chicago.): Illinois

8. Michigan State University, East Lansing: Indiana, Michigan, Ohio

9. University of Kentucky, Lexington: Kentucky, North Carolina, Tennessee, West Virginia

10. American Printing House for the Blind Louisville, Kentucky: National reference center for visually handicapped

11. University of South Florida, Tampa: Alabama, Florida, Georgia, Mississippi, South Carolina, Puerto Rico, Virgin Islands

12. New York State Department of Education Albany (The three New York Centers are located at Albany, Buffalo, and New York City.): New York

13. George Washington University, Washington, D.C.: Delaware, District of Columbia, Maryland, New Jersey, Pennsylvania, Virginia

14. Boston University, Boston, Massachusetts: Connecticut, Maine, Massachusetts, New Hampshire, Rhode Island, Vermont

☐ CEC-ERIC Clearinghouse on Exceptional Children and Network Coordinator's Office Washington, D.C.

estimates of yearly costs are yet available for the Network operation, but an estimate of close to $5,000,000 of federal and local funds is not an unrealistic figure for present operational costs.

4. Initiation of materials design and evaluation procedures. In the last analysis, materials design and evaluation are the *raison d'être* of IMC's. They were designed for this purpose and are, accordingly, uniquely suited to it. Yet, to date, these processes have not developed apace with other Center activities. The scientific development of instructional materials and their objective evaluation present the most difficult and demanding challenge of all to the Network.

It is important to understand that the teacher is the primary client, that he or she can receive help by contacting her Center director, and that the range of service available is not highly restricted. Indeed, a client may ask for a type of assistance never contemplated and a Center may decide to incorporate such service into its routine. Thus, the Network needs the teacher's help to grow and diversify; teachers need the Network's help to serve handicapped students more adequately. And such help is literally theirs for the asking.

Implementing the Media Program in Schools for the Deaf

Richard L. Darling

If school media programs for the hearing have been a weak and sickly nutrient for the growth of learning, then media services in schools for the deaf can hardly be considered support at all. Mrs. Cory's study has shown the sad plight of school libraries and instructional materials programs in these schools. With a few notable exceptions they were understaffed or without staffs at all; they had collections too small for their function; they were maintained by annual expenditures too small to do the job; they were poorly housed; and, as a result, had little to offer the learner. Approximately two-thirds of the schools she studied were so far below any minimum standard of media service that it is doubtful whether they had any impact at all.

When we consider that these schools educate children with the most severe handicap of all educable children it is obvious that media services in schools for the deaf have been even more deficient than Mrs. Cory's study reveals. At first glance, it would be easy to say that they are not so different from schools for the hearing which have only a few examples of good media services, the majority

Reprinted from *American Annals of the Deaf*, November 1967, by permission of the publisher.

having the same inadequacies or no service at all. However, in order to accomplish the same educational goals, media services for the deaf need to be three times as extensive as those for the hearing. The new standards resulting from Mrs. Cory's study reflect that fact. Public school systems with extensive programs for deaf and other handicapped children have begun to weight them as equivalent to three other children for funding their education. Not even the architects of the best media services can afford to be complacent. In schools serving deaf children, where the problems of education are so much greater, the effort has to go beyond what we today consider as standards of excellence. A Knapp School Library Project in a school for the deaf, if it were to be a demonstration of desirable levels of service, would go far beyond the programs Miss Sullivan discussed at lunch today.

The educational media program essential to the education of deaf children, and indeed for all children, is a service that brings to the support of their learning all educational media, so organized and so deployed that they can derive the maximum benefit from each medium, and augmented benefits from combinations of media. To accomplish this goal, each school needs a single, unified educational media service of high quality, supported by auxiliary services from higher governmental and organizational levels — state, regional, and federal. The school media program should combine in a unified service all types of instructional materials and equipment systematically organized so that they can be related to the instructional program in a variety of desirable ways — for group instruction and for independent study, for basic learning and for reinforcement, and to achieve learning experiences in various content areas to which they may contribute.

Whether we are discussing schools for the deaf, or schools in general, there are certain significant developments in our society with which we must be concerned. In less than a generation we have seen a revolutionary change. New and improved transportation and communication have brought boundaries closer to one another. Through communication satellites we see and hear men who are continents away. Supersonic planes, under construction or on the drawing boards, will soon make New York and Paris as close to one another as Lincoln and Omaha. Modern medicine has made possible a huge population in our growing cities and improved agriculture has provided their subsistence, so that ever increasing numbers of the world's population are urban dwellers. This is the kind of world for which we are educating our children.

In the past several years we have seen education responding to this altered world in which our young people must live. National professional associations and groups of scholars have developed new curricula in their subject fields, and, in some cases, systems of educational media to be used in their presentation. The schools have responded by accepting innovation in curricula and in organizational patterns for instruction on an unprecedented scale. But they have not moved as rapidly in adopting new methods and new technology which would facilitate needed change. It seems to me, an outsider in education of the deaf, that schools for children with impaired hearing can lead the way in using technology to achieve recognized educational goals for all children while accomplishing their own specialized goals. This they can do by utilizing all media in an innovative and exemplary manner.

Other speakers at this conference have described their concept of the instructional materials center, exemplary programs of materials and activities in schools for the deaf. However, at the risk of redundancy, I wish to review the components of a comprehensive media program in order to develop some ideas related to its services that are essential to achieving the goals of improved education.

THE MEDIA PROGRAM

The modern educational media program has been created from preexisting components augmented by newer ones. On the most basic level it has been developed through the merging of traditional school library and audio-visual services, but when the media program approaches fuller development, it also includes advanced electronic technology, including television and computer-assisted instruction. The most striking characteristic of a good educational media program is the diversity of its services with the most far-ranging variety of media – printed, audio-visual, and transmitted. A brief and incomplete examination of the materials provided by a comprehensive media center demonstrates its diversity.

The media program should include materials for listening, for viewing, and for reading, each type used for its contribution to the study of a specific topic, or to the learning needs of a particular child. Each type should be accepted for its own integrity and for its value in education.

A large portion of the collection, though by no means a majority, should consist of printed materials. This should be as true in schools for the deaf as in other schools. Because of the special problems in reading of most deaf children, the collection of printed materials should include disproportionate numbers of books which are easy to read but have a high interest level. Nonetheless, they must cover the full range of the curriculum at varied levels of difficulty.

The collection will also include other types of printed materials, such as magazines and newspapers, both in paper and microfilm form. The need for larger collections to meet individual needs and interests mandates provision of many items on microfilm, a trend that is only beginning in schools, but is sure to grow. Like schools for the hearing, schools for the deaf should make increased use of paperbacks, both for their usefulness in expanding collections quickly and inexpensively, and for their great appeal to the young. Programmed books and programmed materials for use in teaching machines, with their capacity for immediate reinforcement of learning, have an important role in remedial study and in independent learning. Media centers in schools for the deaf will also include special materials developed for their students, such as the Project LIFE materials and others. Not to be overlooked are large-type books, prepared for the visually handicapped, but of proven value in reading instruction for all children needing greater security and self-confidence in their learning process.

The collection of auditory and visual materials is even more varied than the collection of printed materials. Even a partial list gives a picture of its scope. It includes 16mm motion picture films, which have been used primarily for group instruction, but are equally effective for individual study. In schools for the deaf 16mm films may be primarily captioned films, but research and observation have shown that regular films, when carefully selected, can be used effectively in the education of hearing-impaired children. Project Discovery has demonstrated how both teachers and students will use 16mm motion picture films when both the films and projectors are easily accessible.

The 8mm film may soon be, if it is not already, even more important than 16mm. Mounted in cartridges for ease in use and handling, 8mm film loops are ideally suited to individual study by students. As you know, many 8mm film loops have been developed specifically to meet the needs of deaf children, such as those prepared under Dr. Stepp here in Nebraska.

Filmstrips are another medium well-suited to individual study. They may be particularly valuable when accompanied by suitably amplified disc recordings, or by tape recordings carefully prepared by the teacher or the media center staff.

Slides and slide sets, related to the curriculum and especially to speech and reading instruction, should be included in the media collection. Slides have the added advantage that they can be easily produced locally to fit clearly identified needs.

Disc recordings, tape recordings, and Language Master cards can be especially useful in the education of children with some residual hearing. Indeed, these materials, and the equipment to use them, should be available for constant use to every teacher of the deaf. In our Montgomery County program for children with hearing impairment, a Language Master is part of each teacher's classroom equipment.

Transparencies, popular and useful in all educational programs, have proven themselves particularly valuable in schools for the deaf. Speakers at these Lincoln conferences have identified the closer attention the teacher can give to the students, and the greater visibility of the teacher to the students among the virtues of transparencies and the overhead projector. But equally important in the child's education is the fact that this is a medium he can readily create himself, while with many media, and particularly print, the child is all too prone to copy and report what he has read or heard. When he has the opportunity to create transparencies, slides, or films to report his learning, he is forced to analyze, digest, and synthesize in order to create something new and different. That synthesis is the very essence of learning.

The media collection also includes maps, charts, and globes, centrally inventoried so that the entire school may use them, but often housed in classrooms needing them most frequently. A good program will also include study prints and art prints in profusion.

For the elementary level students, who usually do not have access to science laboratories, the media center provides simple science equipment, exhibits of rocks, and other realia and models. It supplies models useful in social studies as well as those in science.

In order to provide services with these kinds of materials, the media center must supply the necessary equipment. The media center inventory should include projectors, tape recorders, record players, bioscopes, listening stations, individual and small group viewers, Language Masters, radio and television receivers, and other necessary equipment. The media program provides materials, equipment to use them, and knowledge of their use.

MEDIA CENTER FACILITIES

Though concepts in the planning and design of schools are changing, the design of media centers has changed even more rapidly to enable teachers and students to use media in new ways. The traditional school library often provided just one reading room. The traditional audio-visual center was actually on most occasions, only a viewing room. Today's media center provides facilities for a variety of activities, large group, small group, and individual, and for use of the full range of media.

The present emphasis on independent study has led school planners to question the value of large reading rooms and of separate viewing rooms. Instead they are designing several smaller rooms in the media center for small group and independent study, and every classroom is equipped to accommodate whole class viewing.

Within the media center, the arrangement in furnishings have changed. The traditional school library multi-student tables have been replaced by individual study carrels. Many students, perhaps most, given a choice, prefer to work in small areas, or alone in the semi-isolation provided by a carrel. They are increasingly used for both elementary and secondary grades. For elementary school students, schools have removed the traditional library's rows of tables and replaced them with low tables, stools, and other furniture designed for young children. The media center is often carpeted, and in the elementary grades the floor is where many children sit.

The media center must provide areas to accommodate both listening and viewing activities by small groups. Carrels, equipped with electrical outlets, or with built-in electronic devices should be purchased or locally designed, so that the students may use the full range of media easily in individual study.

One of the most important areas in the media center is the materials production areas where students, teachers, and media specialists produce such instructional material as transparencies, slides, tapes, and motion pictures. The production area needs careful planning so that the necessary equipment can function properly. Equipment located there may include copying machines, ammonia transparency makers, camera copying stands, paper cutters and dry-mount presses, spirit duplicators, and other machines used in production. The room's design should provide appropriate counters and work tables to handle the equipment, and storage cabinets for film and other needed materials. The production area should also include a photographic darkroom.

To implement a media program, however, attention to the center is only half the job. Planning classrooms for multi-media is equally important. In residential schools the dormitory is a third area vital in the use of media in learning. Each classroom must be equipped for projection with appropriate screens, darkening shades or blinds, and have projectors and other electronic equipment for group and individual use. The residence hall should include facilities for independent study using varied media.

It is not necessary, here, to go into the detailed planning of facilities, which has or will be discussed by others on this Symposium. I only wish to remind you that there are many other aspects of facilities which need careful attention in implementing a media program, such as shelving, storage, and so forth. Schools which plan to use closed-circuit television, and all schools should in the near future, need to include television facilities as part of the media center.

ORGANIZATION AND SERVICES OF THE MEDIA PROGRAM

In order to encourage maximum use of all media, each one needs to be as accessible as possible to all students and teachers. Differences in format do enforce differences in the way media are used and shelved, but they should all be housed where students have free access to them. Teachers and students should find, in the media center, one catalog which indexes all media in a single alphabetical file, with subject, title, author and artist where appropriate, approaches to the materials. Both students and teacher, searching for material on a given topic, should expect to find all media related to it indexed in one source, and, to the extent possible, shelved in close proximity. Needed equipment should be nearby for ready use.

Organization can help in implementing a media program, but organization of the center itself is not enough. Utilization of media to the full benefit of children requires a particular attitude toward learning and toward children which only the school administrator can develop. The reluctance of teachers to let pupils go freely to media centers to do independent study and research is a major problem in all schools. Many teachers actually enjoy the child's dependence upon them. Teachers of the deaf, I fear, have been even more reluctant, perhaps understandably, to permit their students the freedom to go independently to other learning centers except with an entire class. But just such freedom is essential if children are to be self-sufficient in the learning process. A full media program is possible only when children are encouraged to be self-reliant. The principal and superintendent must create the atmosphere through work with the school faculty that gives teachers confidence in permitting pupils the requisite freedom for learning outside the classroom.

Media service, to be most useful, must concentrate on the needs of pupils and teachers. Neither the rigid programs of traditional school libraries, nor the emphasis on group instruction of traditional audio-visual programs provides a satisfactory pattern for today's media program. The media specialist must work closely with teachers, assisting them in planning units of instruction so that media may contribute effectively to teaching and so that they can do follow-up work with students in the media center. Another vital service to teachers is continuing inservice education in the use of media to upgrade the quality of teaching.

With students seeking the media center for identified study and research needs, the media specialists should give them the close individual guidance in reading, listening, and viewing that is essential for maximum benefit from materials. The time formerly used for extensive and often wasted library lessons for classes, should be devoted to helping students locate materials, or finding materials for them, to assisting them in assessing the value of materials for their assignments, and to teaching them the values, strengths, and limitations of each medium.

Above all, the media center must provide flexible procedures and extended services. Lengths of loans should be geared to student assignments, and not to the calendar. It should be possible for students to check out materials for use at home, in study carrels within the school, or in the dormitory for long periods of time. The media center, especially in resident schools, should be open for service in the evenings, on weekends, and at any other time children may need materials.

The services of the center should permeate the entire school, reaching to classrooms and dormitories, and should not be a service that merely waits for users to come. With the advent of dial access and increased use of closed-circuit television, there is no reason that all media resources cannot be available to students and teachers wherever and whenever they are needed.

At the risk of repeating myself to the point of tediousness, let me repeat again that media production is a service program as well as facilities. We all chuckled this morning because, in some schools, the copying machine was in the Principal's office or locked in a closet. We should be equally shocked, even horrified, to discover schools where only media personnel and teachers have access to production facilities which can do so much in the development of learning in pupils.

MEDIA PERSONNEL

The media services essential for modern education in all schools, but especially in schools for the deaf, require a new type of media professional. He must know curriculum and learning theory. He must know educational media and their value and uses in education. He must have the ability to bring administrative techniques and creative imagination together to develop media services that meet the needs of today's schools.

In order to help us implement media services, institutions of higher education will have to initiate new kinds of programs for educating media specialists, programs which fuse the best aspects of library and audio-visual education. In the meantime we should use summer workshops and federally supported institutes to update or retrain many of our present workers in the field and to provide needed skills to our classroom teachers.

Better education of media specialists will help, but it is no substitute for numbers. The new American Association of School Librarians — Department of Audiovisual Instruction Standards which Dr. Faris discussed this morning, call for one media professional for each 200 students in schools for the hearing, with one supporting staff member for each professional, including media aids, technicians, artists, and so forth. In schools for the deaf three times as many staff members at the professional level should have special competencies and understanding of the education of the deaf.

There are those, I am certain, who will consider these standards unreasonably high. They are high if we are talking about staffing traditional school library and audio-visual programs. We have all seen programs run by a single person, which were in truth overstaffed, but we are not talking about those programs. We are talking about media programs of sufficient quality and so plentifully supplied with media and facilities that they add a new dimension to the learning opportunities of students, and to the professional ability of teachers.

Mrs. Cory described new media standards for schools for the deaf. They are higher, and rightly so, than standards for other schools. You have an opportunity, using those standards and the increasing federal aid funds, to be pacesetters in improving the quality of American education. You can prove the value of even the newest techniques — dial access, television, and computer-assisted instructions. By using these standards you can develop the most exemplary media services provided for any children in the United States and for those who need it the most. I hope you will do it.

Media Production Facilities in Schools for the Deaf

William D. Jackson

We are in the midst of a technological revolution and a cultural explosion that has engendered pronounced changes in education. Schools are inundated by surging enrollments, creating a shortage of qualified teachers at a time when the need for fully educated citizens and highly trained manpower was never greater. Paradoxically, educators are not only confronted with these problems, but must administer an ever expanding and changing school program in the midst of constant change and innovation when society demands certain things remain unchanged. It is these demands in the form of customs, traditions, regulations and even laws which affect the rate of innovation in education.

American educators often very progressive in their views in many areas sometimes have been very conservative, even rigid, in thinking about their own practices. During the early 1700's, for instance, when educational technology was at a pre-industrial state, schools did not have blackboards or other teaching apparatus, but reportedly, some flourishing schools boasted of owning a globe. Instructional materials were homemade as were all the school supplies. Goose-quills for writing required the services of an expert technician, in most cases the schoolmaster. Very often a teacher was hired on the basis of his ability to cut and mend quills rather than his ability to teach.[1]

The introduction of new educational apparatus to American education, such as the steel pen for writing in the late 1830's, the pencil in 1861, and the fountain pen in 1880, had little impact on classroom instruction until cheap writing paper became commonplace. Such devices as the Spelling Stick were no longer novelties and a host of new machines such as the stereopticon and lantern slide projector were introduced near the turn of the century.

Reprinted from *American Annals of the Deaf*, November 1967, by permission of the publisher.

The *American Education Monthly* as early as 1870 reported that facilities and teachers were indispensable and good apparatus was scarcely less so. Furthermore, it was indicated that teachers should have proper implements to work with if work was expected to be done. Unfortunately such support was slow in coming as was the long awaited technological revolution in education.

Recent enactment of federal legislation has enabled schools to initiate new programs and approaches to learning at a more rapid pace than anyone dreamed possible a few years ago. Schools for the deaf are also experiencing this phenomena and have reaped a bonanza of unexpected benefits, especially in terms of Title I and other federal programs. Captioned Films for the Deaf, U.S. Office of Education, has initiated procedures to equip all classrooms for the deaf with an overhead projector, a remote controlled filmstrip projector, two screens, and two projection tables. Increasing availability of captioned films media kits (such as "Sights and Sounds" complete with recordings, filmstrips, teachers' guides and student workbooks), single concept 8mm cartridge films with projectors and carrying case, overhead transparency masters, and other curriculum materials is overwhelming school personnel responsible for the instructional program in their respective schools. Traditionally the school librarian has assumed responsibility for all book materials, but the concept of an Instructional Materials Center (IMC) includes both books and non-book materials, such as study print collections, filmstrips, films, records, and related media. Consequently educators have been confronted with a controversy in regard to the role of the librarian and the audio-visual specialist in the IMC. Dr. Ray Wyman has suggested that perhaps the traditional librarian and the traditional Audio-Visual specialist should be replaced by a team of specialists.[9]

A recent survey by Mrs. Patricia Cory indicates that few schools for the deaf have adequate libraries in terms of books or facilities.[4] More significant, however, is the fact that only two schools out of the thirty in the survey employed professionally trained librarians and supporting secretarial help. There is no reason to believe the situation would differ greatly if a survey had been made of all schools for the deaf. In all probability, competition for professionally trained librarians will become more acute and it will become extremely difficult to keep qualified personnel. The shortage of trained library personnel is evident in all areas of industry, government, and education. Educators of the deaf will be competing for all types of personnel, skilled and unskilled, professional and non-professional, trained or untrained – in order to fill existing vacancies. New positions are often left unfilled because qualified people are not available, nor does it seem likely that such conditions will be alleviated in the very near future. Consequently we must investigate new approaches and ways of doing things whereby maximum utilization can be made of the time available for instruction. This means greater use of technology in the form of new media. It means accessibility to equipment, facilities and materials, provisions for individual study, flexibility in programming, and freedom to innovate. We must overcome the *caretaker* attitude concerning the acquisition and utilization of instructional materials. Too many of our librarians and A-V personnel are *keepers of things or gadgeteers*. They take immense pride in acquiring more books, films, filmstrips, or other media so it can be cataloged and stored on shelves or in a closet inaccessible to teachers and students. The *gadgeteer* derives his pleasure from the *care and feeding* of elaborate and expensive devices which are too complicated for anyone else to operate. Unfortunately these people often supervise the purchase of expensive equipment and commercially prepared teaching materials. Selection may be on the basis of personal preference, availability from a local dealer, or may otherwise reflect a lack of knowledge and experience. Hopefully the situation will improve as a consequence of the summer media institutes, inservice training and workshops conducted at individual schools, and recognition by administrators of the need for a carefully planned, systematic approach to media acquisition, production, and utilization.

There are a multitude of commercially produced instructional materials available today, and indications are that production of the traditional teaching aids such as books, pictures, charts, filmstrips, records, and related media will continue to grow at a rapid rate. A multiplicity of such materials is highly desirable but more often than not the colorful and attractive commercially prepared materials incorporate vocabulary, language, or concepts which are not suitable for use with deaf children. Commercial materials are designed for a mass market and are, of necessity, general in their treatment of a given subject. The necessity for preparation of instructional materials at the local level is very apparent. Commercially produced materials cannot and do not fit every teaching situation or satisfy a sufficiently large number of teaching needs.

Last year, the Texas Education Agency received a grant to evaluate and redesign a series of overhead transparencies for use by schools for the deaf. These transparencies were designed explicitly for public school classes and were correlated with textbooks for specific subject matter areas and at designated grade levels. Preliminary evaluation by teachers using them at the Texas School for the Deaf indicates considerable modification is necessary before many of them can be used. The original transparency, in some cases, must be redesigned to break the concept down into smaller bits. Sometimes the terminology and language is too advanced. This criticism is almost universally true of all media, including captioned films.

Most schools for the deaf have various resources available which are not commonly associated with the library or audio-visual program but have wide application in the production of media. Darkrooms, cameras, enlargers, lettering equipment, printing facilities, and drafting equipment are readily available in most schools for the deaf as are spirit duplicators, copying machines, typewriters, and other types of office equipment. Such equipment could be used effectively for the production of instructional materials, but it is unusual to find more than a typewriter and spirit duplicator assigned to the teachers' workroom. More often essential equipment is located in the principal's office or locked up in a closet somewhere. The vocational principal usually does not allow anyone but the instructor of printing or photography to use cameras or darkrooms assigned to that department nor does the business manager allow anyone to use the Thermo-fax copier or other copying equipment in the administrative area. The librarian, if the school is fortunate enough to have one, is assigned a work-room or storage room in which a few projectors, a paper trimmer, or related equipment and materials are carefully hidden from view, discouraging teachers or students from using them. Oftentimes a principal or supervising teacher requires that certain equipment and materials be shared by all the teachers and students, consequently no one uses them. An audio-visual coordinator, if he is on the scene, probably requires everyone to fill out forms in quadruplicate before he will replace a lamp in a projector or perform some menial task that any normal teen-ager could be taught to do in a few minutes.

Is it any wonder that classroom teachers of the deaf are pleading for more pictures, charts, chalkboards, and spirit duplicator masters rather than films, filmstrips, transparencies or other media? Why aren't teachers producing more of these latter materials at the local level? Perhaps the answer is that we have not provided the logistic support, encouragement, or leadership whereby the creative talents of our classroom teachers could be utilized more effectively.

Schools for the deaf have several characteristics in common which must be considered in developing a rationale or framework of reference for the local production of educational media. These are:

1. An enrollment of under 500 students with dormitory facilities on the campus.
2. A teaching staff of less than 100.
3. Curriculum structured into levels such as:
    (a) lower elementary
    (b) upper elementary
    (c) high school
    (d) vocational
4. Class size varying from a maximum of 10-12 downward to one or two children.
5. Education of the deaf requires special equipment and different approaches to teaching not common to public school education.
6. Schools and classes for the deaf are often isolated from schools or classes for hearing children and from other schools for the deaf by geographical location in a city, town, or state, and within buildings in a school district.

Development of facilities for media production might be initiated by stages which could be characterized as follows:

PHASE I

No full-time media specialist, but one or more staff members attend a summer media institute. Plans are formulated for inservice training and workshops in media production and utilization. The Administration investigates the feasibility of establishing an IMC and determines possible sources of funds for materials and equipment. Consideration is given to space requirements, staff, and administrative procedures necessary for the operation and supervision of a media center.

PHASE II

Satellite media centers are established in the various departments of buildings utilizing existing equipment and facilities such as teachers, workrooms, departmental libraries, or conference rooms.

An evaluation of existing materials including books, filmstrips, and related library materials should be completed. An up-to-date inventory should be made of all available equipment including typewriters, duplicators, projectors, and screens to determine their location and condition. Responsibility should be given to a full-time staff member to coordinate the overall planning and to expedite the cataloging of available instructional materials. Procedures should be initiated for the repair and maintenance of existing equipment. Attention should be given to the problem of storage and distribution of materials and equipment. Funds should be made available for purchase of new equipment and supplies.

PHASE III

A media specialist is employed to develop a comprehensive media program. Funds are made available for acquisition of needed instructional materials and supplies. All classrooms are equipped with two screens, an overhead projector, remote controlled filmstrip projector, projector stands, and other equipment such as 8mm and 16mm motion picture projectors. The traditional library and audio-visual functions are centralized into one facility which includes the IMC, media production, and administration of the overall media program. The satellite media centers become more functional with the addition of a dry mounting press, paper cutter, dry copier, preview facilities, storage for films, filmstrips, and supplies. It is assumed a spirit duplicator and typewriter are already available. Student assistants would be utilized as projectionists and to position equipment when needed.[3] Procedures are initiated for preventative maintenance on all equipment, which includes ordering and stocking of spare lamps and having personnel available who know how to replace lamps and make minor repairs.

Darkroom facilities and related graphic arts services in the vocational department should be exploited to the maximum. Cardboard frames for overhead transparencies, graphic illustrations, and a variety of printed materials, including full color illustrations, could be produced in the print shop. Drawings and other artwork could be enlarged or reduced with the process camera and inexpensive offset plates could then be made. Such artwork if printed on translucent paper could be used as masters for making overhead transparencies with a thermal copier, diazo machine, or other copying devices. The same masters could also be used to make a spirit master which would allow a teacher to make additional paper copies. Students could then have a paper copy of whatever the teacher was using on the overhead.

FACILITIES

Faris, Moldstad and Frye have suggested a minimum of 1260 square feet be provided for a materials production program.[6] Therefore, a room 30 x 42, approximately the size of a traditional public school classroom, centrally located in the vicinity of the library, and accessible to the staff would be adequate for media production in most schools for the deaf.

Such a room should have a sink with hot and cold water available, good ventilation, light control and a minimum of two 20 amp electrical circuits with two or more receptacles on each wall. Provision should also be made for a small darkroom about 8 x 10 feet in size with storage cabinets, or a small closet for storage of supplies and equipment.

BASIC COMPONENTS

An analysis of production techniques indicates certain elements or activities are common and essential to a successful media program. These activities can be categorized into six basic areas: (1) illustration, (2) preservation, (3) identification, (4) duplication, (5) photography, and (6) display. An unlimited variety of instructional materials can be produced when all six activities are combined, but elimination of one function will reduce the potential of the other five. Effectiveness of the program is also dependent upon the adequacy of the facilities, equipment, materials, and qualifications of personnel involved with media production.

Illustration. Textbooks, teacher-manuals, magazines, and other printed materials are the largest source of illustration for classroom teachers. Clip books and other commercially prepared artwork are also available but seldom found in a school for the deaf. Student artwork and drawings, tracings, paste-ups, layouts, and visual material prepared by staff members are often used for school newspapers, yearbooks, and other publications.

The media production center should have all types of resource materials for artwork — classified and indexed and copyright free when possible — in a form which can be reproduced in any type format. The basic equipment required for this area would be a drawing table with a good light, some storage shelves, and a cabinet for art supplies.

Preservation. Most teachers of the deaf spend hours each day looking for pictures, preparing charts, or making some type of graphic aid. These materials are easily torn and mutilated, hard to store, and difficult to replace. Dry mounting of pictures, lamination, color lifts, felt board materials, cloth backing of charts and maps, and a combination of these techniques can all be accomplished inexpensively with a dry mounting press.

The overall cost of dry mounting materials will vary depending on size of staff and availability of equipment. One dry mounting press would suffice initially; however, it is difficult to dry mount and laminate at the same time. An additional press would allow a number of teachers to dry mount and laminate simultaneously. A tacking iron should be provided with each press, along with a pair of ferrotype tins, a masonite board about 16" x 20" for laminating, a paper trimmer, and a large work table or counter.

Identification. Lettering, captions, and labels are used with all types of visual materials. The need for simple, inexpensive, legible lettering which can be done quickly, accurately, and easily with a minimum of training and experience is generally acknowledged as a major problem by classroom teachers. The typewriter, varityper, and other mechanical devices provide excellent copy if they meet the need and are available. There are, however, several types of the lettering systems, devices, and materials which can alleviate this problem and which can be purchased rather inexpensively from most school and art supply stores. Some of these lettering devices are:

1.   adhesive backed letters
2.   cardboard, plastic, or ceramic letters
3.   stencils with guides
4.   special pens and templates, such as Wrico, Letterguide, and Leroy, and
5.   devices which print labeling on colored plastic tapes.

A sign making machine, used by variety stores to make signs and price cards, could be used most effectively to make quick and easy multicolor flash cards, or other visual aids. Ink is rolled onto metal type with a brayer, then a piece of cardboard is pressed against the type, resulting in a quick print job. This technique is more practical than hand lettering when several copies of an item are needed. IBM has a reconditioned electric typewriter with a large sans serif type face called the "Directory Style," which will reproduce very nicely on thermal copy transparencies, and is large enough to read when projected on a screen.

Duplication. The extent of commercially prepared spirit duplicator masters is almost limitless. More significant, however, has been the decline of the mimeograph during the past few years and the almost unprecedented acceptance of the spirit duplicator by classroom teachers. Availability of materials, ease of operation, and accessibility provide an unbeatable combination which has been further enhanced by the appearance of the thermal copier. This device allows a person to make a transparency for the overhead and a spirit master from the same original black and white copy. Addition of a photocopier and diazo processing equipment offers unlimited possibilities for producing visual materials. Thermal copiers require black and white copy, and the diazo process requires a translucent paper or film positive in order to make a transparency. The photocopier is a useful device for getting a black and white film or paper copy from books or other printed materials. This black and white film or paper positive makes an excellent master for all types of duplication including printing.

Photography. Advent of the 10-second Polaroid picture ushered in a new era for photography. Anyone can take pictures of professional quality without experience or knowledge of photography. Not only is this true of still pictures, as exemplified by Polaroid and the instamatic line of cameras and film by Kodak, but it is also characteristic of the new developments in other areas of photography. The new Super 8mm format for motion picture films and new cameras with automatic controls and zoom lens are other instances. A similar breakthrough was achieved in development of new 35mm single lens reflex cameras with thru-the-lens metering systems. A media production center should have one Model 100 Polaroid camera, a good 35mm SLR with thru-the-lens metering — complete with closeup lens and copying attachments, a copy stand, lighting equipment, a tripod, and an 8mm camera with zoom lens. Other equipment, such as the photomodifier, is necessary for enlargement or reduction of illustrations, unless an enlarger and darkroom facilities are readily available. The Heiland Repronar is also very useful for slide duplication and filmstrip production. An inexpensive single frame 35mm camera can also be used to make filmstrips inexpensively.

Display. The preponderance of bulletin boards, charts, and a host of other static displays in schools and classrooms for the deaf is graphic evidence of attempts to communicate. Generally the display is indeed static and the message is lost in the haphazard arrangement of pictures, captions, and construction paper. Magnetic boards, chalkboards, pegboards, even projection screens can be considered as display devices. One of the most unique and useful types of display utilizes the hook and loop board. A small piece of nylon fish hook tape can be used to suspend a heavy object on the vertical surface of the board. The usefulness of the hook and loop board is virtually unlimited for classroom displays, photography, and numerous other applications. An airbrush and portable air compressor would be necessary for shading backgrounds on displays or to add color to visual materials. Of course, some hand tools such as a hammer, saw, and drill would be extremely useful.

The need for quality "software" is the most difficult problem confronting educators today. Making the rounds in computer circles is the slogan "GIGO" or *G*arbage *I*n, *G*arbage *O*ut. Will we provide adequate facilities for media production and insist upon quality *software* for our deaf students, or are we going to provide them with "GIGO" materials?

REFERENCES

1. Anderson, Charnel. *Technology in American Education 1650-1900.* Department of Health, Education, and Welfare, U.S. Office of Education, 1962, p. 53.
2. Brown, James W., and Norberg, Kenneth D. *Administering Educational Media.* McGraw-Hill Book Company, New York, 1965, p. 357.
3. Coleman, Larry. "Who Will Do the Production." *Educational Screen and Audiovisual Guide,* Vol. 46, pp. 18-19, March, 1967.
4. Cory, Patricia B. *Report on Phase I, School Library Programs in Schools for the Deaf.* Department of Health, Education, and Welfare, U.S. Office of Education, Captioned Films for the Deaf.
5. Davis, Harold S. *Instructional Materials Center: An Annotated Bibliography.* Educational Research Council of Greater Cleveland, Staff Utilization Project, Cleveland, Ohio, 1965.
6. Faris, Gene, Frye, Harvey, and Moldstad, John. *Improving the Learning Environment.* Department of Health, Education, and Welfare, U.S. Office of Education, 1963, p. 148.
7. *Instructional Materials.* Illinois Curriculum Program, Office of the Superintendent of Instruction, Administration and Supervision Series, Bulletin A-3, Springfield, Illinois, 1961.
8. McLuhan, Marshall. *Understanding Media: The Extensions of Man.* McGraw-Hill Book Company, New York, 1964.
9. Wyman, Raymond. "The Instructional Materials Center: Whose Empire." *Audiovisual Instruction,* Vol. 12, pp. 114-116, February, 1967.

Remedial Labs Try to Cure Classroom Troublemakers

"Passive and shy in the classroom, Ricky was arrested for stealing bicycles and a shotgun. During the first half of third grade, he was constantly in trouble and this was reflected in almost all areas of his school work."

Bill's teacher said, "he wants to do something big – he is disruptive in his efforts to gain an abnormal amount of adult approval and attention."

Mary was described by her teacher as being significantly below grade in reading and in math. "She tries, but can't achieve to her ability. She is listless, withdrawn and fearful."

These and other children come to the Phoenix Facility for Diagnosis and Change of Student Behavior Center in need of help, many with lack of motivation. About 70 per cent come from broken homes. Many are over-aggressive, defiant, socially isolated.

A majority are significantly below grade level or are non-readers. They omit or add words, have poor enunciation and comprehension, and ignore punctuation.

"We believe that communication difficulties and poor self-image underlie many of their problems and lead to a downward spiral, in which the student continually experiences failure, ultimately gives up, and becomes a troublemaker in the classroom and at home," comments Facility director, Mrs. Helen Armstrong.

"Unless something is done to return the children to a positive learning situation," she commented, "they become social and emotional dropouts."

The program got underway in January 1968 with 33 students. Since that time, the Center Facility has processed about 103 students in three groups. The cost of the program will be about $166,000 per year, over a three-year period. This includes salaries for the staff of four counselors, two reading specialists, secretary, clerk and four teacher aides, under the administration of an overall project director.

Students referred to the Center spend three weeks in intensive observation, testing and counseling.

The Center's operations include several phases:

Selection and testing: "We want to know as much about the student as possible before we get him," said Miss Jean Kennedy, Supervisor, Grades 5 and 6. "We like all test results sent in with the student, including IPAT (Psycholinguistic), the EPIC ABS Affective Behavior Test, Otis, Peabody, W.I.S.C. and others, including perception and behavior."

The referring teacher is asked to observe the student carefully in the class-room situation, and note his observable behavior characteristics on an Affective Behavior Checklist. Teachers are shown videotapes of standard behavior norms to help them observe the students objectively.

Orientation: Each student coming to the Center is placed under the direct responsibility of a counselor who will guide him through the program and on through the follow-up programs at each school. Parents are included in the orientation.

Counseling: "We stress psychological counseling, the learning process and growth, rather than course achievement," said Grade 3 and 4 supervisor, Mrs. Jo Pitts. "This develops a positive attitude toward the school situation and helps the child better understand himself and the efforts being made for him.

"We want to listen sympathetically to the child and not offer advice or criticism in any way. It is imperative that we look for the positive characteristics to reinforce. We don't say, 'you can do better, Johnny.' We remind him when he has four out of five wrong, that he has one correct."

Prescription: After more testing, evaluation and counseling, an individualized prescription is prepared for each child. This is a form which defines his deficiencies and prescribes specific reading tapes and lessons. This prescription will follow him back to the school once he has left the Center.

The heart of the Center is a language laboratory built around some 300 reading tapes, carefully planned to correct reading deficiencies in perception, phonics, visual/auditory discrimination, comprehension, oral fluency, word attack, or hand-eye coordination.

"We know that many of the students' social and psychological problems are related to reading difficulties," explained Mrs. Pitts. "These children are not mentally defective. A few perform above grade level, but three-fourths below. Once we correct the underlying cause, reduce tension and stress, the behavior problem melts away and the child can move ahead with his class."

Follow-up: After the student has completed three weeks at the Center, he goes back to his school. There he spends about one period a day working closely with a teacher aide who handles follow-up programs at each school.

Teacher aides review the prescription form from the Center, together with his tape assignments, reading level, reading interest, and daily activities. The student listens to enrichment tapes and may watch filmstrips.

Teachers fill out behavior checklists after three weeks, the end of the program, and at the end of each semester. This data is sent back to the Center and, on alternate weeks, the aide goes to the Center to discuss students in her care.

The program does not terminate for the student at a specific date. It is designed to be an ongoing effort until the objectives have been reached. Some students, explained Mrs. Armstrong, have been with the program over a year.

Where Do We Go From Here?

Stephen D. Berry and Charles L. Miller

Are those responsible for public education actually in control? Where do we go from here?

Few would argue that education and training are the most valuable resources in any nation or that they are the foundation of our economic, social, and political strength. Yet, education is following — not leading. It is reflecting too often and not projecting often enough.

The greatest burden for new directions belongs with the educator, but the constituent of education must also be accountable and wary of being sold more of the same unless satisfied with past purchases.

Have we analyzed the available literature and educational research findings and projected attainable and measurable goals for our educational systems, or do we give lip service to them, reflecting smugly, albeit unconsciously, upon what we call our past achievements? Are we growing in our educational contribution to a dynamic and volatile society or are we a helpless giant being dragged and cudgeled by that same society?

This article attempts to deal with these questions in light of experience with two innovative and exemplary projects nearing the end of their tenure under federal support.

BACKGROUND

As early as 1958 educators in an Illinois suburban area* recognized the need for certain cooperative efforts among the local school districts. Audio-visual specialists were interested in forming a cooperative film library, while counselors and testing specialists were interested in developing local standardized tests. Thus, the superintendents worked extensively on forming several such cooperative ventures. The area subsequently became a junior college district, a separate division of the Illinois Education Association, a special education cooperative, and a Title II cooperative. The districts agreed to cooperate on the operation of several Title III ESEA projects.

Because of problems involving the financial structure of the various districts, early efforts at many cooperative ventures came to only partial fruition. Some of the communities in the area were "bedroom communities" whose only tax base was residential; others enjoyed large industrial parks and business districts with a resulting tax base placing them in an enviable position.

Reprinted from *Theory Into Practice*, October 1968, by permission of the publisher.

However, with the advent of ESEA, local administrators were able to test the feasibility of these cooperative ideas at an operational level. Several proposals were put into tentative discussion form for consideration and refinement. Two projects of primary concern here are the Instructional Resources Center (Project #OE 66-590) and the Diagnostic Learning Center (Project #66-1545).

INSTRUCTIONAL RESOURCES CENTER

The Instructional Resources Center was designed to have three major thrusts:

1. *Curriculum Materials Division.* Most teachers are not aware of the materials available to them in the wide varieties of format or structure. A representative collection of instructional materials and resources as broadly based as possible was established in the Curriculum Materials Division. This collection consists of more than 10,000 items and is continually being expanded. As many as forty to fifty teachers, representing literally every area of the curriculum and every grade level, visit the library per week. To date, it has not been possible to determine the economic effect of the information carried back to the home district. One might suspect, however, that more usable materials are requested for purchase.

2. *Study and Consultation Division.* This division was established to provide teachers with the help of special consultants in the solution of special instructional problems; to provide the funds necessary to permit teacher visitations to any school system in the country using the particular technique or process in question; and to provide resources and facilities necessary for curriculum committees and teachers' workshops to develop their ideas for instructional improvement. The result has been over forty separate projects, involving several hundred teachers, in such curriculum areas as reading, music, physical education, ETV, sex education, science, mathematics, and social studies.

3. *Special Production Division.* Teachers receive help from this division to develop their own ideas about how a certain type of information should be presented and how materials should be designed. The staff includes the services of artists, photographers, and graphic art specialists to translate teachers' ideas into usable audio-visual and printed instructional materials. In the past two and one-half years, 12,000-15,000 individual pieces of visual materials have been produced each year, including 35mm slides, filmstrips, transparencies, posters, still pictures,

*This area is composed of four townships (Wheeling, Elk Grove, Schaumburg, and Palatine) in the northwest quadrant of Cook County, Illinois. Described as one of the most rapidly growing populated areas in the United States, it is served by two high school districts, eight elementary districts, and a Catholic and Lutheran parochial school system.

curriculum guides, and student manuals. Production of 8mm and 16mm films and video and audio tapes is also possible. While the quantity and quality of the materials is quite impressive, the significance is the fact that creative teachers now have available the supporting paraprofessional talent they have needed for so many years.

DIAGNOSTIC LEARNING CENTER

The Diagnostic Learning Center was established to probe into the causes of severe learning difficulties in children of apparently normal abilities. In the cooperating school districts, these children were either being overlooked or handled as discipline problems in many schools because no resources were available for analyzing their special learning problems. Furthermore, no professional assistance was available to teachers for the use of specific techniques and materials.

A staff of psychologists, diagnosticians, guidance counselors, and learning specialists was assembled to study these special problems. Evaluation indicated that measurable progress had been made with many of these children, but the data also revealed several other factors:

1. Approximately 80 per cent of the children tested academically and psychologically were socially maladjusted and needed therapeutic as well as tutorial assistance.
2. Teachers were threatened when confronted with lack of success with these children.
3. Parents, although receptive to the program, had great difficulty in dealing with their own problems, some of which were at least partially responsible for their child's maladjustment.

Based upon these findings, the staff is now oriented toward providing psychological therapy in individual and group settings for both the children and their parents. Teachers can also participate in specially designed workshops to broaden their understanding of these children and provide some insights into the weaknesses inherent in the present instructional practices, as well as the whole educational structure.

WHO WILL BE RESPONSIBLE?

The future of these two projects is uncertain. Federal support under Title III ESEA for both the Instructional Resources Center and Diagnostic Learning Center will terminate June 30, 1969. The burden of continued support of successful programs sponsored under this title of P.L. 89-10 falls squarely upon those school systems initiating them during the past two and one-half years.

Through sophisticated assessment of the educational needs of the community and continued evaluation of existing programs, the local school district is responsible for seeing that tax dollars have not been wasted. The time to determine the feasibility of phase-in is prior to application for funds — not prior to the withdrawal of those funds.

Title III officials have been insisting that phase-in plans be included in all new fund applications. Local officials insist that they cannot plan for phase-in until the value of the program has been proven because of the many demands placed on the local tax dollar. Yet, other programs of less financial strain and with less evaluative information are being supported with local funds. Existing programs are continued with little thought given to their worth. Serious evaluation might free local funds for support of more innovative and proven programs.

State and local educational systems are not facing their obligations. These obligations require more than simply continuing successful Title III programs — the need is to determine, from the best data available, the demands which will be placed on the working citizen of the next ten to twenty years and to develop appropriate educational programs. School systems must build in evaluation methods for continuous assessment of needs and practices.

Educators must be prepared to learn new techniques of instruction and be kept informed of new knowledge of learning behavior; subject matter knowledge is not enough. Teacher training must emphasize the learning process and the use of instructional technology, individualized instruction, self-actualization, and other equally important processes to get maximum return for the quantity of input.

The school districts sponsoring the two projects described above are no exception to the general educational rule of planning as the immediate need arises. They find themselves in the awkward position of not quite knowing the appropriate action for continuing the support of successful parts of those two programs. Possible formulae are being examined that include additional federal support, state assistance, and financial involvement of the business world. The pressure of immediacy is most disturbing. There are unanswered questions regarding the future, and no immediate action is being initiated.

These comments are not intended as an indictment against school systems directly involved with the projects described. In fact, they are very likely among the most forward-looking systems in the nation with highly trained and diligent teaching and administrative staffs. Rather, these comments are an indictment against the developmental programs of education in general and the educational heritage which they exemplify.

Organizational bodies must be established within education to reassess existing programs and proposed developments for the future. This cannot be an occasional matter prodded by an impending bond issue, tax referendum, or population explosion. Management in both industry and government has found it necessary to utilize professional specialists who may know little about the eventual product but have the necessary tools to determine the future market. Educators must also turn to these specialists, rather than fool themselves into thinking there exist specialists who have evolved from the teaching and administrative ranks. We do have specialists in some areas whose greatest talent lies in the analysis of needs assessment data and program design. Education should capitalize on both areas of specialization.

CONCLUSION

Those responsible for education are making the decisions affecting educational programs. However, they are not in control. To be in control, one must know what is ahead and what response will be required. Neither the educator nor the constituent has this kind of control at present.

The past has been our only lighthouse. Some excellent things have happened, some of which are still with us. Certainly, we cannot ignore the past, but glancing backward too often results in running into the unexpected future. As long as these encounters are not too damaging, we are not jarred into reality. Use of educational television might be a very appropriate example — ETV, a series of applications of old principles through a relatively new medium, has literally fallen on its face. We must consciously and deliberately use past experience and available expertise to probe the future beyond the present limitations we have established. We must be held accountable for our actions.

We view education as our greatest resource, yet we are not finding the means by which it can be replenished. Greater energies must quickly be brought to bear from all quarters of society to enable us to see and understand this emerging dichotomy, before the gap widens.

How to Design a Working IMC

David S. Porter

From the beginning of the development of educational specifications for Bridge School, through its design on the architects' planning boards and the actual construction and equipping of the building, the Instructional Materials Center has been conceived as the "heart" of the school's operations. Far from

Reprinted from *Educational Screen and Audiovisual Guide,* November 1967, by permission of the publisher.

being a mere repository of reading materials, it has been designed as a live, working center where teachers and pupils alike can find, or have created, the resources they need in the teaching-learning process.

One of the Instructional Materials Center's tasks is to make teaching more effective through the use of teaching aids and the most up-to-date techniques. This is accomplished by stimulating interest in, explaining the value of, and providing instruction in the use of educational media. The Center is in existence to provide a means of securing, selecting, understanding, and explaining the function of each piece of material planned for educational use.

The Center's aims are:

To draw together printed and technological materials in one area for greater circulation.

To provide a wider selection of teaching paraphernalia.

To provide special help in selecting materials to strengthen the learning process.

To adapt materials to many different levels of instruction.

To bring about better coordination of staff in the use of materials.

To provide a work area for independent study, planning, and production of materials.

To set aside areas in which to preview, investigate, and listen to individual learning aids.

To provide a place to produce software and hardware.

To get the best materials into the right hands at the most opportune time.

The Bridge School Instructional Program augments the Lexington Curriculum Scope and Sequence Guides with added current curriculum research, and the Instructional Materials Center is the depository for curriculum guides, sequence charts, planned goals for students, and other system wide material.

THE "HEART" SPECIALIST

To carry out the work of the Center, the Instructional Materials Specialist:

Builds collection of materials to support and supplement the subject matter.

Evaluates and brings to the attention of teachers a wide variety of new materials.

Selects, orders, and shelves library and audio-visual materials at the pupil and teacher levels.

Helps teachers prepare and produce instructional materials.

Trains and supervises parent and student assistants.

The Center's major aim is to provide the necessary materials and services in the shortest period of time, to place teaching materials at the disposal of teachers and pupils at the time of greatest value, and to anticipate future demands for materials.

To carry out effectively the prescribed role of the Center, the Instructional Materials Specialist is a member of the school's Administrative Cabinet and is called upon to make recommendations dealing with the operation of the program.

IMC "OPEN DOOR" POLICY

As a member also of the school's Curriculum Cabinet, the actual day-by-day subject matter planning becomes the Specialist's concern, along with the responsibility for assisting in curriculum discussions. In such a position, the Instructional Materials Specialist can be of service to pupils and teachers alike.

With all that is known about individual differences and learning rates of children, it is vital to make available materials which provide for a wide range of pupil experiences. With a wide range and extensive volume of materials housed in one area, the potential for creating interest and stimulating successful ventures is endless.

The nonbook hardware housed in the Center provides a powerful means for grasping knowledge. Pictures, films, filmstrips, tapes, recordings and television, although housed in the Center, circulate to the classroom areas. Instructional equipment, used by both pupils and teachers, has become a viable means of extending the horizons of knowledge.

Items such as projectors, learning carrels with tape playback equipment, facilities for taping, viewing and listening, once thought of as "gimmicks" or gadgets, have survived the curiosity period and proved to be necessary learning tools. Innovation in teaching methods stimulates innovation in instructional media and traditional library materials have been combined with audio-visual media in keeping with the planned instructional flexibility of the school.

The organizational plan of the school with its adaptations of instruction, various rates of progress, individual and group self-direction processes, and vertical and horizontal structure has caused many demands upon the "Center" for materials that are not usually requested in more conventionally structured schools.

The need for unique materials to meet specialized program requires creative thinking.

Programs based on student reactions to demonstrations and discussion topics stimulate questions needing immediate responses. For this reason the Center must function under the "open door" policy which affords the pupils the opportunity to visit at any time during the day for immediate assistance in finding the appropriate resources in their quest for learning. However, prescheduled visitation is also provided to give the students instruction in finding materials in the quickest, easiest, and most exact methods. Free reading and browsing are encouraged also.

STUDENT INDEPENDENCE STRESSED

While the word, both printed and spoken, is the primary tool of communication, research has shown that learning takes place faster and more effectively if nonverbal materials are used in conjunction with the verbal media. When confronted with a variety of possible approaches to teaching, through knowledge of the different materials available, teachers take many different avenues to reaching the goals they set. To provide for individual differences, teaching machines have been used. To plan for a certain learning experience, projectuals, films, filmstrips and other group demonstration media have focused on the main idea sought. Taped and recorded works have provided new experiences in listening skills. But, beyond this, the pupil is permitted to select, handle, and evaluate materials independently in an area provided for this function.

The potential that can be realized with the use of the study carrel has not yet been fulfilled. Although many of the thoughts are still not on paper, constant discussion and trial runs have taken place. Plans are being drawn to program experiences for the slow learner with the use of tapes, science materials, and projectors. Special class pupils are listening to stories and will eventually be introduced to listening skills through programmed material. The bottleneck to these programs, as with most programmed items, is planning, production, and availability of materials that meet the needs of the child at the time he needs them.

By means of a simple form, teachers and pupils have the opportunity to list books and other materials that they would like to have housed in the Center. Many items which have been commercially unavailable have been produced in the Center's production area. Another simple form is used for requesting materials and services for a specific time. The use of multiple and detailed forms has been discouraged to expedite the Center's services.

Implementation of the aims of the Center has engendered a large volume of work. This volume, however, has been handled quite adequately by the Center's full-time Instructional Materials Specialist, a part-time aid, and a corps of approximately forty parents. With this valuable aid, many services have been offered which improve the educational program of the school.

The Bridge School Instructional Materials Center will continue to serve as the "heart" of the school, with *service* as a key word, *interpretation* as a duty, *involvement* as an aim, and a *living workshop* as the goal.

AUTHOR INDEX